FAMILY RELATIONSHIPS IN THE EARLY YEARS

KAY OWEN AND
CHRISTOPHER BARNES

FAMILY RELATIONSHIPS IN THE EARLY YEARS

1 Oliver's Yard
55 City Road
London EC1Y 1SP

2455 Teller Road
Thousand Oaks
California 91320

Unit No 323-333, Third Floor, F-Block
International Trade Tower
Nehru Place, New Delhi - 110 019

8 Marina View Suite 43-053
Asia Square Tower 1
Singapore 018960

Editorial arrangement © Kay Owen and Christopher Barnes 2023
Chapter 1 © Kay Owen and Marco Antonio Delgado Fuentes 2023
Chapter 2 © Christopher Barnes and Kay Owen 2023
Chapter 3 © Christopher Barnes 2023
Chapter 4 © Christopher Barnes and Kay Owen 2023
Chapter 5 © Helen Simmons and Christopher Barnes 2023
Chapter 6 © Kay Owen and Carol Fenton 2023
Chapter 7 © Carol Fenton and Kay Owen 2023
Chapter 8 © Jenny Boldrin 2023
Chapter 9 © Kay Owen 2023
Chapter 10 © Christopher Barnes 2023
Chapter 11 © Trevor Cotterill 2023
Chapter 12 © Emma Twigg and Christopher Barnes 2023
Chapter 13 © Michelle Appleby 2023

Editor: Delayna Spencer
Editorial assistant: Esme Sawyer
Production editor: Rabia Barkatulla
Copyeditor: Sarah Bury
Proofreader: Brian McDowell
Indexer: Adam Pozner
Marketing manager: Lorna Patkai
Cover design: Wendy Scott
Typeset by: C&M Digitals (P) Ltd, Chennai, India
Printed in the UK

Library of Congress Control Number: 2022950648

British Library Cataloguing in Publication data

A catalogue record for this book is available from the British Library.

ISBN 9781529772111
ISBN 9781529772104 (pbk)

At Sage we take sustainability seriously. Most of our products are printed in the UK using responsibly sourced papers and boards. When we print overseas we ensure sustainable papers are used as measured by the Paper Chain Project grading system. We undertake an annual audit to monitor our sustainability.

For all members of Team Hickson, whether there by reason of birth, choice or association, but especially for Henry and Lewy.

KO

To Vanessa, Maia and Espen – for the happiness, love and inspiration you bring to my life, and my Mom and Dad – for giving everything so that we could follow our dreams.

CB

CONTENTS

AUTHOR BIOGRAPHIES

Dr Kay Owen is a Chartered Psychologist, Senior Lecturer in Education and Childhood at the University of Derby, and editor of *Play in the Early Years*, published by Sage in 2021. She teaches primarily on the BA (Hons) Early Childhood Studies Programme and contributes to other programmes in the Institute of Education. Her research interests focus on the importance of play and creativity and on children's socio-emotional development.

Dr Christopher Barnes is a Chartered Psychologist, Associate Fellow of the British Psychological Society and Senior Lecturer at the University of Derby. His research focuses on parenting and child development in diverse and clinical contexts. He teaches Developmental Psychology across the BSc (Hons) Psychology Undergraduate Programme.

Michelle Appleby is Assistant Programme Leader for MA Education. She teaches on this programme as well as the BA (Hons) Education Studies at the University of Derby. Her research interests include early years professionalism, international education, alternative forms of education, the psychology of learning, understanding and managing behaviour, as well as learning in Higher Education.

Jenny Boldrin is a Senior Lecturer on the BA (Hons) Early Childhood Studies degree at the University of Derby and the Academic Lead for the BA (Hons) Early Childhood Studies online top up. Jenny's professional experience lies in the early years sector where she spent time working with private nurseries and as part of the workforce team for a local authority. She has a particular research interest in the early experiences of previously looked after children and the ways in which professionals can work to support them and their adoptive families.

Trevor Cotterill is Programme Leader for Special Educational Needs and Disability (SEND) and teaches on SEND, Education Studies and Further Education Collaborations programmes at the University of Derby. His research interests include autism, the role of neurobiology and cognition in relation to autism, and ADHD (attention deficit hyperactivity disorder).

Dr Marco A. Delgado-Fuentes has been an advisor to UNICEF, the Inter-American Development Bank and various other agencies in Mexico and Latin America. He has also developed the Mexican National Curriculum for children under the age of 3. His lines of research include intercultural childhoods, social involvement in services for young children, the transition from preschool to primary school and policy development for services for young children and their families. Currently, he is a Senior Lecturer at the University of Derby, a member of the Scientific Advisory Group for the Development of Initial Education (Mexico) and SIG convenor of the British Educational Research Association.

Carol Fenton is a Senior Lecturer on the BA (Hons) Early Childhood Studies programme. Prior to joining the University of Derby, she worked as a primary school headteacher. Carol has researched colour vision deficiency, the effects on children's social and emotional development, and the importance of continuing professional development in developing quality education in Higher Education. She is a member of the Early Childhood Studies Degrees Network (ECSDN) and has been instrumental in the development of new workforce initiatives.

Dr Helen Simmons is a Senior Lecturer in Education (Childhood, Youth and Families) at the University of Northampton. Helen has undertaken research into and published on leadership in early childhood and early childhood policy, and her most recent publication provides a feminist post-structuralist analysis of modern motherhood. Helen is Vice Chair for the Early Childhood Studies Degrees Network (ECSDN) for Policy, Lobbying and Advocacy and is a Senior Fellow of the Higher Education Academy. Her research interests centre on the sociology of childhood, children's workforce development and critically reflective practice.

Emma Twigg is the Programme Leader for the BA (Hons) Early Childhood Studies degree at the University of Derby. Currently, Emma is progressing with her PhD on 'Early years practitioners' representation of children who have been exposed to domestic abuse'. Emma has previously written chapters on child protection and safeguarding and journal articles on the role of creativity in the early years.

PREFACE

Kay Owen and Christopher Barnes

British society has seen many changes over the years and, despite seeing shifts in com-position and functioning, the family unit has remained of central importance, especially in relation to raising children. Families are complex social groups, and those of us who work with children and families recognise that no two are the same. They may differ in terms of the number of people or the number of generations they comprise, the bio-logical or affectional bonds between members, as well as the place and way they live. We recognise also that the family unit is in a constant state of flux – new babies are born, relationships fracture and new relationships are formed, or sometimes families are rocked by trauma and adversity. All of these will alter the way in which the family func-tions and the environment in which children are raised. The main purpose of this book, therefore, is to consider some key aspects of family life in the hope of isolating factors that affect the experiences and potential outcomes for young children.

To help readers engage critically with the theory and research covered, this book begins with a consideration of how the family unit has changed in recent generations, and some of the ways in which it varies throughout the world.

Due to their importance, the roles, relationships and dynamics within the family unit have been extensively studied and researched. We have therefore endeavoured to provide a synopsis of some key theorists and seminal studies. For example, in Chapters 2 to 4, we provide an overview of classic parenting, developmental and attachment theory. This offers the reader a solid introduction to the topic area and a platform from which to explore wider issues known to impact the family during the early years.

ACKNOWLEDGEMENTS

The writing team sends their love and thanks to those family members who have become our best friends and the dear friends who are now integral members of our families. Our thanks also to colleagues at the University of Derby for their support and encouragement.

1

FAMILY: CONCEPTUAL, HISTORICAL AND CULTURAL HERITAGES

Kay Owen and Marco Antonio Delgado-Fuentes

Overview

We are all so used to our own family structure that sometimes it is hard to imagine that no other family is exactly like ours. In this introductory chapter, we will consider how and why families might differ, and begin to evaluate the ways in which this affects young children. In doing so, we hope to provide you with some context and concepts that will help you to critically engage with the chapters that follow.

The chapter will...

- Discuss ways in which 'family' can be conceptualised
- Consider some different ways families are conceptualised around the world
- Explain how families have changed and diversified in Britain over the years
- Investigate the composition of modern British families
- Question how these factors may affect children's relationships.

Key terms

Collectivist and individualist cultures; dependent/non-dependent children

---

Introduction

If we were to ask you to describe your family, some of you would describe a traditional household comprising a married couple and their biological children. Others, however, would probably mention people who are not biologically related but who are thought of as 'family', maybe even omitting some of your 'blood relations'. If we broaden the question to consider how our grandparents would have answered, or what friends from cultural backgrounds different from our own might say, it is immediately clear that families take many different forms and can vary across time, between cultures and due to circumstances.

Statistics and Definitions

Before we begin to discuss the issues, it is important to consider commonly used terms and the prevalence of different family groupings. These statistics are the most recent at the time of writing (2022), but the Office for National Statistics (ONS) 'Families and Households' offers frequent updates.

- **Dependent children** are those aged under 16 years living with at least one parent, or aged 16 to 18 years in full-time education, excluding all children who have a spouse, partner or child living in the household.
- **Non-dependent children** are those living with their parent(s), and either aged 19 years or over, or aged 16 to 18 years who are not in full-time education or who have a spouse, partner or child living in the household.
- **Married and cohabiting couple families** include both opposite-sex and same-sex couples.

In 2021 in the UK, there were:

- 19.3 million families – a 6.5% increase over the decade from 2011.
- 3 million lone-parent families, which accounts for 15.4% of families in the UK; the proportions ranged from 13.1% in the South East of England to 17.8% in the North East of England.
- 3.6 million 20 to 34-year-olds living at home with their parents; this represents 28% of people in this age group, an increase from 24% a decade ago.
- 12.7 million families that included a married or civil partnership couple (an increase of 3.7% since 2011) and 3.6 million families that included a cohabiting couple (an increase of 22.9% over the same period).
- An increasing number of households containing multiple families (about 1.1% of the population) (ONS 2022).

What makes a family?

Traditionally, family was a kinship group, in which adults (predominantly heterosexual and married to one another) took care of their own biological children (Giddens, 1993). However, this definition has progressively shifted due to changes in social attitudes, expectations, and government policy (Evans, Jenkins & Pereira, 2009). Sociological and economic circumstances have also influenced family arrangements. For example, in recent years, rising property prices have led to an increase in multiple families, or multiple generations of the same family, sharing a house and it is expected that more young people will live with their families as the cost of living soars over the next few years. So, while married or civil-partnership couples with biological children remain the most prevalent family format in Britain, there are lots of other forms, including cohabiting parents, stepfamilies, lone-parent families, and couples who live apart.

Time to consider

Consider the following attempts to define 'family'. The first two concentrate on composition:

i   A social group, typically consisting of one or two parents and their children.
ii   A group of persons related by descent or marriage.
iii   All the members of a household living under one roof.

(The Free Dictionary, 2022)

A family is a married, civil partnered or cohabiting couple with or without children, or a lone parent, with at least one child, who live at the same address. Children may be dependent or non-dependent.

(ONS, 2021)

The United Nations Convention on the Rights of the Child (1989) concentrates instead on the functions of the family:

(i)   The family is an institution in which the child should experience compassion and happiness in order to support their holistic development and maintain positive well-being.

- Do you find any of the definitions acceptable/unacceptable?
- What would you add or remove?

Now consider the following definition of a household:

A household is one person living alone, or a group of people (not necessarily related) living at the same address who share cooking facilities and share a living room, sitting room or dining area. A household can consist of a single family, more than one family, or no families in the case of a group of unrelated people.

(ONS, 2019)

- Is a household different from a family?
- If so, what is the main point of difference?

Epochs of British Family Life

Historically, blood ties were seen to confer a moral obligation to care for children, thus creating both a genetic and ethical basis for the biological family unit (Powell & Smith, 2018). However, the form and nature of this unit has seen many changes over the years.

Prior to the Industrial Revolution, most of the population lived in large extended family groups within rural locations, or in nuclear units geographically close to the family (Laslett & Wall 1972). Families were largely self-reliant, working the land together and aiming to provide for the needs of all. Within this system, as people's physical strength and health deteriorated, they could assume the role of caring for the very young or undertaking less physically demanding roles. However, in the UK, the process of industrialisation happened rapidly, leading many to move from rural to more urban locations throughout the 18th and 19th centuries.

Work in the cities was primarily in the mills or factories and for able-bodied males, although there were also some jobs (on negligible pay) that were considered suitable for women and children. Men therefore went to work while the women stayed at home to care for children. While many attempted to relocate with kin, conditions were cramped, meaning there was little room for the extended family or for those who could not be economically productive (Anderson, 1971). The nuclear family thus became the predominant economic and social unit within this period and care of the elderly and infirm passed from the family to the State.

During the two World Wars most able-bodied men of child-rearing age joined the forces. With the men gone, women were called upon to work outside the home, and often to parent alone. Female competence in both of these roles, and the satisfaction some women gained from employment, led to a rejection of post-war suggestions that they should all return to being 'housewives', and provided the impetus for women's increasing participation in the workforce.

Female emancipation, prolonged life expectancy and the increasingly secular nature of society have also influenced how people view and respond to relationships, making them increasingly disinclined to tolerate unsatisfactory partnerships. This, along with capitalism, the need for a mobile workforce (Seccombe, 1995) and even climate change (Edwards, Gray & Hunter, 2009) have altered the conditions that favoured long-term marriages and led to higher rates of divorce and marriage dissolution. As a result of all these changes, the contemporary family is more varied than ever before. In Chapter 5, Simmons and Barnes consider contemporary views regarding male and female parenting as underlying these are deeper cultural beliefs about gender and gender roles. The following Case Study should help you to reflect on this.

The Muxes in Mexico – a Special Case

Several cultures recognise more than two genders, and this impacts upon the family group. We are going to look at one example – the Muxes, in Oaxaca, Mexico.

The indigenous people of Mexico, the Zapotec, have been at the centre of many anthropological studies. Some claim that, particularly in the area around Juchitan, society has been organised as a matriarchy. Certainly, it is the women who tend to own and manage the property, the traditional market stands as well as trade and money. They also decide when love and marriage relationships start and end, and, in cases of separation, they keep the property. Males are traditionally fishermen.

Zapotec people recognise a third gender, the Muxes. These are men who may dress as women permanently, occasionally, or not at all, sometimes changing their manner of dress depending upon whether they are in public or at home. They can establish love and sexual relationships with women, men or other Muxes, and can work in either typical male or female occupations.

Their fluid nature enables families to be adaptable as they help raise and educate children but, because they are independent and autonomous, they can also own property and possess wealth. Muxes therefore tend to be highly valued in society. Most families would like to have at least one Muxe, as they offer their families the best characteristics of both males and females, and ensure family members' economic and emotional wellbeing.

Although modern life has transformed certain traditions, gender roles have remained largely intact, and Muxes seem to have survived the often-violent impositions of the colonial era, which tended to view the indigenous people's sexual behaviour and nakedness as contrary to their values (from Mirande, 2012; Urbiola Solís, Vázquez García & Cázares Garrido, 2017).

Time to consider

- Do you think contemporary attitudes towards LGBT and the trans community have changed our understanding of families?
- Do you think the UK, as a society, has a unified opinion about these changes?

European Variations

Across the European Union, the decade to 2020 saw an increase in the number of households comprising lone adults, childless couples and what are termed 'other types of household', which are mainly economically independent adult children living with one or more parents, elderly people living with family members, or economically independent adults sharing a home (Eurostat, 2020). While we are inclined to assume that living conditions in all EU nations are broadly similar, this same survey revealed some differences between Member States regarding households with children. At one end of the spectrum – in Ireland, Poland and Portugal – over a third of households contained at least one child, whereas at the other end of the spectrum – in Sweden, Finland and

Germany – fewer than one in four households contained children. In Finland (83.9%) and Greece (79.2%), most children lived in a household with an adult couple, but this was much lower in Latvia (46.6%), Serbia (48.2%) and North Macedonia (40.9%). It is therefore clear that the composition of households and of family groups varies across nations. This will affect who the children of that country live with, the likelihood that they will have siblings or neighbourhood playmates and, thus, their experience of childhood.

Countries also differ in terms of how they view society and, subsequently, the values and beliefs they hold about 'family'. We shall consider one such cultural difference next.

Collectivist and Individualist Cultures

Broadly speaking, **collectivist cultures** (e.g. China, Korea, Japan) are traditional societies which emphasise compliance and social cohesion (Janssens, 1993). Community, family and concern for the broader society are all extremely important. Therefore, family and group goals are more important than individual needs and desires. Chinese culture also advocates filial piety, meaning that individuals are expected to show respect for their parents and elders by conforming to these norms and demonstrating obedience and care for the family (Yu-wei, 2021).

Historically, the Chinese culture has always placed great emphasis on academic achievement (Ho & Hau, 2008) and on self-regulation. Both of these were considered to be best encouraged by an authoritarian approach to parenting (Liu, Xiao & Hipson, 2018), often involving what Western eyes would consider to be relatively harsh discipline and punishment (Liu & Wang, 2015). Comparative studies have suggested that, in order to ensure that children achieve the required goals, Chinese parents express less warmth (Cheah et al., 2015), provide few verbal or physical expressions of love for their children, and do not encourage autonomy (Supple, Ghazarian & Peterson, 2009).

In recent years, China's economic policy has changed, leading to greater engagement and interaction with international communities. Large cities now contain greater ethnic diversity and, subsequently, a broader range of cultural ideals. There appears to be evidence that parenting practices are changing in China's urban communities. However, there is also a growing awareness that much previous research and many research conclusions were based on comparisons with predominantly white, North American samples and, as such, may have failed to fully understand the Chinese context (Chuang et al., 2018).

Generally speaking, the UK, USA and much of Western Europe place considerable emphasis on personal drives and achievements. They are therefore known as **individualist cultures** and are associated with more individual-focused and independent lives (Wilding et al., 2020). If we consider modern Sweden as an example, historically, Swedish parents had also adopted a largely authoritarian style. However, changing social attitudes precipitated a more relaxed approach (Sorbring & Gurdal, 2011) with children increasingly being regarded as having an equal right to express their opinions. Legislation has helped to cement negative attitudes towards physically disciplining children (Durrant, Rose-Krasnor & Broberg, 2003) while encouraging an awareness of children's rights and the need for gender equality (Eklund & Lundqvist, 2021). Increased egalitarianism has subsequently led parents to change from being primarily directive to supporting children's developing autonomy. In 2012, Putnick, Bornstein and Lansford found parents in Sweden to be warm, loving and respectful towards their offspring.

Time to consider

Xiu and Maja are both 2 years old. Xiu lives in a rural area of China. His family have a traditional lifestyle, with dad providing for the family by working in agriculture and mum caring for the home and family. Xiu's dad is considering moving to the city to find better-paid work. Maja lives in Gothenburg, Sweden. Her parents both work at the university there, so Maja attends the local nursery.

- How do you think the culture they are being raised in will impact Xiu and Maja?

The culture in which a person is raised will be one of the factors that influences the way they see themselves. While collectivists regard themselves as being part of a closely linked community with common needs and mutually supportive goals (Yeh, Arora & Wu, 2006), individualists view themselves as unique and more loosely tied to the group (Lykes & Kemmelmeier, 2014). The example we have looked at shows that the prevailing culture does much to shape the way in which adults raise children. Where there is a belief in cohesion and uniformity, parents encourage children to maintain close relationships with kin. However, where the main focus is on the individual, relationships are looser and independence is encouraged. Similarly, while some cultures embrace and honour elderly family members, in the West, they more commonly live apart, sometimes in institutions.

Beyond Culture and Economy: Natural and Human-made Events

Although countries have their own prevailing culture, sometimes events bring about major changes in family structure. Kinship ties are powerful in sub-Saharan Africa, but the AIDS pandemic left many children living in single-parent families, or in a home without either of their parents (Fauk et al., 2017; Mathambo & Gibbs, 2009). In other areas, warfare or civil unrest have cost thousands of lives. For instance, the United Nations estimates that over 1 million children have been orphaned in Syria. Undoubtedly, the COVID-19 pandemic will produce family rearrangements worldwide, particularly in regions without recourse to vaccines or medical care (Ayuso et al., 2020; Waters, 2021).

Events within the family, and the specific needs of the individuals within it, will also shape many aspects of family life. Later in the book you will have the opportunity to consider some of these in more detail, such as the impact on the family of having a multiple birth (Chapter 9), a preterm baby (Chapter 10) or a child with autism (Chapter 11).

Time to consider

- Do you think that the COVID-19 pandemic has had consequences for the British family unit?
- Do you think there have been any beneficial effects?
- Is any action required to address the issues that have emerged?

Children's Conceptions of Family

When asked, younger children's views of families tend to revolve around the traditional image of a mother and father caring for their children. However, as they get older these concepts change to reflect their own lifestyles and experiences (Powell & Smith, 2018). Children also become progressively more concerned with the quality of the relationship, forming bonds with those adults who provide nurturance and care. This may lead, for instance, to the caring and supportive stepfather being regarded as 'family', while the absent or abusive biological father is not.

The multicultural society in which we live contains a rich variety of traditions and beliefs. It is therefore important that those working with children listen to the child's voice and accept that their experience and notions of family are valid. For instance, many children may have family friends whom they think of as 'auntie' or 'uncle' even though they are biologically unrelated. Anthropology uses the term *fictive kinship* to refer to such people. In some instances, this is based on a spiritual kinship (Cook & Williams, 2015; Marino, 2020), such as that which might be established during religious ceremonies like Christian baptism (Coster, 2016).

Parenting

We need to remain similarly aware that ideas of what constitutes 'good parenting' vary to some extent between cultures. For instance, research suggests that in Western and European societies, 48% of children who are exposed to harsh, authoritarian parenting display symptoms of anxiety and developmental delay. However, in the Middle East, and in Arab cultures where harsh discipline is often part of the cultural norm, only 11% of children display these adverse effects (Mousavi, Low & Hashim, 2016). Similarly, within rural Chinese communities, practices such as harsh discipline and shaming children for negative behaviour are not considered psychologically damaging (Smetana, 2017). However, studies also suggest that it does not necessarily provide the hoped-for improvements in children's wellbeing or educational development (Xia et al., 2015).

Final reflection

While we are inclined to think of 'family' as being a relatively homogeneous concept, we have seen that it is constantly changing and evolving. The way in which we conceptualise family is shaped by the cultures in which we are raised, and by the political forces shaping our society. Changes at a national or international level, such as the pandemic, may change the composition of the family unit, or the way in which it operates. However, each family group is also in a constant state of flux as it is comprised of individuals, each of whom has their own specific blend of thoughts, behaviours, desires and requirements which will shape the experience of those closest to them.

Key points

- Notions of family differ between cultures and within cultures across time.
- The family is an ideological cultural construct, for which there are many definitions.
- The primordial human group in which young children develop offers them the first experiences of belonging to a group and a culture.
- Family continues to be fundamental for children and their development.
- Child-rearing practices are socially constructed and these change over time and are diverse across and within cultures.

Further reading

Office for National Statistics (ONS) – www.ons.gov.uk/peoplepopulationandcommunity/ birthsdeathsandmarriages/families/bulletins/familiesandhouseholds/2021

The Office for National Statistics (ONS) has up-to-date information about the composition of British families. This 2021 version was published in March 2022.

Rana, R., Sood, R., & Bhardwaj, S. (2021) Women and children's well-being in Indian nuclear families during the COVID-19 pandemic. *Journal of Childhood, Education & Society*, 2(2), 178–193. https://doi.org/10.37291/2717638X.202122108

This paper provides insights into the impact of global events on the family unit.

2

CLASSIC PARENTING THEORIES

Christopher Barnes and Kay Owen

Overview

This chapter will consider three of the most prominent theoretical works that have contributed to our understanding of parenting: *good enough parenting* (Winnicott, 1953), *parental styles* (Baumrind, 1971) and *the process model of the determinants of parenting* (Belsky, 1984). We outline the key features of each theory as originally presented, and then evaluate them in light of contemporary research. The theories are presented chronologically to demonstrate how thinking has evolved over the years, and readers are invited to reflect on the relevance of these theories from both a critical and applied perspective.

This chapter will...

- Outline three important parenting theories
- Consider the modern relevance and application of each theory
- Discuss how these theories relate to individual, interpersonal and social contexts.

Key terms

Determinants of parenting; good enough parenting; parental style

Introduction

It is generally accepted that parents and caregivers are one of the primary influences in children's lives, as they organise, structure and place limits on what children can do. Parents fulfil multiple and important functions (Sanders & Turner, 2018), including:

- protecting and nurturing the developing child
- ensuring the child has their basic health needs met
- providing emotional support and love
- enabling the child both cognitively and socially.

As we shall see, parents play a major role in shaping how a family functions (Matejević, Todorović & Jovanović, 2015) and how members relate to one another, thus influencing a child's development across all major domains of functioning (cognitive, socio-emotional and physical). Although parents generally occupy the dominant role (Isaeva & Volkova, 2016), the relationship between parent and child is reciprocal (Tang et al., 2016), with children's behaviour and individual differences impacting the parent and the way in which the parent and child interact. However, thoughts about the balance between these factors differs between theorists.

Time to consider

Before you read about the theories, consider the following:

- What do you think determines the way a person parents?
- Do you think child development is due to parental characteristics, child characteristics, the family's environmental context (home and community), or a mixture of these?
- What other familial, community, cultural and societal factors might influence individual development and the parental relationship?

Winnicott (1953): Good Enough Parenting

Winnicott (1953, 1960) introduced the term 'good enough parenting' to combat the damaging pressures within Western society to become a 'perfect parent'. He noted that many parents believed society expected them to meet their child's every need and they unconsciously strove to conform (Pedersen, 2016).

Winnicott suggested that instantly meeting children's every need is counterproductive because the small frustrations caused by waiting actually aid development. For instance, an infant initially conceives their mother as being a part of themselves. Through having to wait (a short time) for their mother to attend to them when they cry, the child learns that they are a separate being and develops the notion of external reality. Similarly, through encountering minor misfortunes and handling them appropriately, the child learns resilience, coping and life skills – all of which would have failed to emerge had the parent intervened immediately.

According to Winnicott's theory, parents initially sacrifice their own needs and desires in order to accommodate those of their newborn. However, over time (often due to fatigue!) parents fail to maintain these exacting standards and in doing so lapse from being 'perfect parents' to being 'good enough parents'. Attaining the correct balance between over-parenting and neglect is difficult but necessary in order to achieve healthy cognitive and emotional development, and ultimately raise a child with a more rounded character. It is important that the parent remains emotionally available to the child and works to foster two-way communication, but it is only by stepping back a little that parents enable their children to learn tolerance and become independent. Besides basic physical, nutritional and protective needs, the child also requires their emotional needs to be met in the interests of long-term development, optimal functioning as an adult, and security. This broadly requires the provision of:

- consistent and unconditional love
- reasonable and consistently enforced boundaries
- rich and varied stimulation (Hoghughi & Speight, 1998).

As the infant grows, their level of dependence changes: from 'absolute dependence', through 'relative dependence', culminating in 'towards independence', a state where they can manage without maternal care. Winnicott also used the term 'holding' to emphasise not simply the act of physical holding but the environment (e.g. the area, the level of home stimulation or impoverishment) in which children are 'held' and raised. He attested that these factors impact both parenting and, subsequently, child development.

Winnicott (1960) suggested that child development and the establishment of parent–child relations have three key components:

1   'Come into being' – child development is impacted by family characteristics and whether environments are favourable or unfavourable; this incorporates the quality of parental care they receive and the child's inherited potential (not simply their biological potential but the family's socially inherited factors too).
2   'Living with' – refers to establishing a mental representation of the relationship, first between the mother and infant and then later with the father too.
3   'Continuity of being' – whereby the infant grows into an individual through successful adaptation and established relationships.

Critical evaluation and applications

Many would argue that the pressures to be a perfect parent have increased in modern society (Simmons, 2020a) and this has precipitated a rise in intensive or 'helicopter' parenting, where children are closely monitored and overprotected. Furedi (2001) and Shirani, Henwood and Coltart (2012) suggest that parents do not allow their children to learn through creativity, risk taking or free play due to the social pressures exerted upon them. Indeed, the stress placed upon parents to behave or raise their children in certain ways has resulted in some becoming paranoid parents who feel the need to provide overly structured and adult-initiated activities constantly throughout the child's day. Naturally, most parents have their children's best interests at heart, but when this leads to intensive parenting, many more negative outcomes may be seen for children (Schiffrin et al., 2015). In fact, work by Caputo (2007) proposes that children of intensive parents appear to be risk averse and lack self-control. However, children of 'good enough mothers' are more likely to be confident with risk-taking behaviour, will experiment with their play and are able to self-regulate their own behaviour.

Time to consider

Do you think Winnicott's theory is still relevant and representative of families today?

Baumrind's (1971) Typology: Patterns of Parental Authority

Diana Baumrind's seminal work in the 1970s was based on her extensive observations of parents interacting with their preschool-aged children. She found that there are certain key features that consistently distinguish between effective and ineffective parenting styles (Baumrind, 1971; Hart, Newell & Olsen, 2003). Typically, effective parenting includes:

- acceptance and involvement
- control
- autonomy granting

Her work initially identified three distinct parenting styles:

- Authoritarian
- Authoritative
- Permissive

But Maccoby and Martin's (1983) analysis of parental warmth and responsiveness later led them to add a fourth style:

- Uninvolved/neglectful/disengaged (Fan & Zhang, 2014)

These child-rearing methods have differing attitudes towards control, respect and relationships (Mehrinejad, Rajabimoghadam & Tarsafi, 2015). However, when reviewing Baumrind's work, Maccoby and Martin (1983) went further and argued that the two most important areas of parenting are the degree of:

- warmth, support and acceptance (responsivity/support) and
- parental control and expectation (demandingness)

Table 2.1 Summary of parental attributes and style

	Responsive/Supportive	Unresponsive/Unsupportive
Demanding	*Authoritative*	*Authoritarian*
	High warmth	Low warmth or cold
	High control	High control
Undemanding	*Permissive*	*Neglectful/Disengaged*
	High warmth	Low warmth or cold
	No control	No control

Authoritarian parents possess strict ideas about behaviour, expect obedience and are generally themselves the product of authoritarian parents (The Dunedin Study, n.d.). They are highly demanding (Pellerin, 2005), low in responsiveness and warmth, and not very child-centred. Their interactions with their child are generally controlling, power-assertive, coercive, sometimes degrading and high in unidirectional communication. There is little discussion as it is expected that the child should follow orders without question. Children who question this authority may be threatened with punishment, or actually, punished.

Research has consistently discovered negative outcomes for children raised in authoritarian households. These outcomes are primarily related to emotional and behavioural difficulties, including aggression, defiance and anti-social behaviour (Farrant, 2014). Children are more likely to be unhappy and unfriendly to others, may cope less well with life stress and may have adverse life outcomes, including poorer academic attainment. They are often disliked by their peers (Deković & Janssens, 1992), increasing the likelihood of their involvement in bullying – as either bully or victim. Older children are characterised by personality traits that are closely linked to mental health disorders, such as anxiety and depression, and include low self-worth and suicidal ideations (King, Vidourek & Merianos, 2016).

Authoritative parents have ideas about behaviour and discipline which they are willing to explain and discuss with their children. They are highly demanding, but also responsive, warm, attentive, patient, sensitive and are more likely to take a child-centred approach. Research suggests that this parental style is most prevalent among adults who have themselves been raised by authoritative parents (Belsky et al., 2005) and who have formed a secure attachment with their child. In interactions with their child, they make reasonable demands and consistently enforce them. This approach imparts autonomy to the child (Alwin, 2004), allows their natural skills and abilities to flourish (O'Connor & Scott, 2007) and teaches them how to negotiate with others, respect rules and boundaries, and foster positive emotional connections with their family and peers (Yeung et al., 2016). In conversation, parents allow bi-directional communication that encourages the child to express themselves, and when disagreement occurs, they will engage in a joint decision-making process.

As these children age, they are generally much more competent socially (Baumrind, 1991; Deković & Janssesn, 1992; Miller et al., 1993; Weiss & Schwarz, 1996) and academically. They are also more self-assured, display fewer problem behaviours and are able to cope with everyday stressors. Children who have a secure relationship with authoritative parental figures are more resilient when faced with new and unfamiliar challenges, are more able to regulate their own behaviour and emotions (Doinita & Maria, 2015) and approach learning opportunities with confidence (O'Connor & Scott, 2007).

Permissive parents are very responsive to their children but make few demands. In conversation, they allow communication to flow freely and their interactions tend to be child-centred. However, they do not set or enforce rules or discipline (Wischerth et al., 2016), meaning that, ultimately, the child can do almost whatever they want. These apparently lax parental behaviours are generally because the child is loved so much. As a result, the child knows they have freedom and sees no need to seek parental permission for actions.

It is not uncommon for children raised using this parental style to be impulsive, to lack self-control and to achieve poorly at school. As they age, these traits and the lack of rule-setting make them more likely to engage in delinquent and aggressive behaviour (Sarwar, 2016).

Neglectful/disengaged parents are both undemanding and unresponsive towards their children. They show little interest and have little involvement in their children's lives, often being too wrapped up in their own world and issues. Their interactions with their child tend to be rejecting or neglecting and uninvolved. Children therefore largely lack support or guidance and take responsibility for their own behaviour and wellbeing.

Children raised using this parental style frequently have attachment problems as infants and toddlers, and struggle with peer relationships throughout childhood. As they get older, they often exhibit antisocial behaviour, poor self-regulation, substance abuse, risky sexual behaviour, low academic and social competence, and have a tendency to internalise their problems. They find it difficult to make emotional connections or to demonstrate appropriate behaviour and self-control in public (Hughes & Cossar, 2016; Lang et al., 2016).

Parental style is often apparent in how parents talk to their child. Table 2.2 provides an example.

Table 2.2 A typical conversation over a toy between a parent and child by parental style

Parental style	
Sibling 1	'Can I play with that toy now; you've had it for ages?'
Sibling 2	'No, you can't, I haven't finished with it yet!'
Sibling 1	'Mummy/Daddy, they won't share.'

	Authoritarian Authoritative	Permissive	Neglectful	Disengaged
Parent	'Give your sister that toy!'	'Can you please share?'	'Would you like to share?'	*Ignores Child*
Sibling 2	'But why?'	'But why?'	'But why?'	*Siblings continue to argue over toy*
Parent	'Because I said so. Do it right now or else!'	'You need to share because you have had your turn and your sister would like a turn now.'	'Oh, OK. Well share it if you want to.'	*Groans* 'Do what you want, I don't care.'

Critical evaluation and applications

The children

It is now widely acknowledged that effective parenting supports children's holistic development, not only during childhood but throughout life (Kooraneh & Amirsardari, 2015). Indeed, a study by Kaufmann et al. (2000) isolated parenting style as being the major determinant of successful socio-emotional adjustment regardless of the child's sex, ethnicity or socio-economic status. Baumrind regarded authoritative parenting as liable to achieve the best outcomes, and this perspective has been largely supported by subsequent research.

The parents

Metsäpelto and Pulkkinen (2005) discovered that adults who exhibited extroverted behaviours were willing to consider new ideas, had low levels of anxiety and were more likely to adopt an authoritative and nurturing approach to parenting (Desjardins, Zelenski & Coplan, 2008). In contrast, many permissive parents appear to be introverted and display high levels of anxiety (Ghani, Roeswardi & Aziz, 2014), which encourage them to over-indulge and please the child rather than set clear, and potentially unpopular, boundaries. Authoritarian and neglectful parents are also more likely to score highly for narcissism, making them less aware of the child's emotional needs, less empathetic and frequently unresponsive. They may also become overbearing or overly expectant of the young child (Hart et al., 2017) and harsh parenting practices are more prevalent where these have been experienced in their own childhood (Belsky et al., 2005). However, Rudy and Grusec (2006) found that an authoritarian style was associated with higher self-esteem for Middle Eastern families in Canada, but not for Anglo-Canadian families. Interestingly, permissive parents often develop insecure attachments with their children, as they frequently lack the self-esteem and social skills necessary to enforce rules (Ebrahimi et al., 2017).

Challenges

It is important to note that there have been several important challenges to Baumrind's theory. First, it is now widely accepted that the relationship between parent and child is always bi-directional and that the type of parental style adopted by the caregiver can be influenced by the child (Bates & Pettit, 2007). For instance, children who are perceived as being attractive by their caregivers are more likely to illicit positive responses, including affection. In addition, as 'attractive' infants age, this is further reinforced through positive reactions from a range of adults (Langlois et al., 2000). Conversely, when children are regularly disobedient, angry or difficult to manage, it becomes more challenging for parents to adopt an optimal (authoritative) style (Crouter & Booth, 2003).

Second, there is an issue of generalisability, particularly across cultures. Baumrind's theory was based on the principles of Western culture and, in this sense, a more individualistic (**individualism**) understanding of child development. This means there are problems when attempting to apply her theory to other types of cultures, such as **collectivist** ones (Hofstede, 1980, 1983) (see Chapter 1). Indeed, in Baumrind's original research, and then in later research by Dearing (2004), authoritarian and other similarly restrictive parenting practices have been found to be associated with positive outcomes for African American school children. Furthermore, Chao (1994) suggests that an authoritarian parental style does not have a negative effect on Chinese children. In fact, these children are likely to see strict parenting as an expression of love, parental involvement and a tool to promote harmony within the family.

Third, research has demonstrated that caregivers of lower socio-economic status (SES) are more likely to use an authoritarian child-rearing style (Shaw et al., 2004), while those of higher socio-economic status are more likely to be authoritative. There have been several suggestions as to why this is the case, although it is primarily attributed to Westernised beliefs that caregivers from lower economic groups value conformity, whereas higher economic groupings promote autonomy (Luster, Rhoades & Hass, 1989).

Time to consider

- Based on Table 2.2, what sorts of conversations do you think will happen during adolescence?
- Do you think Baumrind's parental styles would be apparent when the child is newly born or during their first year of life?
- Is it possible for children, once they have grown up, to adopt a different parental style from that of their own parents, and what factors might be important in determining this?

Case Study – Lucy's homework

Lucy is 8 years old and attends junior school. She has been finding her work a challenge recently and has not been able to keep up with all her homework. Lucy's parents have been told that she is 'only just meeting expectations' for English and Maths. They have been advised to fit in regular homework sessions after the school day has finished. Lucy's parents have said she will not be allowed to play with friends, watch television or have treats until the work has been completed. The following week Lucy returns home from school and is just about to start her schoolwork when there is a knock at the door. It is Lucy's friends, who live nearby, and they want to know if she can play.

- Using the information in this chapter, how do you think a parent with each of the four named parental styles (authoritative, authoritarian, permissive and disengaged) might respond?
- What conversations might occur?

The Determinants of Parenting: A Process Model (Belsky, 1984)

In 1984, Jay Belsky proposed a model of parenting that comprised three main domains:

- *Parent-related* characteristics (Domain-1), this includes factors such as the parents' own upbringing, their psychopathology (e.g. the presence of mental health issues such as depression) and personality.
- *Child-related* characteristics (Domain-2), this includes factors such as the temperament or characteristics of the child.
- *The family's social context* (Domain-3), this includes factors such as the degree of social support available to the family, their socio-economic conditions, and the quality of the relationship between parents.

Whereas Winnicott's and Baumrind's theories place responsibility primarily with the parent, as you can see, Belsky suggests that competent parenting is influenced by a variety of factors that individually and collectively shape how adults treat their children (Sherifali & Ciliska, 2006). He also proposed that parenting behaviours may change according to circumstances. For instance, a happy, financially stable adult who loses their job may miss their colleagues and become preoccupied by money worries. As a result, they might be less engaged or more short tempered with their child, and the child may respond by withdrawing, or arguing back, triggering further negative responses from the parent. Parenting, Belsky suggests, is therefore a process rather than a fixed commodity, as every change in circumstance or behaviour has a knock-on effect. The way in which someone parents is thus determined by both internal and external factors (Taraban & Shaw, 2018) that will differ both between individuals and across time (McCabe, 2014).

Belsky's original model, which illustrates this process, is redrawn in Figure 2.1.

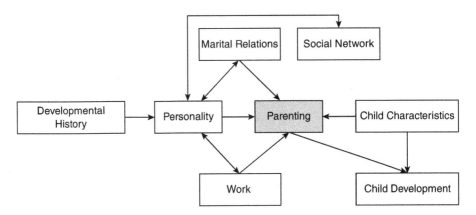

Figure 2.1   Belsky's process model of the determinants of parenting (Belsky, 1984)

The characteristics of the parent

Belsky (1984) suggested that the most important determinant of parenting is the *personal psychological resources* of the parents, as they enable the adult to safeguard both the child and their shared relationship. These resources originate in the parents' own childhoods, as their developmental history shaped their personality and psychopathology in the same way that they are now shaping their child's. The relationship that they had with their own parents will influence how they view both themselves, and relationships with other people. Those who were, for instance, subject to maltreatment when they were younger are liable to carry the psychological and emotional scars into adulthood.

> In general, supportive developmental experiences give rise to a mature healthy personality that is then capable of providing sensitive parental care which fosters optimal child development. (Belsky, 1984: 86)

Belsky, and most other modern researchers, divide parenting into positive or negative attributes. Positive parenting is underpinned by warmth, limit setting and scaffolding (Waller et al., 2015), while negative parenting is inconsistent, harsh, and controlling (Chang et al., 2003). As the relationship with parents has such an impact on a child's sense of self, and their notion of what constitutes socially normative behaviour, many patterns of behaviour are reproduced when people have their own children. When combined with genetic predispositions, this means that people often replicate the parenting style and characteristics of their own upbringing. Evidence now confirms that both positive (Capaldi et al., 2003) and negative attributes (Belsky, Conger & Capaldi, 2009) pass from parent to child, as do some aspects of personality (Belsky & Jaffee, 2006; Prinzie et al., 2009), cognitive-affective processing (Lorber, O'Leary & Kendziora, 2003; Mence et al., 2014), and susceptibility to depression (Wilson & Durbin, 2010).

Whereas mature and psychologically healthy individuals optimise outcomes for children, mentally ill parents, for instance those with episodic mood or personality disorders, often struggle to parent safely, thus increasing the risk of children being maltreated or taken into care (Kohl, Jonson-Reid & Drake, 2011) Similarly, untreated maternal depression is linked to maladjustment in infants and pre-schoolers (Goodman & Garber, 2017), and the children of women who abuse substances have been shown to suffer higher rates of emotional or behavioural difficulties (Risser et al., 2013).

The characteristics of the child

The child's temperament can influence the way in which they are parented, as we discussed in the section on Baumrind's typology (Baumrind, 1971; Cui & Conger, 2008). However, other characteristics of the child can impact on parenting style and behaviour too. For instance, caring for a child with a learning disability is potentially both stressful and demanding, which can result in more punitive child-rearing practices (Hayes & Watson, 2013).

The family's social context

The family's social context can be a valuable source of support, as support from the extended family, a marital partner or the parents' social group will enable the parent to address challenging circumstances and safeguard the child (McCurdy, 2005). Witnessing a positive relationship between their parents promotes wellbeing in children (Cui & Conger, 2008; Tan, Gelley & Dedrick, 2015), in part because it models emotion regulation, but also because it determines the emotional climate of the family and shapes all emotion-related parenting practices (Morris et al., 2017). Thus, children who experience warm, positive relations within their family display more positive and prosocial peer behaviour at school and in their daily life (McHale & Fivaz-Depeursinge, 2010). On the other hand, a fractious (see Chapter 6) or abusive relationship (see Chapter 12) between parents can negatively influence outcomes for children, as can social and economic disadvantage.

Action for Children (2023) estimate that there are currently 3,900,000 children living in poverty in the UK. A lack of money can mean children living in unheated housing and going to school hungry, as well as having to do without the resources or experiences financially secure families enjoy. Poverty is also often linked to insecure accommodation (The Children's Society, 2023) that necessitates frequent changes of home, school, and consequently, friends. Unsurprisingly, therefore, poverty has been found to damage adult mental health and wellbeing (Shields-Zeeman & Smit, 2022) and all aspects of early child development (Roos, Wall-Wieler & Lee, 2019).

Critical evaluation and applications

Belsky's (1984) model was pioneering in its day and has, to a large extent, stood the test of time. There is now broad general agreement that parental behaviours are shaped, not only by the adult's personality, but also by the needs and personality of the child, and by the family's circumstances. Whilst each of these undoubtedly contributes to the way in which people raise their children, Belsky contended that it is the parents' current characteristics which are the most important as they not only impact parenting behaviour, but also shape the home environment. Even in difficult circumstances, optimal parenting is possible as long as the parents' psychological resources are intact.

There are, however, several issues with Belsky's model. For instance, he does not specifically define how developmental outcomes are assessed, yet his early work carries an expectation that parents will take ultimate responsibility for generating improvements against unknown criteria. This criticism needs to be balanced against a substantial body of research that illustrates the importance of parental personality and caregiving behaviours for children, particularly in relation to things such as psychological resilience. Furthermore, research consistently suggests that the children with the most favourable outcomes tend to live in cohesive, supportive, two-parent families, where there are no major pathologies (Zeitlin, Ghassemi & Mansour, 1990).

Parental Cognitions

While the theories and studies reported in this chapter have focused on many important aspects of the parent–child relationship, there has been less emphasis on the role parental cognitions may play in shaping parent–child interactions. Parental self-efficacy beliefs (Bandura, 1997) are those the parents hold about their ability to successfully perform parenting tasks and activities and can be both domain general (applying to parenting broadly) or domain specific (applying to a specific context). Reviews (Coleman & Karraker, 1997; Fang et al., 2021; Jones & Prinz, 2005) have illustrated that parents who feel more efficacious are likely to display greater parental competence and positive parenting practices, strategies and behaviours (Coleman & Karraker, 1997). Evidence also suggests that parents who feel more competent in their role are less likely to experience parental depression (Jover et al., 2014; Porter & Hsu, 2003) and stress (Dunning & Giallo, 2021; Gordo et al., 2018), and cope better with difficult life demands (Cooklin, Giallo & Rose, 2012). Indeed, our own work proposes that parents who perceive themselves as more competent in the parental role have higher self-esteem and greater attachment (Barnes & Adamson-Macedo, 2007), which is the strongest predictor of a good quality of life (Knibb, Barnes & Stalker, 2016).

Final reflection

In this chapter we have considered three major theoretical approaches to parenting: good enough parenting (Winnicott, 1953), parental styles (Baumrind, 1971), and the determinants of parenting (Belsky, 1984). The information and research presented suggests that parenting is shaped though a multitude of individual and environmental circumstances which collectively influence the developing child. The poorest outcomes are associated with neglectful or overly punitive parental behaviours, whereas responsive, loving, caring and supportive parents enable children to flourish. We must take care, however, not to assume that there is a uniformly 'right' way to parent, as much depends on broader social and cultural norms.

Key points

- Parents are generally seen as the primary agents who constrain, organise and structure their children's experiences and personalities.
- The link between individual characteristics (of the parent and child) and the social context have been identified as important factors in shaping the parental relationship.
- Parenting is a complex, bi-directional and dynamic process which is likely to impact on development right across the lifespan.
- The parental relationship is part of a broad and complex array of factors that shape the future development of children and the life-long consequences of the behaviours they go on to adopt.

Further reading

Belsky, J., Conger, R., & Capaldi, D.M. (2009) The intergenerational transmission of parenting: introduction to the special section. *Developmental Psychology*, 45(5), 1201–1204.

Hoghughi, M., & Speight, A.N.P. (1998) Good enough parenting for all children: a strategy for a healthier society. *Archives of Disease in Childhood*, 78(4), 293–296.

Hughes, M., & Cossar, J. (2016) The relationship between maternal childhood emotional abuse/neglect and parenting outcomes: a systematic review. *Child Abuse Review*, 25(1), 31–45.

Taraban, L., & Shaw, D.S. (2018) Parenting in context: revisiting Belsky's classic process of parenting model in early childhood. *Developmental Review*, 48, 55–81.

Each of these articles provides deeper insights into the work of the individual theorists mentioned in this chapter.

3

DEVELOPMENTAL THEORIES AND THE FAMILY

Christopher Barnes

Overview

Over the last 120–150 years, many developmental theories have been created and conceptualised. These theories have been used to help us to understand individuals' development across their lives and the importance of parent and child relationships. While we covered parenting-specific theory in Chapter 2, this chapter goes further. It highlights the range of classical and contemporary developmental theories to aid your understanding of the context in which parenting and family relationships occur. You will read about the major theories of development in turn. First, we examine the Psychoanalytic theories, which cover Psychosexual and Psychosocial theories. Next are the Learning theories of Behaviourism and Social Cognitive theory. Third are the Cognitive Developmental theories, which include Piaget's theory of cognitive development and Vygotsky's socio-cultural theory. Finally, we will cover the Developmental Systems theories. There is also Ethological and modern Evolutionary theory which will be covered in the chapter about attachment. We will consider the importance of each theory in turn, identifying its core features and the classic experiments used to test its assumptions, evaluating each one and illustrating how they have been applied to real-world contexts.

This chapter will…

- Provide a definition of what development is and some of the core principles and origins of developmental theory
- Outline some classic and contemporary psychological theories
- Emphasise the key strengths and weaknesses of the classic and contemporary theory.

(Continued)

> Key terms
>
> Development; family; Psychoanalytic Theory; Learning Theory; Cognitive Developmental Theory, Developmental Systems Theory

Introduction

In this chapter, 'development' is defined as the process by which people grow and change over the course of their lifespan. It can be understood through the changes and similarities that children and adults display, and it relates to any of the major domains of functioning – biological and physical, cognitive and socio-emotional (Bornstein & Lamb, 2017).

Development occurs most rapidly during early life, which perhaps accounts for why there is a multitude of theories and perspectives on offer to explain it. It is important to note that many classical theories took opposing positions when explaining how development happens. These positions have to a large extent been described as 'conceptual splits' (Overton, 2006). The split approaches include:

Nature vs Nurture – whether development is largely influenced by nature (such as a person's genetics) or nurture (such as a person's experience from interacting with the environment).

Activity vs Passivity – whether people actively shape their own development or are passively being shaped by forces beyond their control.

Continuity vs Discontinuity – whether development happens in a stable, gradual way without any sudden changes (continuity) or in a 'stage-like' way where we see significant jumps and advances to new levels of functioning (discontinuity).

Universality vs Context-specificity – whether changes during development are common to all people (universal) or different across people from different cultures, in performing particular tasks, in specific contexts or in individuals (context-specific).

The table below will help you to identify the similarities and differences between developmental perspectives on the basis of these core conceptual splits. You may find it helpful to take note of this before you go any further.

Scientific Origins of Developmental Psychology

Most people would agree that the *scientific* origins of the study of human development began with the work of Charles Darwin (1809–1882), a British naturalist who is best

Table 2.3 A summary of the major developmental theories in relation to the core concepts

	Psychoanalytic	Behaviourism / Social Learning Theory	Piagetian	Sociocultural theory	Ethological / Evolutionary	Developmental Systems Theory
Nature-Nurture	Both	Nurture	Both	Both	Nature	Both
Activity-Passivity	Active	Passive and Active respectively	Active	Active	Active	Both
Continuity-Discontinuity	Discontinuous	Continuous	Discontinuous	Continuous	Both	Both
Universality-Context specificity	Universal	Context Specific	Universal	Context Specific	Universal	Context Specific

known for his theory of evolution. Darwin drew parallels between child development and human evolution, prompting many scientists to begin theorising about child behaviour. Following Darwin, the 'normative period' was pioneered by Granville Stanley Hall (1844–1924), who is widely thought of as the founder of the child study movement (Cairns & Cairns, 2007). Hall's most significant contribution was to devise, along with his student Arnold Gesell (1880–1961), a theory that explained development in evolutionary terms, and as a process of maturation that was genetically determined. Hall and Gesell used the normative approach to develop methods that would enable scientists to measure a wide range of characteristics (e.g. everyday knowledge, interests and fears), believing this would offer a standardised way to establish (by age) what typical development should be like. Gesell's work expanded this approach into other areas, such as motor abilities and social behaviours. At about the same time, the French psychologist Alfred Binet (1857–1911) was also using a normative approach to study development. Binet and his colleague Theodore Simon (1948) were commissioned to identify children with learning difficulties in order to remove them from standard education and place them in special education classes. In doing so, they developed the very first intelligence test. The scale they produced was later translated into English at Stanford University and became known as the Stanford–Binet Intelligence Scale. The scale and the score it produced for a child were found to accurately predict their school achievement. A lot of attention was then focused on this approach and, in what would be considered controversial nowadays, it was used to understand and compare people of differing genders, ethnicities and family backgrounds.

An overview and evaluation of each major developmental theory now follows.

Psychoanalytic Theory

Psychosexual theory (Sigmund Freud)

Psychoanalytic theory was pioneered by Sigmund Freud (1856–1939), who proposed that personality development, and the way parents manage their child's instinctual impulses, will affect the traits they later display. As part of his theory, Freud outlined three concepts of personality that comprise the individual (Freud, 1930). They are the Id, Ego and Superego (Freud, 1917, 1923).

The Id is the term Freud used to describe the part of personality that is driven by our instinct, the Ego is the term for the rational part of our personality and the Superego encompasses our internalised moral standards. Freud notes that the Id is present from birth; it functions only to serve and satisfy our innate biological instincts. The Ego is the conscious part of personality that relates to the child's ability to perceive, remember, learn and reason, and has the job of finding socially approved means of gratifying the child's instincts. Therefore, as the Ego matures, the child becomes better at controlling their irrational Id and finds more appropriate ways to gratify their needs. The Superego, on the other hand, is the seat of conscience; it develops between the ages of 3 and

6 years and is involved in the process of internalising the moral values of the child's parents. Once the Superego emerges, the child can understand whether they are good or bad by themselves and don't need their parents to tell them so. These three components – the Id, Ego and Superego – gradually develop and are integrated across a series of five psychosexual stages: Oral, Anal, Phallic, Latency and Genital. Each stage covers a period from birth up until 12 years of age.

Psychosocial theory (Erik Erickson)

Erickson revised Freud's theory and termed it a 'psychosocial theory'. He emphasised the socio-cultural rather than sexual determinants of development (Erickson, 1950). It is worth noting that while Erickson accepted many of Freud's ideas, he differed in two important ways. First, he saw children as having an active role in their adaption to their environment rather than being passive reactors to biological urges and moulded by their parents. Second, Erickson placed much less emphasis on sexual urges and far more emphasis on social and cultural influences.

Evaluation of psychoanalytic theory

Psychoanalytic theory has largely been criticised because of its *lack of scientific method*. Freud used a limited sample of mainly adult women who had known psychological problems. In addition, Freud did not use any actual data to test his theories, his theory could not predict a person's development and he did not write up his observations until some time afterwards. However, there are two important benefits of Freud's work. First, while the theories have been difficult to test, he was one of the first people to emphasise the importance of unconscious processes underlying human behaviour. This insight is now supported by modern psychological research. Second, Freud also made links between early life experiences in the family and the impact they could have on later development.

Learning Theories

Behaviourism (James Watson and Burrhus Skinner)

Learning theory can be split into two predominant theoretical positions – what we can term 'classical behaviourism' and 'social cognitive theory'. Behaviourism was created largely because these theoreticians wanted a way to approach human development that was objective and rooted in concrete observations of overt behaviour. This was in stark contrast to the methods used by the psychoanalytic approach, which was based on speculation about unconscious motives or unobservable behaviour that was not testable or replicable in some way. Therefore, behaviourists wanted to use very precise and testable methods. They used controlled experiments to determine how children react to various environmental influences. Two of the most well-known and influential proponents of behaviourism were James Watson (1878–1958) and Burrhus Skinner (1904–1990).

Watson's (1913) work was based on Pavlov's (1927, see 1960) research and they believed that development was the result of learned associations between external stimuli and observable behaviour. However, whereas Pavlov conducted his work with animals, Watson was able to demonstrate that human infants' fears and emotional reactions were acquired rather than inborn. In one of his many experiments, Watson presented a 9-month-old child with a gentle, white rat and, over months, each time the infant reached for the rat, they would bang a loud steel rod with a hammer. The child eventually began to associate the white rat with the loud noise. The resulting learnt behaviour meant that even the sight of the rat became sufficient to produce a fear response in the child (Watson & Rayner, 1920). Watson termed this type of learnt behaviour *classical conditioning*.

Skinner also made an important discovery. He proposed that animals and humans repeat acts that result in a favourable outcome and suppress those that lead to unfavourable outcomes. He termed this phenomenon *operant conditioning* (Windholz, 1987). Actions that increase the chance of something happening came to be known as 'reinforcers'. Reinforcers can be positive when something pleasant is given, or negative, when something unpleasant is removed. Similarly, punishers can be positive or negative. They are classified as "positive" when something is added to the situation, even if it is unpleasant or aversive (for instance: spanking). Something would be termed a "negative punisher" when something pleasant (for instance: a toy that is being fought over) is taken away. Therefore, operant learning is associated with external stimuli (reinforcers and punishers) that impact our behaviour and in which voluntary acts or operants become either more or less probable based on the consequences they produce.

Social cognitive theory (Albert Bandura)

Bandura's social cognitive theory (1977, 1989, 2006) is the other major learning theory and his contribution was to introduce the importance of motivation and self-regulation to our understanding of human behaviour. In contrast to the classic behaviourists, Bandura suggested that people were not just passively controlled by brain mechanisms that respond to the external environment. Instead, he proposed that individuals use their senses, motor control and cognitive abilities to actively achieve tasks and complete activities, and to give their life meaning (Harré & Gillet, 1994). Bandura was also instrumental in highlighting the importance of *observational learning* for children. Indeed, he suggested that much of children's behaviour was the result of their observing others. The term originates in his classic studies, often referred to as the Bobo doll experiment (Bandura, Ross & Ross, 1963), whereby children who witnessed aggressive behaviour re-enacted this behaviour when prompted.

Evaluation of learning theories

One of the strongest benefits of learning theories is their precise and testable nature (Horowitz, 1992). However, too much emphasis is placed on the environment as the key determinant of human behaviour and too little on the role of cognition. Nevertheless, Bandura's work did go some way to address this issue. For example, whilst classic behaviourists saw learning as a passive process, Bandura emphasised the importance of mental processes that impact learning and behaviour. Therefore, social cognitive theory is different from classic behaviourism as it focuses on how children learn through observation, and how they attend to, retain, reproduce and motivate themselves to produce behaviour.

Cognitive Developmental Theories

Cognitive developmental (Jean Piaget)

Jean Piaget (1896–1980) is one of the most well-known and influential developmental psychologists of all time. Piaget thought of cognition (or intelligence) as being part of a biological system and similar to other systems within the human body. For Piaget, cognition was always organised and adaptable. The main component of cognitive development was what he referred to as 'schemas' – organised patterns of thought or action that the child constructs to make sense of some aspect of their experience. He believed that children actively construct new understandings of the world around them and they do this from the time they are born through interaction with their environment. Therefore, when a child observes things that go on around them, they will test out new objects, make connections or associations between events and become inquisitive when their current understanding does not explain a new experience.

During his early work, Piaget began to devise a theory of cognition (Piaget, 1952) based on observations of his own children (and others) in real-world situations. Through these naturalistic observations, Piaget proposed four developmental stages: sensorimotor, preoperational, concrete operations and formal operations. Together, these stages cover the period from birth up to 12 years. They are outlined below. In this chapter, the focus will be on the period from birth to 8 years. Therefore, only a brief mention of the later stages will be made.

Sensorimotor stage (birth up to 2 years)

The first stage of cognitive development is what Piaget referred to as the *sensorimotor stage*. From the outset, Piaget proposed that babies are born with an ensemble of 'innate' schemas. These schemas can be thought of as like reflexes because they are believed to be rigid cognitive structures. As the baby engages in reflex behaviours, they acquire knowledge about the world around them. But innate schemas do not remain innate for very long. In fact, in functioning for the very first time they change – they assimilate, they encounter disequilibrium and they accommodate – and become *acquired schemes*.

Time to consider

Let us consider a real-world example of how a schema becomes modified and adapted in a newborn. Initially, babies will suck (the schema) on anything in order to pacify themselves. But as they get older their schema changes and they become selective about what they really want (i.e. they suck to gain something they really want – food). In this way, their schema changes and adapts as their understanding and interaction with the world increases.

- Can you think of any other examples of behaviours that become modified and adapted in the early years of a child's life?

Let's now skip ahead to when babies reach 8 to 12 months. Piaget believed that at this age infants start to understand their physical world and achieve one of the major milestones of the sensorimotor stage, *object permanence*. This is when the infant realises that objects continue to exist even when they are outside the infant's sensory capabilities. As the child reaches 18 to 24 months of age, they are able to hold mental representations that are more complex and flexible and persist over time. The child is no longer dependent solely on the direct input of information from the world and instead has begun to develop more complex ideas and concepts.

Preoperational stage (2 to 7 years)

In the second stage of cognitive development, Piaget suggested that children begin to possess and use systems of mental representation and symbolic thought (e.g. using language, memories and imagination) (Müller & Racine, 2010). The goal for children is to achieve operational thought, even though they still lack the ability to grasp some concepts of situations and events. The most prominent limitation on a child's thinking at this stage is their inability to see the world from anything but their own point of view (i.e. egocentrism). One of the most famous studies to demonstrate this was Piaget and Inhelder's (1956) 'Three Mountains Task', in which children were presented with a model of three distinctly different mountains and were shown photographs of the model from different viewpoints and asked to choose the picture that best represented the scene from Piaget's perspective. As Piaget sat at a different angle to the model from the child, his view of the model was different from the child's. In almost all cases, children under the age of 8 selected the photograph from their own viewpoint. Piaget believed that this demonstrated that the child was incapable of taking on the perspectives of others or seeing the world in a different way.

Concrete operations (7 to 12 years)

The third stage of cognitive development is where the child achieves reversible thinking (that some things or actions can return to their original state) and the ability to decentre (where a child can consider more than one aspect or perspective of a situation). Therefore, during this stage we see the emergence of operational structures, where operations are internalised actions that are reversible. Operational thought means we possess the ability to internally know about an object or an action's reversibility and do not need to see it enacted. For example, the child may know that ice can melt into water but that it can also return to ice if frozen again. However, the child's thoughts at this stage are not yet fully formed and thought is limited to concrete physical reality. While the child can deal with representing objects internally, these objects need a real exist- ence and cannot be more abstract. For example, if you posed a problem to a child and said Lucy is taller than Kacey-Jo; Lucy is smaller than Maia; who is the smallest? Then the child would have real difficulty working this out in their heads. However, if you gave the child three dolls (Lucy, Maia and Kacey-Jo) and asked them the same question then they would have no difficulty because the objects are real.

Formal operations (12 years +)

The fourth and final stage is formal operations. Piaget (1972) suggested that during this period the child develops the ability to think abstractly without the need for things to have a concrete reality. During this stage, thought becomes more like that of adults and children become able to solve problems in their head, working through the validity of any given propositions and conceiving other worlds or possible realities.

Socio-cultural cognitive theory (Lev Vygotsky)

Vygotsky (1978, 1987) was a Russian psychologist who, similar to Piaget, saw children as being active in shaping their own development and as explorers of their environ- ment. However, the main difference between these two theoreticians was the way they viewed the process by which children think and learn. For Vygotsky, collaborative dia- logue was key, and this was achieved through social interactions with more knowledgeable others (experts), such as adults or older children. He recognised that collaborative dialogue was necessary for children's acquisition of things like cultural values, beliefs and problem-solving strategies (Vygotsky, 1962, 1978). In contrast to Piaget's views, children were not independent thinkers. Children's ability to think and grow was viewed as a socially mediated process wherein communities and parents play a crucial role in moving development forward (Vygotsky, 1978, 2004; see also Rowe & Wertsch, 2002).

In addition, Vygotsky (1978) believed that, as a child acquires the skills they need in life, there will naturally be some that fall just beyond the child's ability. He also noticed that children tend to do better during activities when supported by someone who is more knowledgeable. Vygotsky (1978, p. 86) termed the distance between the actual development level of the child, (which is determined by independent problem solving), and the level of potential development achieved through adult guidance or the collabo- rative assistance of more capable peers as the 'Zone of Proximal Development' (ZPD;

1978, p. 86). Therefore, when children are close to mastering a particular ability, they can achieve success if they are supported by someone who has already mastered the skill, or guided by someone who is able to provide a supportive framework (often referred to as *scaffolding*). Support or guidance can enable children to be successful in an otherwise unachievable activity. Therefore, when educators or parents work with children, they should aim to do activities slightly above the child's developmental level as this will drive development forward.

However, Vygotsky placed more importance on the role of language, in contrast to Piaget. Piaget believed that thinking came prior to language, and that even though preschool children talk to themselves a lot, he felt their use of language was relatively unimportant. Vygotsky, on the other hand, believed that language was an integral part of cognitive development. Vygotsky suggested that much of the interaction between parent, sibling or educator relies on talking and listening (Eun, 2010). He believed that the 'self-talk' preschool children engage in regulates their behaviour and internal thought process. Specifically, Vygotsky referred to this self-talk as *private speech*, stating that repeating or imitating phrases heard from more knowledgeable others was key to the child's ability to solve problems. As the child gets older, the overt private speech becomes internalised and more adult-like, whereby people become able to have conversations with themselves in their own heads.

Evaluation of cognitive developmental theories

In much the same way as *psychoanalytic theory*, Piaget has been criticised for using an approach (at least in his early work) in which he did not use set questions, have a standard method of presenting his tests or use tests that were relatable to the child. He may also have inadvertently 'led' children to express views that were not their own by using misleading questioning. He also failed to account for or address the sorts of social factors important when learning (e.g. collaborative dialogue with more knowledgeable others), such as those identified by Vygotsky (1979).

One of Vygotsky's greatest achievements was to define the ZPD, which can be applied to any learning scenario and any age group. However, he was much less clear about how development (more broadly) happens. (Chaiklin, 2003, pp. 42–46). Nevertheless, Vygotsky emphasised the importance of the 'experts' that surround the child and their role in enhancing the child's development. While it is important to recognise that Vygotsky drew attention to the social transmission of knowledge across the generations, he neglected to account for the impact of children's biological endowment on their cognitive development.

Time to consider

Potty training and sleeping through the night are things we have all had to master and some of you may even have first-hand experience of getting your own child to use the toilet or to sleep through the night! This exercise is designed to help you think about the major developmental theories covered so far and to apply them to a real-life setting. So, consider the following questions:

- How would each of the major developmental theories conceptualise the issue of toilet training or sleep training?
- Using one of the theories, what tips or methods would you suggest to help parents to toilet train or sleep train their child?
- What, theoretically, might explain the failure of your tips or methods?

Developmental Systems Perspectives

In contemporary developmental science, developmental systems theory (DST) is a broad-based perspective that has been built over time, and formed from a wide range of other theories (including, Developmental Contextualism [Lerner and Kauffman, 1985], Life-span Developmental Theory [Baltes, 1987], Action Theory of Human Development [Brandstadter and Lerner, 1999], Life-course Theory [Elder, 1998], Bioecological Theory of Developmental Processes [Bronfenbrenner, 1979], Dynamic Systems Theory (DST) [Thelen and Smith, 1998], Holistic Person-Context Interaction Theory [Magnusson, 1995], Epigenesis [Gottlieb, 1992], and Holistic, Developmental, Systems-Oriented Perspective [Wapner, 1981]). The resulting perspective has coalesced into a single unified position that shares a series of guiding principles we will cover in the sections below. However, it is important to point out that DST is not a 'theory' in the hypothetico-deductive sense (Moore, 2016) (i.e. where a theory may be created from observable and testable methods and allow for predictions to be made that can be independently verified), and is better thought of as a framework (Godfrey-Smith, 2001) for understanding human development.

This perspective, as noted by Overton (2013), sees humans as active in shaping their own development, that they can be relational, spontaneously active rather than just reactive, adaptive, self-creating, self-organising and self-regulating. This framework also attempts to establish the nature and components of development at the individual level (set within the person's domains of functioning; physical, cognitive and socio-emotional), as well as accounting for inheritable and evolutionary factors. Furthermore, the DS perspective is said to adopt relational positions (Overton, 1998; 2006). This means that theorists are interested in understanding the sorts of reciprocal and multi-directional relationships that exist within a person (e.g. between biological and psychological systems), as well as between people and extending to their wider contexts and environmental settings. In this sense, there are no split conceptual positions from a DS perspective as they are not trying to argue whether development is caused by inborn factors versus environmental ones. Therefore, unlike classic theories (such as behaviourism) DS theory does not dichotomise development in this way. Instead, DS theory accepts that both aspects (e.g. nature and nurture) play a role to varying degrees and that this may vary from attribute to attribute.

Shared components

There are in total four shared components or principles that underly this perspective, including:

i   Change and relative plasticity,
ii Relationism and integration across the levels of organisation,
iii Historical embeddedness and temporality, and
iv The limits of generalisability, diversity and individual differences.

In the first of these components (**change and relative plasticity**) it is proposed that people have an ability to change, adapt or recover (sometimes in response to adversity) across the entirety of their lifespan. Though any potential for change may be constrained by past developments (e.g. if the child has experienced severe trauma) or contextual conditions (e.g. if the child lives in an area of high deprivation) (Lerner and Kauffman, 1985).

The second component is **relationism and integration of the levels of organisation** (Bronfenbrenner, 1974; Zigler, 1998). This means that the basis for developmental change is the result of the relations between the multiple levels of organisation and that change can happen through the relations across these levels. These levels span right from within the individual; their inner biological (genetic) and psychological (e.g. attitudes, beliefs or emotional states), to the social relations between people, at community and sociocultural level, set within both designed and natural environments. In addition, a DS perspective refers to the relationships between factors and across the levels of organisation as 'relational units' or 'change units'. This means that factors from any level of organisation can impact on variables from any other and it is these inter-level linkages that should be the focus of analysis.

Next is the notion of **historical embeddedness and temporality**. This component proposes that all levels of organisation within the developmental system are integrated with historical change. This means that developmental patterns (e.g. onset of language or acquisition of numeracy skills) may be different from one historical period to the next. Furthermore, when developmental change happens it is important when it occurs during the lifespan (temporality). For example, things such as childhood trauma can be more detrimental to later development the earlier in life they occur.

The final component is **the limits of generalisability, diversity and individual differences**. As we discussed in Chapter 1, development is affected by the social, cultural and political environment in which the child is raised. These environmental factors provide a backdrop, and the attitudes, beliefs and behaviours of those directly involved in child rearing then lead to individual differences.

In this book, we illustrate how DS theory has been used to understand individual development in the early years (see Chapters 12 and 13). For those readers interested in seeing an application of DS theory to parenting and child development the work of Lerner is a useful starting point (Lerner et al., 2002; 2014). Though research also exists that has explored the role that parents and/or caregivers play in:

i   The experience of grief and the loss of primary relationships (e.g. parental) (Alvis et al., 2022),

ii   Parent–child relationships following a premature birth (Blackburn & Harvey, 2019),

iii Parents' involvement in schooling (Li, Wang & Liu, 2020).

Evaluation of developmental systems perspectives

Perhaps one of the more major contributions of DST is the attempt to resolve the conceptual splits embedded within most of the other major developmental theories. The DST resolves the split through its adoption of relational positions (Overton, 1998; 2006). This means that rather than explaining development from the perspective of one extreme theoretical fixed position (e.g. Nature or Nurture), a DST perspective seeks to explain how much of one or other position accounts for any given attribute (e.g. Language development).

Furthermore, as documented by Griffiths, P.E., & Tabery, J. (2013) DS perspectives are criticised for the fact that predictions cannot be made when using it (Tooby et al., 2003, p. 860), and that it makes causal analysis impossible. However, DS proponents argue that it is not a theory in a hypothetico-deductive way (i.e. we can make hypotheses on the basis of the theory and test them in some way), and that instead it needs to be thought of as a framework. Using DST as a framework allows us to map more precisely the complex nature of an individual's context and understand the factors that exist both within and between a person's developmental system.

Final reflection

In this chapter, we have considered some of the major theoretical approaches to development. The theories highlight the capabilities of children, how they change across their lifespans and the role parents play in fostering their child's development. While each theory has its own pros and cons, they offer us a critical insight into parent–child relationships, and useful ways of thinking about the context in which they take place.

Key points

- The major developmental theories have focused largely on early childhood. They offer us diverse perspectives to aid our understanding of development and family relationships.
- Theoretical approaches have often taken up conceptually 'split' positions: nature vs nurture, activity vs passivity, continuity vs discontinuity and universality vs context-specificity.
- Developmental systems theory attempts to resolve the inherent problems and conceptual splits found in the other major psychology theories of development.

Further reading

Bornstein, M.H., & Lamb, M.E. (eds) (2017) *Developmental Science: An Advanced Textbook.* London: Psychology Press.

This textbook is one of the leading publications in the field of developmental science, that offers readers a comprehensive overview of human development.

Griffiths, P.E., & Tabery, J. (2013) Developmental systems theory: what does it explain, and how does it explain it. *Advances in Child Development and Behavior*, 44, 65–94.

This article offers readers further critique and discussion of developmental systems theories.

Lerner, R.M., Rothbaum, F., Boulos, S., & Castellino, D.R. (2002) Developmental systems perspective on parenting. *Handbook of Parenting*, 2, 315–344.

This article provides an insightful application of developmental systems theories to parenting.

4

ATTACHMENT AND ATTACHMENT DISORDERS WITHIN THE FAMILY

Christopher Barnes and Kay Owen

Overview

Attachment relates to the strong bond that children form with a primary caregiver. It is commonly regarded as a major developmental milestone and something that shapes future relationships. In this chapter, we explore the main theoretical approaches to attachment and discuss how researchers and clinicians have attempted to measure it. We also consider factors that can make, or break, the attachment bond and what impact the quality of the bond has on a child's development.

This chapter will…

- Provide an overview of attachment theory
- Outline some of the major ways of measuring and differentiating attachment relationships
- Illustrate factors that may impact attachment formation
- Outline attachment-related disorders.

Key terms

Attachment; secure attachment; attachment disorder; strange situation; sensitive period; separation anxiety; internal working model, parental sensitivity

---

Introduction

In Chapter 3 there was an opportunity to read and think about the major developmental theories. One theory we mentioned there but did not discuss was ethological theory, which explains development from a bio-evolutionary perspective. It suggests there is:

- **a critical period** – some behaviours can only emerge at a fixed point of development. If conditions are not met at that point, it is not possible for the behaviour to develop later.
- **a sensitive period** – there are times when the infant is particularly sensitive to environmental influences, and these are the best times to develop specific behaviours.

The Development of Attachment Theory

Early research into attachment was conducted with animals. Lorenz (1935) researched geese and Harlow (1958) researched monkeys. They concluded that infants attached themselves to an adult who they then relied on for support. When separated from their primary carer, the infants became withdrawn and unhappy, and later struggled to integrate with others of the species. Both Harlow and Lorenz believed that this was adaptive – in other words, it was an inbuilt drive necessary for survival.

Bowlby was aware of the application of ethological theory to explain this aspect of animal behaviour and he proposed that children also display a wide range of pre-programmed behaviours, which are designed to meet human needs and ensure survival. In the first year of life, he suggested, one of the greatest needs is relationship formation. These ideas were popularised by the famous *Attachment and Loss* series of books (Bowlby, 1969, 1973, 1980; Bowlby, May & Solomon, 1989). However, Bowlby continued to expand his theory of attachment beyond this point, often working with Mary Ainsworth, whose scientific investigations helped him to revise and evidence his claims.

Bowlby believed that children have an inbuilt 'attachment behavioural system' which seeks out a person who is available, attentive and responsive. He suggested that as soon as they find someone who meets these criteria, babies are instantly and visibly happier, more confident and more playful. However, the opposite is also true. When left alone, infants become anxious. They cry, call out for their attachment figure and may attempt to locate and cling to them. If the attachment figure is repeatedly unresponsive or unavailable, the child, in an attempt to safeguard themselves, may become *detached* and move from reliance on others to self-reliance. Bowlby's major contention, therefore, was that, dependent on the family setting, children may form a secure and lasting attachment to a primary caregiver, or an insecure one that can cause complications in future relationships.

Bowlby and Ainsworth worked from the Tavistock Clinic in London, as did James and Joyce Robertson. The Robertsons were social workers, and they became concerned by the distress they noticed among young children when they were hospitalised and separated from their carers. They coined the phrase *separation anxiety* to account for this phenomenon, which was integrated into attachment theory (Robertson & Robertson, 1989). The Robertsons made a short film called *A Two-Year-Old Goes to Hospital* to create broad public awareness of childhood attachment.

Phases of Attachment

Bowlby suggests that there are four distinct phases of attachment:

Phase 1: Pre-attachment (up to 6 weeks) – Ethologists believe that certain types of behaviours will help the individual to survive and develop typically (Gottlieb, 1996). One of the best examples is the newborn's cry, but others are a newborn's gaze, smile or grasping. Crying is seen as an innate mechanism that is biologically programmed to attract caregivers and which caregivers are biologically programmed to respond to. So, the infant's cry ensures their needs are met. It also increases the likelihood of contact and the prospect of forming primary emotional attachments.

Phase 2: Attachment in the making (6 weeks to 6–8 months) – In this phase, we see that infants prefer those who are familiar (such as a parent) to strangers. They display a range of behaviours when they are around this person that may include babbling, smiling or laughing. At this point, they understand that their actions can result in a response from their caregiver.

Phase 3: Clear-cut attachment (6–8 months up to 1.5 years of age) – It is at this point that infants become attached. The child will often demonstrate separation anxiety when the caregiver leaves their proximity. They may also use the caregiver as a secure base from which to begin their exploration of the environment.

Phase 4: Reciprocal relationships (1.5–2 years onwards) – Infants typically go through rapid changes in their cognitive and communicative abilities during this period. They are able to gauge and understand caregiver behaviour, feelings and mood, which aids the formation and development of their relationship.

Bowlby (1969, 1973; Bowlby et al., 1980) also suggested that there are four defining features of the attachment bond:

1   Proximity maintenance (the desire to remain close to the attachment figure).
2   Separation distress.
3   Safe haven (retreating from danger to a place close to the caregiver).
4   Secure base (using the caregiver as a safe place from which the child can explore the world).

Measurement and Stability of Attachment

Mary Ainsworth initially researched 'maternal deprivation' while working at the Tavistock Clinic with Bowlby, but later continued her research in Africa and America. She noted that, while there were some important differences in how children behaved when separated from their mothers, it was their behaviour at the point of separation which was the most telling. Perhaps one of the most well-known experiments regarding attachment is Ainsworth's *Strange Situation* (Ainsworth et al., 1978). The experiment explored how infants used their caregiver as a secure base, and how they responded to moments of separation and reunion with their caregiver. The Strange Situation is composed of eight discreet episodes (or phases). These are detailed in Table 4.1.

Table 4.1 The Strange Situation (Ainsworth): episodes, events and observed action or behaviour

Episode	Present/Duration	Events	Action/Behaviour observed
1	Caregiver, baby and researcher (30 seconds)	The researcher shows the caregiver and baby into the laboratory room and then leaves.	None
2	Caregiver and baby (3 minutes)	The caregiver is seated and asked not to interact. The baby is sitting and playing.	Using the caregiver as a secure base
3	Stranger, caregiver and baby (3 minutes)	The stranger enters the room, they (i) sit quietly, (ii) talk to the caregiver, and then (iii) approach the baby (spending 1 minute for each). The mother exits the room.	Reaction to the stranger
4	Stranger and baby (≤ 3 minutes)	First **SEPARATION**. The stranger's behaviour is oriented towards the baby, and they offer comfort if required.	Separation anxiety/ distress and how the baby reacts to the stranger
5	Caregiver and baby (≥ 3 minutes)	First **REUNION**. Caregiver greets/ comforts baby if needed. The stranger leaves the room. After a short while, the caregiver leaves room, saying 'bye-bye'.	Reaction to the caregiver during the reunion
6	Baby (≤ 3 minutes)	Second **SEPARATION**. Baby is alone.	Separation anxiety/ distress
7	Stanger and baby (≤ 3 minutes)	The stranger enters room and orients their behaviour to the baby, offering comfort if needed.	Whether the baby can be comforted by a stranger
8	Caregiver & Baby (3 minutes)	Second **REUNION**. Caregiver greets/comforts baby if needed. The stranger leaves the room.	Reaction to the caregiver during the reunion

Key: (≤) time spent is equal to or less than indicated; (≥) time spent is equal to or more than indicated.

The work of Ainsworth et al. (1978) identified three distinct patterns of behaviour which were organised into attachment categories. A fourth was added later by Main and Solomon (1986, 1990), with Mary Ainsworth's approval. Each category has its own distinct set of infant behaviour characteristics that indicate the quality (security) of the attachment relationship. You may see them referred to by different names, so we have provided the most common ones here:

Secure – About 60% of children fall into this category. They use their caregiver as a secure base and feel able to play and explore their environment in the knowledge that they have support if needed. They may engage with the stranger while their attachment figure is present. When separated they become upset but believe their attachment figure will be responsive to their calls. Upon reunion, they actively seek them out and clearly demonstrate they are glad to see them again. Any distress is quickly overcome.

Insecure, anxious-avoidant – About 15% of children regard their attachment figure as being non-responsive and unreliable. They avoid or ignore their caregiver, explore very little and are unresponsive to the stranger when their caregiver is present. They may appear unconcerned when the caregiver leaves the room and once again ignore or avoid them during a reunion. They have learned that their carer will either reject or ignore them and so have *detached* from their caregiver and devised a strategy that allows them to be close enough for protection, but far enough away to avoid overt rejection. Ainsworth and Bell (1970), surprised by the children's apparent calm, investigated further. By monitoring heart rate, they discovered that the infants were actually extremely distressed, but by avoiding direct contact, they prevented the distress from becoming overwhelming.

Insecure, resistant/anxious-ambivalent – About 10% of children appear 'clingy' in that they do not leave the side of the caregiver, and do not use them as a secure base. When the caregiver leaves the room, they usually become distressed, but some may appear resentful, and others seem resigned to the carer's absence. When reunited, they may cling to the caregiver or combine this behaviour with anger, throwing tantrums and in some cases using physical aggression. This is the least well understood of the attachment styles.

Disorganised/disorientated – In the late 1980s this fourth category was added after Ainsworth, and some of her graduate students, noticed that there were children who did not fully fit into any of the existing categories. This attachment style is marked by confused behaviour that fluctuates between wanting to approach their caregiver and completely withdrawing. The children often have flat, emotionless facial expressions or show tense movements of the sort that usually indicate stress. Approximately 15% of children are said to fall into this category, although this may be higher in populations considered to be 'at risk'. It is also thought to be allied to maternal depression. Many of the mothers were bereaved, often having lost their own mothers (Main, 1977).

Measuring attachment: Q-sort

The Attachment Q-sort (AQS or Q-methodology) provides an alternative procedure to the Strange Situation to assess a child's attachment category. It was designed to measure the interaction between a child and their caregiver (Waters & Deane, 1985) and involves looking at prototypical secure base behaviour (i.e. the balance between a child's independent exploration and how much they seek proximity to their primary caregiver; (Cadman, Diamond & Fearon, 2018). Unlike the Strange Situation, the Q-Sort process is conducted under safe and low-stress conditions, typically in the home environment, and is unlikely to involve any artificially created attachment-related stress situations (Cassidy & Shaver, 2008). Instead, the child and carer are observed during their spontaneous everyday activities over a 1-2 hour period. Variations of this method include the Attachment Network Q-sort (ANQ), which allows measurement of relationship-specific attachment styles for multiple attachment figures (Kamperman et al., 2020). The Q-sort approach involves the use of 90 cards on which are written statements regarding dependency, social interaction and social perceptiveness. A highly trained observer sorts the statement cards into a predefined number of piles (typically nine), ordered from those that are most descriptive of the child to those that are least descriptive. For example, some cards ask about the level of fussiness when the child returns to the mother after playing, and others about the child's willingness to accept comfort from non-parental adults if the child is upset or injured (Cadman, Diamond & Fearon, 2018). The piles can be arranged in a rectangular order (so that the distribution of cards means each pile contains an equal number) or quasi-normal (where more cards are placed in the centre piles than at the extremes). This latter method results in a more considered approach by the observer who must weigh up which statements are most characteristic of the child. Once the placement of the cards is finished, criterion scores from each individual card are then used to establish the extent of attachment security. This is done by comparing each child's score to a pre-existing value created by experts and that represents the prototypical behaviours of a securely attached child. The benefit of this approach means:

i   a children's tendency to use a parent or caregiver as a secure base is understood,

ii how the secure base phenomenon relates to attachment classifications,

iii what is considered normative secure base behaviour, can be better understood (APA, 2022).

Time to consider

In light of Ainsworth's work, consider the following:

- Are there any problems with measuring attachment using the Strange Situation procedure?

- Do you think attachment formation is possible between children and childcare providers?
- In what ways do you think attachment formation may be impacted if primary caregivers work full-time?

The Impact of Attachment Styles

Research suggests that children who experience warm, sensitive and responsive parenting or early care will develop a secure attachment (Golding, 2008). This allows children to build trust in others and develop positive expectations about future relationships (Delaney, 2017). It also builds security and self-confidence, which enables them to explore the wider world (Bomber, 2007).

On the other hand, insecurely attached children commonly demonstrate ambivalent behaviour, instability, preoccupation, avoidant responses, and there is generally a lack of cooperative communication between parent and child (Golding, 2008; Porter and Hsu, 2003). Insecurely attached children are more likely to go on to develop psychosis and anxiety disorders in later life (Russo et al., 2018).

Time to consider

Why do you think the attachment bond between a child and their primary carer has such a major impact?

The Internal Working Model

Allied to the development of attachment, throughout infancy and early childhood, children are also constructing what Bowlby termed an *internal working model* (IWM). The relationship with their primary carer – whether it is positive (a caregiver who is accessible, dependable and responsive) or negative (a caregiver who is unresponsive and unavailable) – subsequently acts as an unconscious template for future relationships.

Bowlby introduced the concept of working models in *Attachment* (Bowlby, 1969), the first of the *Attachment and Loss* series, with early explanations having much in common with the psychological concepts of scripts and schemas. He suggested that, in an attempt to understand and predict human behaviour, children create mental models based on their own experiences, which they then apply (largely unconsciously) to new situations. As children usually have intense interaction with a relatively limited range of people, these figures provide the basis for the child's mental models which then become internalised.

The IWM has three components:

- Model of self
- Model of others
- Model of relationships.

So, the child who enjoys a secure attachment with a loving and attentive adult develops an IWM that says they are worthy of love, that others are reliable and cooperative, and that relationships bring satisfaction and happiness. However, a child who is rejected or neglected builds an IWM that says they are unworthy, that others are untrustworthy, and that relationships are unsatisfactory.

Once internalised, the IWM is difficult to change. However, as the child grows, their experiences may lead them to develop alternative or conflicting models. They might recognise that their view of themselves or of others is distorted, inaccurate or outdated. Bowlby viewed this conflict as being at the root of most of the psychopathologies he saw in his clinical work and believed that it had to be articulated and addressed before the individual could move forwards (Shaver, Collins & Clark, 1996).

Factors that Impact Attachment Formation

Critical/sensitive periods of attachment

So, what happens in situations where a caregiver is not available, for instance when children are taken into institutional care? One of the most shocking news stories of 1989 was the lack of care children received at an orphanage in the Romanian city of Bacău. Under the leadership of Nicolae Ceaușescu, abortion and contraception were forbidden. This led to an increase in the birth rate and, subsequently, a high number of children being put into state care. Political decisions and the economic circumstances of the country meant that many state-run orphanages went into decline, resulting in children suffering abuse and neglect. Cases such as the orphanage at Bacău triggered research into the impact of severe institutional neglect on developmental outcomes. Some research suggests that even discrete periods of early deprivation can cause changes in brain structure that are long-lasting (Hodel et al., 2015) and can impact later cognitive and socio-emotional development (Greenough et al., 2002). Research specifically focused on institutionalisation indicates that children may also experience behavioural and emotional difficulties, including in relationship formation. However, Gunnar and Reid (2019) suggest that, in cases where children aged between 1.5 and 3 years join an adoptive family, 38% will develop fully formed attachment within three months of joining the family, and up to 90% within the seven to nine months after adoption (Carlson et al., 2014). Furthermore, early intervention involving moving the child from an institution into a high-quality family environment can result in a return to more typical brain growth (Bick et al., 2015).

Parental/caregiver sensitivity

Another factor that impacts attachment is the extent to which a caregiver interprets and responds appropriately to their child (Mesman, Oster & Camras, 2012). Parental sensitivity will often mean that the caregiver will be consistent, responsive and warm to their child. By contrast, caregivers who engage in less physical contact with their child or react negatively to infant distress are more likely to have a child who is insecurely attached. Indeed, work by McElwain and Booth-LaForce (2006) demonstrated that attachment security was related to sensitivity to distress at 6 months of age. Gerlach et al. (2022) suggest that early parental sensitivity may be a protective factor against distal (e.g. poverty, single parenting, migration, low education) and proximal (e.g. parental disagreement or arguments, risk of child maltreatment and/or neglect, child's poor health condition) familial risk factors. In addition, Cooke et al. (2022), in their recent meta-analysis, suggest that parental sensitivity is particularly associated with children's externalising behaviour problems rather than with internalising problems. Externalising problems are observable behaviours such as conflict and aggression, whereas internalising problems are difficulties within the self, such as anxiety or depression.

Individual differences

When children are born prematurely, or possess a developmental disorder of some sort, it may impact on their behavioural development and, subsequently, on the interactions that occur between parent and child. For example, in Chapter 10, we learn about the typical disposition of a child born early and how they may react to their caregiver differently compared with babies born at full-term. In particular, premature babies may exhibit lower levels of alertness, they may have fewer periods of wakefulness (Harrison, 1992), less activity and be less responsive to social stimulation (Crnic et al., 1983a; Eckerman et al., 1994). These sorts of behaviours may make it more challenging to read babies' behavioural cues and respond sensitively to them. Indeed, Larsson, Nyborg and Psouni (2022) suggest that the quality of family interactions and developmental outcomes is more crucial for prematurely born babies as compared to term babies. Therefore, obstacles and challenges in family interactions may ultimately impact attachment and relationship formation. Similarly, infant temperament may also play a part in the type of attachment style children go on to form. For example, work by Takács et al. (2020) indicates that infant temperament during the weeks after birth may have a long-lasting impact on the mother–child relationship. Research by Abuhammad, AlAzzam and AbuFarha (2021) indicates that when an infant is considered to be 'easier', it has a stronger impact on whether mothers understand their infant's needs in an accurate way and in a timely manner.

> ## Time to consider
>
> How might the mental ill health, such as depression, of the primary caregiver impact attachment formation?

Developments and Critiques of Bowlby's Theory

- Bowlby's rudimentary notions of the IWM were developed by Main, Kaplan and Cassidy (1985) and then by Bretherton (1985), while the work of Main and Solomon (1986, 1990) helped to demonstrate that attachment could not simply be classified as secure or insecure. Main and Solomon (1986) proposed the addition of a *disorganised attachment* category to encompass the unusual behavioural patterns often seen among children raised in adverse environments.
- Michael Rutter studied and critiqued many aspects of Bowlby and Ainsworth's work, providing alternative models for viewing attachment. Notably, in his book *Maternal Deprivation Reassessed* (1972), Rutter argued that children could form attachments to carers other than the mother, or to multiple adults. Although it had been the norm for mothers to remain at home with their children when Bowlby initially formulated his theory, he subsequently amended it to incorporate fathers, grandparents and professional carers. This helped to move the theory from being a monotropy to recognising that a child can have multiple attachment relationships.
- Rutter (1979) also challenged Bowlby's assertion about the impact of insecure attachments in infancy, saying that while it would increase vulnerability to psychopathologies, it did not make them inescapable. Instead, he proposed that severe deprivation and poverty were significant predictors of later problems.
- Bowlby postulated that there was a critical period for attachment. Recent research demonstrates that it is more accurate to talk of a sensitive period. For instance, adopted children generally form secure attachments even when they were not adopted as babies.
- Many feel that concepts have been overgeneralised and applied without taking due account of other factors that influence behaviour (Weinfield et al., 1999). Indeed, in everyday life, about a third of children who have a sensitive and responsive parent do not demonstrate the behaviours associated with secure attachment.
- Scholars have also questioned Bowlby's assertions that attachment is instinctive rather than learned, and that the effects of neglect are irreversible (Harris, 1998).

Attachment Disorders

The Diagnostic and Statistical Manual of Mental Disorders, Fifth Edition (DSM-V), describes two main types of attachment disorder:

i   Reactive Attachment Disorder (RAD),
ii   Disinhibited Social Engagement Disorder (DSED).

However, it is important to note that, even though exact prevalence figures are unknown, RAD and DSED are rare clinical conditions (Allen, 2018). Seim et al. (2020) suggest that during childhood, if children are exposed to adverse experiences (such as neglect, maltreatment, deprivation or abuse), it may result in a broad range of psychiatric conditions and/or psychosocial problems (Hughes et al., 2017; Sonuga-Barke et al., 2017), but only in severe cases will it lead to a diagnosis of a Reactive Attachment Disorder or Disinhibited Social Engagement Disorder.

Reactive Attachment Disorder (RAD)

In this type of disorder, diagnoses are typically made after the ninth month of age, with symptoms generally appearing before the child is 5 years old. While the full criteria are listed in the DSM-V, it is important to note that there are certain core features that distinguish it from other similar diagnosable conditions (e.g. autism). In the case of RAD, the child will be emotionally withdrawn towards their caregiver and they will show persistent social and emotional problems. It will also be evident that the child's emotional needs (e.g. comfort or interaction) will have been persistently unmet. Some studies have found that a diagnosis of RAD will more likely result in an increased chance of being classified as having a disorganised attachment pattern (Pritchett et al., 2013).

Disinhibited Social Engagement Disorder

This type of disorder is typically characterised by a pattern of behaviour, whereby the child may actively approach unfamiliar adults. They may demonstrate behaviour that is overly familiar with others or shows a willingness to leave them with minimal hesitation or venture off even when they are in unfamiliar environments (Guyon-Harris et al., 2018). The child may also have experienced extremes of insufficient care, such as social neglect or deprivation, frequent changes of primary caregiver, or being brought up in unusual settings that place limitations on the ability to form an attachment. Recent meta-analyses suggest that children displaying higher levels of Disinhibited Social Engagement behaviour (DSEB) are more likely to have an insecure or disorganised attachment style (Zephyr et al., 2021).

Attachment disorder: Implications for later development and family relationships

Given that these disorders are more likely to occur because of severe adverse experiences, and in some cases because of institutional care, a number of research studies have investigated later outcomes in relation to attachment disorders. For example, Guyon-Harris et al. (2019a, 2019b) conducted two studies using data from the Bucharest Early Intervention Project (BEIP), which was a prospective examination of foster care as an alternative to institutional care in Romania. Their analysis (Guyon-Harris et al., 2019a) suggested that children diagnosed with DSED during early childhood had associated and reduced functioning during early adolescence, such as in familial and peer relationships, academic performance and physical and mental health. Similarly, their second study (Guyon-Harris et al., 2019b) investigated children diagnosed with RAD. They suggest that the variation and trajectory of RAD are impacted by the quality of foster care (including the timing of family placement) and the length of time children spent in institutional care. More recently, research by Zephyr et al. (2021) investigated parental behaviours associated with DSEB in children living with their biological parent(s) and exposed to substantiated maltreatment. Part of their reason for conducting this study was to understand any pertinent factors associated with the general caregiving environment that remain difficult to test when children are in placed environments. Their findings suggest that even when children are from high-risk 'intact' families, and were never institutionalised, they still show DSEB, although this was only to a small extent.

Final reflection

Based on the evidence considered here, the attachment bond between a child and their primary carers would appear to have a considerable impact on the infant's sense of wellbeing and on their future ability to form and maintain relationships. While Bowlby's work has been critiqued by modern scholars, it was undoubtedly a seminal theory that shaped thinking about how adults interact with young children. It is therefore important that those who work with the very young recognise the need to provide reliable and responsive care.

Key points

- The work of John Bowlby – as part of the broader ethological theory – provides a framework for understanding the phases of attachment formation during the first years of life.
- Mary Ainsworth's Strange Situation provided a method to categorise the types of attachment pattern infants form with their primary caregiver.
- Attachment formation may be impacted by adverse childhood experiences, carer sensitivity and individual differences.

- Severe life circumstances may lead to disordered attachment patterns. However, in many of these cases developmental plasticity enables children to recover and experience typical functioning.

Further reading

Gleason, M.M., Fox, N.A., Drury, S.S., Smyke, A.T., Egger, H.L., Nelson, C.A., et al. (2011) Validity of evidence derived criteria for reactive attachment disorder: indiscriminately social/disinhibited and emotionally withdrawn/inhibited types. *Journal of the American Academy of Child and Adolescent Psychiatry*, 50(3), 216–231. DOI: 10.1016/j.jaac.2010.12.012

This article provides a useful insight into the longitudinal impact and outcomes for children with an attachment disorder.

Gleason, M.M., Fox, N.A., Drury, S.S., Smyke, A.T., Nelson, C.A., & Zeanah, C.H. (2014) Indiscriminate behaviors in previously institutionalized young children. *Pediatrics*, 133(3), e657–e665. 10.1542/peds.2013-0212

This study illustrates the potential impact of institutionalised care upon children's attachments.

Oosterman, M., & Schuengel, C. (2007) Autonomic reactivity of children to separation and reunion with foster parents. *Journal of the American Academy of Child and Adolescent Psychiatry*, 46(9), 1196–1203. DOI: 10.1097/chi.0b013e3180ca839f

This article examines the effect of foster care upon children and the factors that may enhance or be detrimental to child outcomes.

Smyke, A.T., Dumitrescu, A., & Zeanah, C.H. (2002) Attachment disturbances in young children. I: The continuum of caretaking casualty. *Journal of the American Academy of Child and Adolescent Psychiatry*, 41(8), 972–982. 10.1097/00004583-200208000-00016

This study looks at some of the differences between socially depriving environments (institutionalised and home) and their impact on attachment formation.

5

MODERN PARENTING: IDEOLOGIES, IDENTITY AND EXPERIENCES

Helen Simmons and Christopher Barnes

Overview

Parenthood is a multifaceted and diverse concept that is impacted by a person's history, political and geographical context, cultural and social norms, individual differences and family circumstances. In this chapter, we explore ideologies of what it is to be a mother and father, how people transition to parenthood and experience being a parent, and how they seek information, as well as access support, through online media.

This chapter will...

- Discuss ideologies of motherhood and fatherhood
- Explore the transition into parenthood and the experiences of parents
- Consider how parents are informed by web-based platforms.

Key terms

Fatherhood; ideologies; motherhood; social media; surveillance; web-based platforms

---

Introduction

There is much talk about what it means to be a parent. The conversations and thoughts we have about parenthood are packaged together with assumptions, ideals and societal expectations concerning what it should look like because parenthood does not exist in a vacuum. It is a dynamic, multifaceted and multi-level role. Parents change across their lifespan, as do the conceptions about what it means to be a parent. In this chapter, we explore some of the broad theories and narratives about parenthood and how they impact our understanding of parenthood. We speak about mothers and fathers separately, with the intention of presenting the unique conceptualisations and challenges they each face.

Motherhood Ideologies

Ideologies regarding motherhood are not a new phenomenon. Constructs of what makes a 'good mother' have existed throughout history. What does vary, though, is the form that these ideologies take. As social constructs, characterisations of effective mothering will vary historically, globally and socially.

Dominant discourses relating to motherhood do have one agreed narrative, the fundamental importance of motherhood. As Wiesner-Hanks (2010, p.95) states, 'many psychological theorists view one's relation with one's mother as the central factor in early psychological development, with some arguing that this is not culturally specific but innate'.

An innate drive to become a mother, an idea some have contested, has become a 'master narrative' - in other words, a 'story' that forms the basis of many other theories and ideas (Kerrick & Henry, 2016, p. 1). This belief in an innate drive to be a mother has, through policy and intervention, subsequently served to 'regulate women's activities and behaviours' (Wiesner-Hanks, 2010, p. 95). Whether a woman becomes a mother or not, through social construction, politics and ideologies, 'motherhood is central to the ways in which [women] are defined by others and to their perceptions of themselves' (Phoenix, Woollett & Lloyd, 1991, p. 13).

The regulation of and political intervention into the lives of women is not just a historical construct, but something very real within the professionalisation (Furedi, 2008; Hardyment, 2007; Phoenix et al., 1991) and surveillance (Simmons, 2020) of modern motherhood. By exploring the ideologies and norms of modern motherhood, it is possible to consider the factors that influence both the development and the potential impact of these constructs.

The science of good motherhood and intensive motherhood

Ideologies of motherhood, whether traditional or contemporary, can be exacerbated by dominant psychological discourses that are embedded in government directives and intervention strategies. Most recently, the idea of a 'good mother' has been defined through the lens of 'scientific motherhood' (Hamilton, 2021, p. 9). With a reliance on neuroscience, an explanation for human behaviour is provided, along with a criterion for effective motherhood, which must be met to ensure the meeting of the developmental milestone, secure attachment and positive behaviour for children.

Described as 'neuromania' (Macvarish, in Lee et al., 2014, p. 166), scientific motherhood is an associated ideology that enforces the idea of standardised norms and holds parents responsible for ensuring their children meet them. In doing so, it therefore also 'negates state responsibility' for child development (Burman, 2008, p. 154).

Hamilton (2021), in her Black feminist analysis of intensive mothering in Britain and Canada, made comparisons between scientific motherhood and intensive motherhood. First explored by Hays (1996), intensive motherhood is an ideology brought about through the 'cultural contradictions' (Hays, 1996, p. 3) of modern motherhood, whereby women are encouraged to be 'good mothers' through ensuring a nurturing home environment while simultaneously meeting modern standards of securing successful career outcomes. Hamilton (2021, p. 18) proposes that scientific motherhood and intensive motherhood call on 'mothers to seek expert advice about an endlessly long list of specific behaviours but also requires that women retain this information to exercise the "right" parenting choices'.

It is important to acknowledge that ideologies, including 'intensive motherhood', have been challenged as coming from a 'place of privilege' (Henderson, Harmon & Newman, 2015, p. 513). In their exploration of the effects of intensive motherhood, Henderson et al. (2015, p. 513) state that:

> This model of mothering has been critiqued for overlooking the very different ways of doing motherhood, including the voices of lesbian, bisexual, or transgendered mothers, those from varying socioeconomic backgrounds, as well as mothers of colour.

Narratives regarding modern motherhood are distributed through structural surveillance (Henderson, Harmon & Houser, 2010; Simmons, 2020) in the form of government intervention and via the media. In their exploration of motherhood ideologies and myths in American magazines, Johnston and Swanson (2003, p. 22) found that 'there are clearly racial and class biases in the social construction of good and bad mothers'. The traditional model of motherhood, according to their content analysis, is white, middle class, educated and does not work outside the home. This model is reinforced through media representation and is 'politically sanctioned', with myths of motherhood presented as 'natural, instinctual, and intuitive, as opposed to cultural, economic, political, and historical' (Hardy, 2000, cited in Johnston & Swanson, 2003, p. 22).

Time to consider

Mothers are being negatively affected by the presence of unattainable standards of perfection, regardless of their beliefs about intensive mothering. (Henderson et al., 2015, pp. 522–523)

- What are your reflections on this quote?
- What factors have added to these 'standards of perfection'?

Experiences of Modern Motherhood

When considering the impact of motherhood ideologies, it is useful to relate to current contexts and information platforms. In modern motherhood, the notion of 'expert' has changed. Historically, mothers may have accessed parenting books and popular parenting gurus as figures of expert advice, outside of their own local networks. This may have included John Bowlby, Donald Winnicott and Penelope Leach, and more recently, Jo Frost and Gina Ford (Davis, 2012; Hardyment, 2007; Simmons, 2020). However, through technological advances, the platforms that mothers have turned to for advice have changed and mothers now look to parenting forums, websites and other popular platforms for support and guidance.

Parenting forums as the modern 'expert'

With online support for new parents, such as *Babycentre* (Babycentre, 1997), *Mumsnet* (Mumsnet, 2000) and *Netmums* (Netmums, 2000), there is more information than ever for new parents. These platforms are often grounded in discussion boards and the sharing of ideas and tips regarding challenging aspects of new parenting (including sleep, infant feeding, care routines etc.). They can therefore provide empowering opportunities for mothers to find agency and autonomy in their role. The other side of the coin, though, is that modern platforms may also bring opportunities for unwelcome judgement, comparisons and increased feelings of inadequacy. Academics such as Lee et al. (2014) are concerned that *Mumsnet* and other such forums provide a space that is at best judgemental and at worst promotes bullying and aggressive attitudes.

Foster, Longton and Roberts (2003), the co-founders of *Mumsnet*, collated many of the postings submitted by parents on a wealth of different subjects. Their reflections offer an insight into the underpinning philosophy embedded into their platform, which is:

> From teething troubles to meddling mother-in-laws [sic], there's not a dilemma faced in the first year of your child's life that you won't find on these pages. (Foster et al., 2003, p. 1)

Case Study – Ruth's reflections

Despite the popularity of parenting platforms, research conducted by Simmons (2020) revealed some apprehension by new mothers regarding how far to trust opinions and views shared online. For example:

Because he was my first, I was very nervous about using anything that wasn't NHS guidelines or anything like that or just other people's advice, I was a bit dubious. So yeah, for him it was more NHS and midwife and health visitor websites and that kind of thing, just to get their sort of, advice. I didn't tend to use the 'mumsnets' or things like that much. It's just too many opinions, you just want to go to one place that's got the information. And that's it, whereas if you start ... one person says one thing, another person says another thing and you're just in a worse state than you were before cos you've just got too much information. (Ruth)

Time to consider

Consider Ruth's reflections as a new mother alongside the philosophy offered by *Mumsnet*'s co-founders.

- How do they compare?

Social media platforms

For some mothers, engagement with social media platforms (Facebook, Instagram, etc.) can help to create a feeling of community, something that was particularly important during the global Covid-19 pandemic, when support and human connection was so limited. However, not all users find social media use beneficial. McDaniel, Coyne and Holmes (2011) suggest that social media platforms can reduce connectedness. They argue that mothers use them to 'look at pictures and status updates but may not receive much support in return' (McDaniel et al., 2011, p. 1515). This reduced connectedness may go some way towards explaining the rise in the phenomenon of 'mommy blogging', as labelled by Beaupre Gillespie and Schwartz Temple (2011, p. 147). This involves the development of interesting websites, through which women share their motherhood experiences and 'online musings' (Beaupre Gillespie and Schwartz Temple, 2011, p. 147) with other mothers.

Research that explored the rise in blogging in recent years, and its links to maternal wellbeing, found that 'blogging predicted feelings of connection to extended family and friends which then predicted perceptions of social support' (McDaniel et al., 2011, p. 1509). Valchanov, Parry, Glover and Mulcahy (2016, p. 51) suggest that through social networking mothers can 'turn to the internet as a source of community, which helps them connect, communicate and share'.

For some mothers, the use of social media platforms can result in a growing feeling of inadequacy, which is exacerbated through images of perfection and idyllic family life that is shared online. Valchanov et al. (2016) make links to ideologies of motherhood, including 'intensive mothering' (Hays, 1996, p. 97), and how portrayals on social media may differ from the private reality. These contemporary constructions of motherhood, according to Valchanov et al. (2016, p. 53) can result in anxiety for mothers who feel:

> they are never "good enough" …[contributing] to the internalization of ideologies, which are then used to assess, describe, and scrutinize personal and societal mothering behaviours.

Henderson et al. (2015, p. 524) consider the implications of such narratives and suggest that:

> Even women who do not subscribe to these ideologies are at-risk [of] experiencing increased stress and anxiety and decreased self-efficacy in the face of the pressure to be perfect and guilt for not living up to high mothering expectations.

The notion that ideologies, including those emphasised via social media platforms, can invade the lives of women, despite a stark awareness that the projection of life embedded into posts and stories do not reflect the reality of everyday life, is worrying. This concern is magnified by Douglas and Michaels (2005) and their argument that the most powerful source of surveillance and pressure within 'new momism' comes via media and social media platforms. The projection of perfection and ideologies of motherhood as natural and instinctive are reinforced through an 'unattainable image of infinite patience and constant adoration' (Douglas & Michaels, 2005, p. 2).

Whatever its impact, the shift in the way new mothers network digitally with family and friends is apparent, and it is important to recognise the influence that those platforms have within modern motherhood.

Focus on research

Research by Simmons (2020) involved several participants sharing their experiences of using social media platforms:

> Our phones are so readily available, and we have these apps you know … we create these groups, and you know, it can turn into a bit of a monster really, that gets bigger than you need it to be. (Kate)

> I think what makes parenting very different these days, like with the whole Facebook thing and social media thing … people put up snapshots and snippets! But you do start to get used to it, don't you, and you start to realise the truth, don't you, cos you know that it can't be perfect all the time! (Louise)

> I've had weeks where I don't look at Facebook and you actually feel well … happier! And generally, people put the best of what they're doing on it and you're thinking 'oh my god, people are living the best all the time!'. So, I find that getting away from Facebook sometimes, that helps. (Gemma)

Time to consider

How do the reflections of the new mothers above compare with the research offered by Henderson et al. (2015)?

Modern Fatherhood

As we have seen during the first part of this chapter, multiple ideologies exist about motherhood, and in this next section, we turn our attention to those that concern fathers. It may be unsurprising to hear that most of the literature about parenthood is weighted heavily towards women. Even when men's experiences are investigated, they tend to be bound up and presented from a joint familial perspective (i.e. of both parents) rather than an individual one. Furthermore, several studies report on the underrepresentation of men in parenting research. Indeed, Phares et al. (2005) reviewed research in the field of developmental and paediatric psychology and found that (of those studies reviewed) only 2% had father-only participants. This is a trend that has continued to be reported in more recent literature (Daniels, Arden-Close & Mayers, 2020; Davison et al., 2018; Leach et al., 2019). The disparity is important to acknowledge since it identifies that fathers' needs are not being fully represented, despite recent changes to parental leave and a move towards greater equality following the birth of a child in the UK. There are several reasons why this might be. For example, historically, much of the parental burden has fallen to women. Research tends to recruit from mainly female-dominant populations unless fathers are specifically targeted. Finally, it may be that men have limited interest or capacity to take part in the research. Whatever the reason, numerous attempts have still been made to conceptualise what fatherhood is. There is unlikely to be one clear answer. Due to the complexities surrounding fathering, there is likely to be a range of multilevel and dynamic factors at play: the individual differences between men, fathers' recent historical past and experiences of being fathered, social and community-based attitudes and pressures towards fatherhood, the cultural and religious beliefs that inform fathering, and the political narratives that shape the broader ecology of parenthood.

Transition to fatherhood

Consequently, as men move through parenthood there is a shift in their status as an individual and the identity that shapes them. In Habib's (2012) review of the 'transition to fatherhood', he outlines some of the key elements in understanding the emergence of becoming a father. Habib highlights several ways of thinking about paternal involvement. Evidence is provided that suggests that (i) *engagement* (time spent in the act of caregiving), (ii) *accessibility* (the time that fathers have available), and (iii) *responsibility* (decision making on behalf of the child) are all implicit and positive indicators of paternal involvement that will likely lead to better outcomes for the child. Alongside this exists an organic but complex and changing role throughout a father's lifespan (Parke, 2000), with Habib documenting five main types of fathering role:

- **Remote** – where the father displays little or no interest in the child(ren).
- **Provider** – the father is seen as the person who earns the main income of the household and in this sense has a more 'traditional' function.
- **Assistant** or **secondary parent** – where the father is seen as a helper to the mother.
- **Shared caregiver** – where the father is seen as equivalent to the mother and shares the tasks and duties they perform.
- **Primary caregiver** – where the father has the main responsibility for the child(ren).

Time to consider

In light of Habib's work, consider the following:

- What do you think determines the type of fathering role a person has?
- Is it possible for men to transition between or occupy more than one type of fathering role?
- What sort of child outcomes might we see for each fathering role?

Naturally, when men transition to the role of 'parent', changes are seen at an individual and social level that may result in both positive and negative outcomes. These changes may impact on things such as the beliefs men have in their competence and confidence to perform the role (Barnes et al., 2021; Trahan, 2018). They may impact how a man attaches and bonds to their child (Warren, 2020), and the extent to which he experiences mental health difficulties as a result of child-rearing – anxiety (Leiferman et al., 2021), depression (Solberg & Glavin, 2018) and stress (Canzi et al., 2019). There is evidence, too, that more needs to be done to understand the sorts of needs men have and how they would like to be supported (Baldwin et al., 2019). Indeed, a systematic review (Baldwin et al., 2018) was conducted to identify fathers' experiences in terms of their mental health and wellbeing. The findings suggest that during the transition to fatherhood men experience significant changes to their identity, confront challenges during the adjustment to this new role and need to overcome any associated negative feelings. There are challenges to the intimate partner relationship too. It is not uncommon for many couples to experience decreased satisfaction in their relationship (Doss & Rhoades, 2017). Nevertheless, where partners do manage to work collaboratively, their collaboration acts as a positive and protective feature that leads to enhanced cohesion and better outcomes for the family unit (Morrill et al., 2010).

There are, of course, societal and community-based expectations and beliefs that shape what paternal identity 'looks like', all of which are bound to the social and cultural norms of the period. Regardless of the era when fathering happens, it is likely to be influenced by a range of complex factors that are dynamic, open to change and determined by the contextual factors at play in his environment. Furthermore, the intergenerational aspects of fathering will also come into effect. For example, research conducted with African American populations suggests that childhood experiences, interactions and relationships with fathers have a knock-on impact on their parenting role, level of involvement with their children and their responsibilities (Allen & Doherty, 1996; Roy & Dyson, 2010). Work by Cooper et al. (2019) further identifies that those men who reported having more positive interactions and involvement with their fathers were in turn more likely to be actively engaged with their children.

When considering the impact of parenting on children, we cannot easily separate fatherhood from motherhood. In most circumstances, even when the family structure is different, the context is dynamic. Nevertheless, Johansson (2011) proposes several ideologies of fatherhood and the way fatherhood has been constructed (i.e. thought or spoken about):

- **Functionalism** – this dominant discourse of family life and parenthood came about and was predominant in the 1950s and 1960s when fathers were depicted as heads of the family and mothers were described as having emotional and expressive functions.
- **Modernity** – as a discourse, modernity places a predominant emphasis on individuals and their move towards equality and democracy within the family relations.
- **Hegemonic masculinity** – is the idea that men's dominance in society legitimises patriarchy and reinforces power structures within the family so that women are subordinate in their role.
- **Inclusive masculinity** – from this perspective and based on the work of Anderson (2009), fatherhood is bound up with masculine identities. This perspective paints a picture of men's masculinity as inclusive and where fatherhood may – in some circumstances – be emphasised by more gender neutralised roles. Therefore, parenthood is seen less as a dichotomised role and instead is thought of as 'just' parenthood.

Discourses about modern fatherhood

For some, there is a contemporary discourse that attempts to define what modern-day 'good' fathering looks like – a man who is emotionally involved with his children and who adopts a role that is more hands-on, nurturing and caring (Busby & Wheldon-Johns, 2019; Henwood & Procter, 2003; Miller, 2010). For others, fathering is about fulfilling a more 'traditional' role where instead they strive to become good breadwinners (Hakoyama, 2020). Though the latter ideology is often thought of as being negative, research suggests that the provider role may just be an alternative way of expressing care and responsibility for the child (Christiansen & Palkovitz, 2001). Thus, a tension exists between the man as a modern father on the one hand (nurturing, caring and involved) and the man as a 'traditional' provider on the other hand (Miller, 2010; Shirani & Henwood, 2011). Furthermore, work by Henwood and Procter (2003) supports the idea that while men (aged 18 to 35) are often open to a shift towards a new type of fatherhood, they still have concerns centred on the provision of both financial security and care, or in negotiating fairness, equity and decision making in the home. However, recent research by Busby and Wheldon-Johns (2019) suggests that while men's domestic duties and contributions to childcare have increased, the distribution of labour is still often inequitable. They go on to argue that the reason for the inequitable balance may be due to the prevailing social norms that are in part led and supported by the law and policy framework of our time. Indeed, Busby and Wheldon-Johns (2019) propose that, whilst there is a political shift towards 'new fatherhood' seeking to reorient work/family balance and their corresponding gender roles, this assumes that there is a desire amongst men to fully shift to an emotionally involved style of care.

Fatherhood online

For fathers, the use of social media, online forums and other platforms can be very nuanced. For some purposes (such as help-seeking), the nature of online platforms may facilitate an easy and more anonymous way for fathers to gain information. In this sense, some researchers believe that, when it comes to information seeking, social media may help men overcome barriers related to the male identity and the masculinities or societal expectations placed on men that might otherwise inhibit them in the offline world (Harris et al., 2020). Laws et al. (2019) discovered evidence for men taking on shared responsibility when it comes to things such as their children's dietary and physical behaviours. However, some fathers may experience difficulties and barriers in accessing or finding web-based information because at times they feel the information they need is conflicting or unusable and is not of sufficient quality. Nevertheless, Jensen, Ammari and Bjørn (2019) report that social media usage tends to be more selective, with fathers preferring sites that offer anonymity or the use of pseudonyms (such as *Reddit*) to those where identity may be more visible (such as *Facebook/Meta*). Furthermore, work by Teague and Shatte (2021) found that when fathers do use sites such as *Reddit*, they are likely to disclose and offer support to others. Their work suggests that some men will offer encouragement to others, and that this provides men with informal and emotional support.

Final reflection

In this chapter, we have considered how both motherhood and fatherhood are conceptualised. The ideologies that define parenthood are bound up and explained through many multilevel factors: the individual (identity and cognitions), community (geographic and neighbourhood), society (cultural and political), and broader historical and lifespan factors.

Parenthood is a dynamic process, where traits and roles can be both stable and transitory throughout a person's life. While living in a digital age facilitates communication, information and accessing support, it is unclear if this facilitates parenting and child outcomes.

Key points

- Ideologies of motherhood, along with a long history of 'expert' advice, have resulted in social and cultural pressures and surveillance, particularly for new mothers.
- Support that recognises that motherhood is not context-free would help to facilitate a more respectful, empathetic and individualised approach.
- Fatherhood comes in multiple forms, from wide-ranging roles (from remote parent to primary caregiver) to personal identities. It is shaped by the context, environment and societally held beliefs of the time.
- There is a lack of research focusing on the needs and individual nuances of fatherhood.

Further reading

Hamilton, P. (2021) *Black Mothers and Attachment Parenting: A Black Feminist Analysis of Intensive Mothering in Britain and Canada*. Bristol, UK: Bristol University Press.

This book provides an intersectional analysis of contemporary mothering ideologies. Essential reading for anyone interested in parenting culture, race and intensive mothering practices.

Simmons, H. (2020) *Surveillance of Modern Motherhood: Experiences of Universal Parenting Courses*. Basingstoke: Palgrave Macmillan.

This book explores the social and cultural pressures within modern motherhood, in relation to different levels of surveillance. It considers the support currently offered to new mothers, with insight into the wider constructs and experiences of modern motherhood.

Baldwin, S., Malone, M., Sandall, J., & Bick, D. (2019) A qualitative exploratory study of UK first time fathers' experiences, mental health and wellbeing needs during their transition to fatherhood. *BMJ Open*, 9(9), e030792. DOI:10.1136/bmjopen-2019-030792

The transition to fatherhood is often not covered to the same extent as motherhood. This article (as well as Habib's earlier written review below) offers you an insight into the experiences of men as they become fathers and the impact it has on them and their identities.

Habib, C. (2012) The transition to fatherhood: A literature review exploring paternal involvement with identity theory. *Journal of Family Studies*, 18(2–3), 103–120.

6

PARENTAL RELATIONSHIPS
Kay Owen and Carol Fenton

Overview

The relationship that parents have with one another does much to shape their personal happiness and to determine the atmosphere within the family unit. This chapter considers some of the factors that can make or break the parental bond, and how family members are affected if the relationship breaks down. The chapter concludes by considering post-separation parenting, and how children respond to being raised by a lone parent.

This chapter will...

Consider how the following impact young children:

- Adult roles and relationships within the family
- Separation and divorce
- Lone parenting.

Key terms

Lone parenting; parental relationships; relationship breakdown

---

Introduction

In Chapter 2 we considered Belsky's 'determinants of parenting' (1984), which suggested that the way in which adults parent their children is a product of who they are, where they are, and what is happening in their lives. If you reflect on your own experiences, you will probably agree that having a strong, supportive relationship with someone you can rely on makes life feel better, while negative, destructive or demeaning relationships make it feel worse. You would probably also agree that whether you feel secure, loved and respected or frightened, lonely and despised affects how you behave and respond to others. Therefore, in order to understand how and why parental relationships affect children, we need to begin by unpicking how the nature of the relationship impacts the parents themselves.

Happiness

Psychologically, happiness (or 'subjective wellbeing') has two main aspects:

- Cognitive (thinking)
- Affective (experiencing).

Happy people report frequent or high levels of love, joy and contentment and infrequent or low levels of anger, frustration and sadness (Nelson-Coffey, 2018). Research suggests there is also a strong correlation between happiness and a sense that life has meaning (Kashdan, Biswas-Diener & King, 2008; King et al., 2006).

This sense of life having meaning is seen as comprising:

- coherence (my life makes sense)
- significance (I have worth and value. My life has importance)
- purpose (I have goals and a direction in my life) (King, Heintzelman & Ward, 2016; Martela & Steger, 2016).

Researchers such as Kamp Dush, Amato and others (Kamp Dush & Amato, 2005; Kamp Dush, Taylor & Kroeger, 2008) have discovered that married people are generally happier than unmarried people, and thus experience more of the positive thoughts and feelings listed above. The phenomenon has been investigated across many nations and by many different scholars, and the results are largely consistent. On the whole, married participants report higher life satisfaction and more positive affective states – not only than those who are unmarried, but also than cohabiting or divorced participants (Diener et al., 2000).

Studies also show that married adults are:

- emotionally healthier
- physically healthier
- economically more secure than unmarried adults (Waite, 2000).

Both men and women report an increase in their happiness and wellbeing in the two years following marriage. However, over time marriage is more strongly associated with wellbeing for men than for women. Indeed, studies consistently show that men's wellbeing seems to improve simply as a consequence of being married (Acitelli &

Antonucci, 1994). Some studies have suggested that the support a spouse can offer is more important for men because women generally have more alternative sources of support. Rather than being an automatic product of marriage, women's wellbeing and marital satisfaction vary according to their perceptions of the support they receive from their husband (Acitelli & Antonucci, 1994) and the quality of the relationship between them (Saphire-Bernstein & Taylor, 2013).

For both sexes, low marital quality is indicated by:

- high levels of marital stress
- low levels of marital harmony

which in combination

- reduce life satisfaction
- increase rates of depression.

We can therefore already see that the quality of the relationship between adults impacts them physically, emotionally and financially, as well as determining how they feel about themselves and the way their life is going.

Roles within Marriage

Berger and Kellner's classic (1964) study argues that the roles within a marriage (or partnership) are socially constructed. People need to learn how to play the role of a wife or husband and the role of a married person. They say that marriage is an ongoing construction in which roles have to be constantly negotiated, affirmed and renegotiated as circumstances change. According to their theory, all relationships are therefore fragile because they are in a constant state of flux. The need to constantly renegotiate what each partner wants and needs from the relationship can easily become acrimonious if one or both partners consider themselves to be carrying an unreasonable burden. Miller and Sassler (2012) noted that the major causes of arguments between couples were money and the distribution of work. They therefore interviewed 30 couples about how labour and responsibilities were distributed within their household. Most men preferred to have a partner who contributed financially to the household, and many couples were actively trying to share the burden of making money. However, when it came to domestic chores, none of the couples felt they were shared equally.

Researchers found that the couples fell into one of three groups:

- *Conventional*, in which each partner accepted the traditional gender role – the man went out to work and the woman cared for the home and children.
- *Contesting*, in which one partner (generally the woman) tried to forge a more balanced arrangement, although often unsuccessfully.

- *Counter-conventional*, in which the female partner provided financially but still performed most household labour.

Even where housework was shared somewhat equally, the women tended to supervise the men's chores. As a result, women retained accountability for its performance.

As previously noted, difficulties frequently emerge when circumstances necessitate a renegotiation of role, for instance, if a woman who has performed a conventional role returns to the workforce as the children grow, or due to her husband's loss of employment. Miller and Sassler (2012, p. 446) said:

> When men aren't working, they don't see domestic labour as a means of contributing. In fact, they double down and do less of it, since it challenges their masculinity. But when men earn more, women – who are almost all working, too – feel obliged to contribute in some way to maintaining the household, generally by cooking and cleaning.

Time to consider

Look again at the factors that lead to happiness and a sense that life has meaning.

- Do you think the distribution of responsibilities that Miller and Sassler discovered will impact any of those?
- Do you think the anomalies they noted are still true, or have roles changed since this study was conducted?

The Impact of Children on Parental Relationships

The need to negotiate and agree roles and responsibilities is ongoing throughout the marriage or partnership, and becoming parents adds a further dimension and a whole raft of additional jobs. This has become increasingly so in recent years as the cultural context of parenthood has shifted and intensified, bringing an expectation that parents will invest significant time and energy into their children's upbringing (Craig, Powell & Smyth, 2014; Wall, 2010). Research suggests that men and parents of high socio-economic status find the transition into parenthood easiest, while lone mothers, who lack strong support networks, find it hardest. In the early stages, new parents experience a rise in wellbeing and life satisfaction. Unfortunately, for the majority this is followed by a decline (Margolis & Myrskyla, 2015) as the realities of sleepless nights and financial demands begin to bite.

Parents therefore report that their change in status has both positive and negative aspects:

- Life has more meaning
- They feel they have an important social role.

However, it also brings:

- financial strain
- sleep disturbance
- greater stress
- lower relationship satisfaction (Doss & Rhoades, 2017).

If we view this in the context of Berger and Kellner's (1964) theory, and Miller and Sassler's (2012) observations about relationship conflict, we can see that becoming parents creates additional financial pressures and many new jobs and responsibilities that need to be negotiated. So, while some find the addition of children cements and solidifies their relationship, for others it greatly increases the possibility of conflict.

Relationship Breakdown

The statistics

People generally enter marriage in the hope and expectation that it will be life-long. Unfortunately, for a variety of reasons, this is not always the case. In the UK, 42% of marriages end in divorce (Office for National Statistics (ONS), 2020b). In numerical terms, 107,599 opposite sex and 822 same-sex couples divorced in 2019. After a dip the previous year, numbers have begun to rise again, and it is predicted that they will increase post-pandemic, as the experiences of lockdown caused many relationships to fracture.

The Office for National Statistics (2020b) records show the following:

- By their 30th wedding anniversary
  - 53% had divorced if they were aged under 20 when they married
  - 23% had divorced if they were aged 30 to 34 when they married
  - 7% had divorced if they were aged 45 to 49 when they married.
- The average age of people divorcing in 2019 was 46.4 years for men and 43.9 years for women.
- The median duration of marriage in 2017 was 12.2 years.
- The peak time for divorce is between the fourth and eighth wedding anniversaries. By the 26th anniversary, the chance of divorcing falls to below 1%.
- 62% of divorces were on petition of the wife.
- 15% of divorces were granted for adultery – the same for both sexes.
- 36% of divorces granted to men and 54% of divorces granted to women were due to unreasonable behaviour.

- 32% of divorces granted to men and 22% of divorces granted to women were granted with dual consent following two years of separation.
- Second marriages are more likely to end in divorce than first marriages.
- Almost half of divorces involve children under 16 years.

The impact of marriage breakdown on adults

The act of separating two lives that had previously been intertwined has both a practical and a psychological impact on those involved. We therefore need to consider both the emotional and legal aspects of divorce. The legal dissolution of a marriage necessitates agreement regarding the care of any children under 18 years and the separation of finances – often including relinquishing the family home. Moving from two incomes to one, and from one home to two, means that both partners generally move to a smaller property, often in a cheaper area and, potentially, away from an established support network. Divorce is thus economically costly to both men and women, but statistics show it is disproportionately costly to women. Nationally, family breakdown was estimated to have cost the taxpayer almost £51 billion in 2017 through effects on health, extra housing support, lost work hours, legal aid and other related factors (Relationship Foundation, 2018).

Humans are social animals and being married makes people feel connected and wanted. Marital breakdown is therefore associated with the loss of the psychological benefits we noted at the beginning of the chapter. Because men derive the greatest emotional benefits from marriage, they experience a greater drop in wellbeing following divorce than women do (Lucas, 2005; Scourfield & Evans, 2014). On average, separation is twice as stressful for married couples as for cohabiting couples, mainly because cohabiting couples are less likely to have children and often have less joint finance. Obviously, much depends on the circumstances of the separation. Where both adults manage a relatively amicable division, there will still be an inevitable sadness and period of reflection, but the process will be far less traumatic than if a partner feels abused, betrayed or marginalised either by their ex-partner or the process. Such circumstances lead to instability, depression, an erosion of self-worth and increased fear of the future. If the legal process becomes highly conflictual, the financial and emotional costs increase for all involved.

However, we must also acknowledge that for those escaping an abusive or highly dysfunctional relationship, divorce may bring enormous relief. Indeed, people who remain in unhappy marriages report lower levels of wellbeing than those who are unmarried (Williams, 2003). The implications for children being raised in an abusive household are considered in Chapter 12.

The short-term impact of marriage breakdown on children

Research suggests that children who live with both biological parents have greater physical and emotional wellbeing, enjoy more positive relations with their siblings and peers, and perform better academically (McLanahan & Sandefur, 2009). Divorce increases the risk of adjustment, and behavioural, mental and physical health problems for both adults and children (Malone, 2010). However, children's responses to parental divorce, in both the short and the long term, have been shown to vary according to their age, the circumstances surrounding separation, and the way in which each parent behaves.

To all intents and purposes, divorce marks the end of the cohesive family unit and the emotional and financial stability generally associated with it. For children, this is often unexpected (Booth & Amato, 2001) and requires them to amend their perceptions and expectations (Bernstein et al., 2012). It therefore inevitably brings a sense of loss and grief similar to that experienced following a death (Shulman, 2005). Research by Kelly (2000) suggests this is mediated by the extent to which they are exposed to parental conflict. In some instances, children's experience of conflict and divorce can increase sensitivity to loss and develop into anxiety and depression. Even when children appear to have successfully navigated the changes in their life, most recall the time of parental separation as one of substantial unhappiness (Emery & Forehand, 1996).

The period of separation and divorce is one of change, distress, uncertainty and heightened emotion for both adults and children (Malone, 2010). Even the very young pick up on and respond to parental distress. Research suggests that the responses to parental separation outlined in Table 6.1 are common (Aggarwal, 2019; Clarke-Stewart et al., 2000; Cohen, 2002).

Table 6.1 Common childhood responses to parental separation

Cognitive – *Due to cognitive immaturity, children may be unable to understand that:*

This new situation is permanent

Their parents' distress is not their fault

The divorce is not their fault

They may also struggle with:

Concentration

Academic achievement (especially boys)

Physical – *Some of these are psychosomatic whereas others are a common response to emotional trauma:*

Sleep disturbance

Nightmares

Stomach upsets

Headaches

Joint pain

Socio-emotional – *The fracturing of the attachment bond may create:*

Clinginess

Increased or renewed separation anxiety

Fear of abandonment

Mood swings

(Continued)

Table 6.1 (Continued)

Behavioural – *Behaviour may be:*
In response to uncertainty or an attempt to get attention from distracted adults
Irritability in infants
Aggression
Temper tantrums
Increased crying
Regression in terms of skills or behaviours (e.g. potty training, thumb sucking)
They may also feel:
Overwhelmed by their parents' sadness
Uncertain
Unloved
Lonely
Rejected by the parent who is not present
Divided loyalties
Anger
Guilt
Grief

Time to consider

Many adults assume that children are naturally resilient and will simply take parental divorce in their stride. In light of the evidence:

- How do you feel children could be supported through the process of parental divorce?
- Who would you regard as having a role in this?

The long-term impact of marriage breakdown on children

Parental divorce can place children at greater risk of mental health issues, particularly depression, in later life and make them more prone to aggression and issues with social relationships (Amato, 2010). However, none of these issues is inevitable, and many children adapt well following the initial impact (Amato & Afifi, 2006). Children's responses vary markedly as a result of their age, the family's circumstances and functioning prior to the divorce, and the way in which the adults in the family deal with this difficult time. The severity and duration of negative responses is also dependent on the presence of a variety of protective and risk factors (Amato, 2000). In the next section we shall consider how adults can mitigate the impact of divorce.

The impact of adult behaviours

Amato (2000) suggests that a child's successful adjustment is shaped by a combination of personal and contextual factors before, during and after the divorce. Research suggests that the legal aspect of divorce has little impact; it is the emotional environment and the practical ramifications of the separation that are of primary importance (Hashemi & Homayuni, 2017). By the time a decision is reached to divorce, children may have been exposed to conflict and negativity for some time (Zineldin, 2019). This is clearly potentially damaging, still more so if it continues into a high-conflict divorce marked by blame, hostility and aggression (Anderson et al., 2010), as adults involved in this sort of battle can often lose sight of the children's real needs and feelings (Amato, 2001; Kelly & Emery, 2003). Parental separation has already destabilised the child's world, but if this is rapidly followed by the sale of the family home (and loss of the familiar neighbourhood), necessitating a change of school (and the loss of friends and familiar routines), the child will usually struggle to adapt behaviourally, socially and academically more than a child who retains some stability in their life. Similarly, parents who pursue a reasoned negotiation regarding their separation and who model conflict resolution enable their children to maintain affectionate bonds with both of them. However, a high-conflict stance, by the couple and/or their extended families, may force the child to 'choose sides' and potentially lose part of their family. Maintaining as much stability as possible enables children to compartmentalise the distress and trauma of the divorce, thus preventing it from becoming a widespread or generalised trauma, with more long-term repercussions.

Unsurprisingly, children who are resilient and have high self-esteem adjust more easily to the changes in their life. Similarly, children who are appropriately informed about the divorce, and the impact it is likely to have on their life, have an increased sense of control, which improves wellbeing and adaptation (van der Wal, Finkenauer & Visser, 2019). Indeed, non-conflictual communication between the parents and clear communications with the child do much to lower the development of anxiety, depression and aggression in children (Herrero, Martínez-Pampliega & Alvarez, 2020). It should also be noted that children who lived in dysfunctional, conflictual, or abusive households actually enjoy higher levels of wellbeing post-separation (Amato et al, 1995).

Post-divorce parenting

Following the breakdown of a relationship, care of the children may change to:

- lone parenting
- co-parenting
- step parenting
- extended family care
- Local Authority care.

Lone parenting is considered here, and some other formats will be considered in Chapter 7.

Lone parents

Lone parents are officially defined as 'A mother or a father living without a spouse but with his or her dependent child or children who are aged under 19 and undertaking full-time education' (Gov.uk, 2010). Prior to the mid-1990s, lone parenthood was generally the result of one parent dying, or the child being born to unmarried parents. Responses to the two situations were very different. A child who experienced the death of a parent was afforded sympathy whereas an illegitimate child was an object of shame. Over the last 30 years attitudes have changed dramatically and lone parenthood is now seen as an established pattern of living in westernised society (Letablier & Wall, 2017).

Information from the Office for National Statistics (2021), Public Health England (2021). Statistical commentary: children living with parents in emotional distress, March 2021 update (www.gov.uk) and Gingerbread (2022) tells us that:

- in 1971 just 8% of UK children lived in lone parent families
- by 2019 this had increased to 14.9%, some 2.9 million families
- London has the highest proportion (19.1%)
- the South West of England (10.9%) has the lowest (ONS, 2020)
- 58% of lone parents with dependent children have only one child, higher than other family types
- only 12% of lone parents have more than three children
- women account for 91% of lone parents with dependent children (a percentage that has changed little over the decades)
- less than 2% of single parents are teenagers
- the average age of a single parent is 38; single mothers average 37 years old; single fathers average 44 years old
- 49% of single parents had their children within marriage and were subsequently separated, divorced or widowed
- lone fathers are around twice as likely to be widowed as lone mothers.
- less than 10% of lone parents have shared care arrangements for their children
- 65% of resident parents report their child has direct contact with its other parent; 85% of non-resident parents reported having contact.

Patterns of lone parenting have changed over the years (Letablier & Wall, 2017). While some will find themselves as the only adult in the house and with sole responsibility for the children, others may return to live with their own parents, move in with a new partner, or share custody with the children's other parent. When we add in other variables, such as the number and age of the children, and other circumstances within the family, we can see how hard it is to generalise about lifestyle or the impact on the children. Furthermore, on average, single parenthood lasts around five years. Lone parenting is thus generally a transitory state.

Dermot and Pomati (2016) note that UK governments have historically viewed lone parents as a political and social problem. Political discourse increasingly positions lone parents as deficient, suggesting that they are less empathetic and responsive (Oyserman, Radin & Saltz, 1994), more likely to adopt neglectful, harsh and uninvolved parenting strategies (Lee, 2009) and lacking the resource management skills of successful families. Campbell et al. (2016) detail some of the adverse health and social outcomes experienced by lone parents and their children:

- They suffer from depression and psychiatric disease
- They attempt suicide
- They suffer from alcohol and drug-related disease
- They experience poor educational outcomes and school behaviour problems
- They experience lower employment rates.

However, Campbell et al. (2016) conclude that much of this is due to the high rates of poverty within this social group, possibly compounded by a lack of contextual support (Waldfogel, Craigie & Brooks-Gunn, 2010). Gingerbread (2022), the support group for single parents, notes:

- 38% of single parents receive child maintenance
- 41% of children in single-parent families live in relative poverty, around twice the risk of relative poverty faced by children in couple families (24%)
- Single-parent households are the most likely to be in arrears on one or more household bills, mortgage or non-mortgage borrowing commitments
- 27% of single parents have a disability, compared with 21% of couple parents.

This issue of lone-parent poverty and low employment rates had been dealt with internationally by governments by the implementation of policies to promote employment. Unfortunately, findings indicate that employment does not always reduce poverty, due to the difficulties of finding lucrative employment that fits around childcare responsibilities. Lone parents are inclined to do without things themselves in order to provide for their children (Dermot & Pomati, 2016), but the worries and stresses of single parenting often take a toll on psychological health and emotional wellbeing, and may significantly impact the approach to child-rearing (Wiener, Devine & Thompson, 2020). When stressors are minimised, research demonstrates that lone parents are equally competent in delivering effective and responsive child-rearing practices as parents in other family structures (Stolz et al., 2017).

Time to consider

Article 9 of the United Nations Convention on the Rights of the Child UNICEF UK, 1989) states: 'Children whose parents have separated have the right to stay in contact with both parents, unless this could cause them harm'.

(Continued)

- What benefits do you think a child might get from this?
- Can you envision any problems?
- Who do you think should make the decision as to whether contact might cause the child harm?

Final reflection

Human beings have a desire to bond, and a harmonious relationship between parents improves outcomes on a range of measures for both them and their children. However, the euphoria of new love is generally short lived and, as life unfolds and circumstances alter, many partnerships fracture. For children, this heralds a period of uncertainty and change that can prove extremely distressing, with the potential to cause long-term damage. It is important for parents and members of the extended family to acknowledge the magnitude of what is happening in the child's life and to do all they can to maintain stability in relationships and life experience. While lone parents are often vilified, research would appear to suggest that problems are connected to broader social issues rather than being inherent within the parent.

Key points

- The quality of the relationship between adults impacts their happiness and life satisfaction, which in turn affects the dynamic within the family.
- Adult roles and responsibilities must be constantly renegotiated, especially when there are major changes such as the birth of children.
- Marriage breakdown is both financially and emotionally costly but is most damaging in cases of high-conflict divorce.
- Children will invariably show emotional and behavioural changes when parents separate. Difficulties are minimised when they are provided with love, support and as much stability as possible by the whole family.

Further reading

Blake, L. (2017) Parents and children who are estranged in adulthood: a review and discussion of the literature. *Journal of Family Theory and Review*, 9(4). https://doi.org/10.1111/jftr.12216

A comprehensive review that considers the reasons and outcomes associated with estrangement between parents and their adult children. Lucy Blake has also produced a variety of interesting papers on the impact of assisted reproduction techniques on family members.

Karandashev, V. (2015) A cultural perspective on romantic love. *Online Readings in Psychology and Culture*, 5(4). https://doi.org/10.9707/2307-0919.1135

An interesting article that considers cultural, historical, psychological and sociological perspectives on love. It concludes that romantic love is a universal phenomenon, but the way in which it is expressed varies according to cultural influences.

Neff, L.A., & Karney, B.R. (2017) Acknowledging the elephant in the room: how stressful environmental contexts shape relationship dynamics. *Current Opinion in Psychology*, 13, 107–110.

This article considers why stressful events and factors such as poverty create strain in romantic relationships.

7
DIVERSE FAMILY STRUCTURES
Carol Fenton and Kay Owen

Overview

Ask a group of early years children to draw their family and they will provide depictions of many different groups. Some may draw a mum and dad, others two mums or two dads, and still others will draw step-parents, a large extended family, or just their grandparents. In this chapter we will consider the dynamics in an array of different family structures and investigate the factors within them that enable children to thrive.

This chapter will…

Consider the prevalence and context surrounding different family formats, particularly:

- Step, blended or reconstituted families
- Custodial grandparents – kinship care
- Same-sex parents and surrogacy
- Discuss research evidence concerning how diversity affects children.

Key terms

Blended families; stepfamilies, custodial grandparents; diversity; kinship care; joint kin households; surrogacy

---

Introduction

As Owen and Delgado-Fuentes discussed in Chapter 1, in the 1950s the British family unit was thought of as a heterosexual, married couple and their biological children. However, social, cultural and political changes have enabled a far wider variety of family units to emerge and the roles within them to change. Attitudinal shifts among the population have also allowed increasing numbers of people to live in a family unit that feels right for them. For instance, few Britains would now expect someone to stay with an abusive spouse, and most are accepting of same-sex couples marrying. Even at a national level, data from the Office for National Statistics for married and cohabiting partnerships now includes both opposite-sex and same-sex couples. A recent report from the Children's Commissioner (2022) shows that family composition differs substantially according to geographical location, socio-economic status, ethnicity and religion. However, as we will see, the extent to which every family 'works' is largely dependent on the personalities of individual members and the dynamic between them.

Children's Perspectives on Family

Bronfenbrenner (1977) devised a model to explain how families exist in a layered nest of systems, each of which will influence the growing child. The child is at the centre, generally supported by adults who are bonded to the child and to one another. Bronfenbrenner referred to this grouping of immediate family as the Microsystem. However, this central unit does not function in isolation. Interactions (which he termed the Mesosystem) connect this inner group to a wider community (Koster, 2018). Beyond this lies the Exosystem (family friends, neighbours, the media), Macrosystem (cultural ideaologies) and Chronosystem (environmental and historical conditions and changes). All of these will have some influence on how a child develops. Although official data are limited, the Children's Commissioner (2022) notes that family members do indeed generally give and receive support from other family members beyond their household. As social attitudes have changed, children have been granted a greater say in who they see from this wider community in the Exosystem, and how they interact with them (V Morrow, 1998). These changes in structure and attitude mean that notions of what constitutes a 'family' are now far less fixed. When asked to list their family, most children include the people they live with (Hill, 2005). However, those who live in *joint kin households* (e.g. two brothers, their partners and children) usually include more relatives in their definition, while some living in nuclear families (i.e. biological parents and their children) do not even include grandparents.

Most theorists and researchers would agree that the group who primarily care for the child have the greatest impact on their development. This relationship is generally life-long – unless one of the parties challenges or severs it (McKie & Cunningham-Burley, 2005).

Time to consider

- Would you agree that the modern family exists in a layered nest of systems as Bronfenbrenner suggests?
- How do you think greater autonomy in childhood might influence a child's emotional and social development?

There is insufficient space to evaluate every family format, but we shall now consider some of the most prevalent and discuss the research evidence surrounding their impact on children.

Stepfamilies and Blended Families

A *stepfamily* can be defined as a family group where at least one child is biologically related to one of the adults, but not to that adult's partner. An example of this would be a divorced or widowed woman living with her children and her new partner.

In a *blended family*, both adults may have children from previous relationships, or they may have additional children together.

Prevalence

The rise in divorce rates over the course of the last century led to an increase in the number of stepfamilies and blended families, but this was followed by a sharp drop between 2001 and 2011. In part, this was due to improved, accessible contraception, which allowed couples to plan their families, often waiting until both had established themselves in a career. Given that younger couples are more likely to separate or divorce, many had not yet had children when these formative relationships dissolved. Therefore, less than 10% of UK children are currently being raised in a stepfamily. Of these, the vast majority of stepfamilies contain children from the women's previous relationships. Only about 10% contain the father's children, and a smaller proportion still (about 4%) contain children from both parties' previous relationships. London and the south-west have the lowest numbers of stepfamilies, and the highest numbers are found in South Wales, the East Midlands and around the coast. Couples who marry are more likely than cohabiting couples to go on to have their own children.

Adjustment

Obviously, the formation of a new family unit brings a new parent figure, often new siblings and a new set of grandparents and extended family members. Letablier and Wall (2017) note that while the parents optimistically view this as a new family, children find the transition less straightforward as they have to find their place in a diverse group, potentially composed of children from a range of different relationships. Difficulties are most evident during the first two years (Dowling & Barnes, 2020; Smart, 2006), but some experts say that it can take as many years as the age of the child at remarriage for the stepfamily to bond properly. In other words, a 7-year-old may be 14 before they feel fully secure in the new unit. Furthermore, research suggests that complex stepfamilies face more adjustment problems than those where all the children are related to the mother (Dunn, O'Connor & Levy, 2002; Hetherington 1999). Young children are the ones who find adjustment to a new family unit the easiest, having had less time to form deeply established relationships and routines in their original household.

Parenting

We know that children are particularly fragile during the period immediately following the breakdown of their parents' relationship, and this means any further changes require delicate handling. Initially, many issues appear attributable to the disruption and conflict associated with the breakup, especially if it has been hostile and/or created major changes in the child's life, such as a change of house and school. When divorce proceedings are highly conflictual, parenting practices often become competitive and marked by rivalry, low cooperation, and negative emotionality (Murphy, Jacobvitz & Hazen, 2016).

It is estimated that approximately 3% of children subsequently divide their time between two addresses (Children's Commissioner, 2022). Where biological parents have re-partnered, children may therefore be parented by three or four individuals. From previous chapters we know that parenting behaviours are shaped by the person's physical, situational and psychological resources (Chapter 3), their own attachment and childhood histories (Chapter 4) and gender (Chapter 5). Everyone has their own specific mix of these, meaning it is likely they will approach the role in different ways (Letablier & Wall, 2017). As we have already noted, instability, inconsistency and uncertainty can all be difficult for young children to cope with (Brand et al, 2017). Establishing as much consistency, regularity and stability as possible will therefore benefit the child.

Obviously, where one parent has custody, the resident biological parent is invariably more influential than the non-resident parent. Koster et al. (2020) and Lee and Hofferth (2017) suggest that children's experiences will vary according to whether they live with their mother or father because resident mothers usually engage in a variety of parenting activities whereas resident fathers spend the majority of time in play. If the child lives mainly with the mother, Kalmijn (2015) notes the relationships with the father may deteriorate, leaving the child feeling that the price of their parents' divorce is a broken relationship with their father. This is particularly prevalent if both parties re-partner and transfer attention from their children to their new partner (Manning & Smock, 2000) or to new children.

Problems and resolution

For children moving into a stepfamily, it is the relationship with the new step-parent that usually causes the most anxiety and difficulties (Cartwright, 2014). Relationships with step-parents are characterised by less closeness and greater conflict than parent–child relationships (Arnold, 1998). Older children in stepfamilies experience higher levels of disagreement, lower levels of interaction and maternal supervision, and a decreased sense of socio-emotional and global wellbeing than children raised in nuclear families (Centre for Law and Social Policy, 2022).

Children who spend time with both biological parents inevitably feel divided allegiances. A sense of loyalty to a birth parent may lead to animosity and rejection of their 'replacement'. Alternatively, children may fear causing anger, hurt or rejection by admitting to their biological parent that they have bonded with the new step-parent.

There is evidence to suggest that when children are worried about losing contact with one parent, they may act out these insecurities in their stepfamily. This sort of behaviour may present step-parents with additional challenges and result in their feeling as though they are the ones who have to pick up the pieces of their partner's previous relationship. Perhaps it is unsurprising that helplines such as Family Lives (formerly Parentline Plus www.familylives.org.uk) receive high volumes of calls from step-parents who are experiencing depression and anxiety. The result of this leads to a strain on their role in the family and may negatively impact their intimate partner relationships or cause feelings of stress and inadequacy.

Research by Jensen, Shafer and Larson (2018) suggests that the mindset of the new step-parent will impact how well the relationship works. Those who enter the relationship prioritising their own biological children are inclined to expect obedience from step-children. Those who regard their partner's children as a barrier in their relationship are likely to report more issues as the years progress. Unsurprisingly, overly authoritarian step-parents are unlikely to forge good relationships with their step-children (Jensen et al., 2018).

It would appear that the key is stability. Friction and relationship difficulties are inclined to escalate when there is repeated re-partnering, as the child needs to adjust to changes in circumstance and formulate a range of new relationships, some of which may only be transitory. Research shows that repeated changes in living arrangements have a more detrimental effect on children than living with non-biological parents and siblings do. Furthermore, the more often changes occur, the more negative the consequences are for children (Coleman & Glenn, 2010).

The happiest relationships seem to result from step-parents getting to know the child, and supporting both them and the biological parent, before assuming a parenting role themselves (Cartwright, Farnsworth & Mobley, 2009). Over the longer term, according to clinical tests, between two-thirds and three-quarters of children in stepfamilies (and even more if the child is living in a well-established stepfamily) do not exhibit any additional emotional or behavioural problems. Indeed, over all our years of working with students, we have heard many express real love and gratitude for the support and guidance provided to them by step-parents.

Time to consider

Imagine a child lives with their parents and has regular contact with both sets of grandparents. Then the parents separate and both re-partner. There are now potentially four parents, eight grandparents, additional siblings, aunts, uncles and cousins.

(Continued)

- What emotional impact do you think this would have on the child?
- How might the child react to new siblings, especially if they were a lone child previously?
- How important are the age and socio-emotional stage of the child?

Kinship Care including Custodial Grandparents

Kinship care is the term used when children go to live with a family member other than their parent, often in order to avoid a move into local authority care. As we will see, most of these children flourish as a result of the move. However, many kinship carers report facing enormous challenges with only minimal support (Harwin et al., 2019; Hunt, 2018).

Statistics compiled by the organisation Grandparents Plus in their 'State of the Nation Report' (2020) show that:

- 79% of kinship carers are the child/children's grandparents
- 9% are aunts or uncles
- 80% are White British or other White
- 1.6% are Black, or Black British-Caribbean
- 1.4% Asian or Asian British.

While some of these kinship carers have made informal arrangements for the child's care, most have either a Special Guardianship Order or a Residency Order. An estimated 200,000 grandparents in the UK currently have grandchildren living with them, with maternal grandmothers being the most likely to assume the role. The reasons for these kinship carers assuming responsibility for the childcare vary. Some have needed to step in because the parent has died, others because the parent is in prison, but the main reasons (in descending order) are:

- neglect
- parental drug or alcohol abuse
- parent unable to cope
- domestic violence
- parental disability/illness
- parental abuse of the child.

Placing children with kinship carers has demonstrably better results than moving them into local authority care, particularly with regard to their identity formation and mental health (Dorval et al., 2020). It enables children to retain family (Brown, Cohon & Wheeler, 2002), cultural and community relationships (Mosek & Adler, 2001), thus reducing the potential disruption and sense of loss that could follow a move away from parental care. It is also less restrictive than foster or residential care, and is the outcome preferred by the children themselves (Department for Education and Skills (DFES), 2007). Unfortunately, children from Black and ethnic minority backgrounds are less likely to move into kinship care, increasing the risk of social isolation and a loss of cultural identity (Lin, 2018).

The impact on children

In Chapter 4, Barnes and Owen discussed the importance of attachment and the Internal Working Model (IWM) for all children. Clearly, children who have faced traumatic events and instability are in even greater need of consistent loving care. Some studies (Bowers & Myers, 1999; Cox, 2000; Edwards & Daire, 2006; Wang et al., 2019) report that children raised by their grandparents have:

- worse physical health
- more behaviour problems
- lower academic scores
- more psychological problems
- insecurity and trust issues
- fears about grandparents dying.

Before jumping to any conclusions, we must remember that many of these children have experienced major family instability and trauma of the sort often linked to subsequent developmental, behavioural or health needs. Thus, there is a need to consider whether these issues are attributable to the grandparents or to the reason the child needed to move in with their grandparents in the first place.

While kinship carers provide increased stability and security for children, they also face more challenges. They are older, generally have lower incomes and receive little formal support despite often being the child's sole carer (Geen, 2004). Many also have their own health issues and the arrival of the children may create over-crowding in the home. In combination, these can reduce the carer's ability to nurture and care for the children successfully.

However, the vast majority of carers who responded to the Grandparents Plus survey (2020) felt that the children had settled well, and most recent studies suggest that children who are looked after by kinship carers usually benefit from loving, stable homes (Wellard et al., 2017) and enjoy largely positive outcomes (Harwin et al., 2019).

The grandparents' perspective

Fuller-Thomson and Minker (2000) report that the majority of kinship carers assume control 'willingly and with relief' following a period of turbulence or crisis. Many grandparents report that, instead of striving for perfection, they feel more relaxed about parenting the second time around and enjoy the fun and laughter children bring. Wang et al. (2019) suggest that there are many other positive aspects for the grandparents:

- They feel they are helping
- It 'keeps them young' and gives them a sense of purpose in life
- It allows them to correct mistakes they made the first time round
- They have more patience, wisdom, time (and sometimes money) than they did when raising their own children
- The experience leads to personal growth.

However, custodial grandparents often find themselves locked in a 'tricycle of care giving', being responsible for their own elderly parents, their children and grandchildren. This brings a raft of social, emotional, physical and financial demands such that other aspects of their lives have to be abandoned or put on hold. Carer requirements often necessitate the carer giving up their job and abandoning their friends, social structure, privacy and financial security. As a result, 86% (Burton, 1992) reported feeling depressed or anxious most of the time. When grandparents have needed to take on their birth children's offspring, the difficulties are often exacerbated by resentment and a deteriorating relationship with their own child. While recognising that all family members benefit from continued contact, the shift in caring responsibilities and the factors that have necessitated the shift mean that the family dynamic is frequently complex and unstable.

As we have seen, the child's move into kinship care is generally in response to very difficult circumstances. The number of children in kinship care families is increasing (Lin, 2018). However, few local authorities recognise or make provision for kinship carers (Farmer & Moyes, 2008). Many carers report feeling ashamed, judged and stigmatised due to the lack of public understanding. This is compounded by the lack of available emotional and financial support. Furthermore, the trauma experienced by the children during their early lives can cause them to exhibit challenging behaviours, further compounding the difficulties. The global Covid-19 pandemic has added a further layer of stress and demands on carers, with the requirements of home schooling and blended learning proving particularly alien to those who were educated very differently and who are often unfamiliar with technology. Charitable organisations supporting kinship carers warn that many are now close to breaking point and that there is an urgent need for more comprehensive support.

Time to consider

Look at the reasons why these children are moving away from their parents' care. You will notice that a lot of these reasons could be classified as adverse childhood experiences (ACEs).

- What issues do you think this might present for the child and for their new carers?

Same-sex Parents and Surrogacy

The last decade has seen a significant growth in the number of people identifying as a gender or sexual minority (Reczek, 2020) and by increasing acceptance of same-sex marriage and same-sex parenting throughout most of the population. Research demonstrates that sexual orientation has little impact on a couple's approach to parenting or on outcomes for children (Biblarz, Carroll & Burke, 2014). A sample of the studies looking at the children of same-sex parents is presented in Table 7.1.

Table 7.1 Sample of studies looking at the children of same-sex parents

Researcher	Findings
Manning, Fettro & Lamidi (2014)	Children fared as well in social and cognitive development tests as the children of different-sex parents. Differences between children were more attributable to socio-economic status or family stability.
Tasker (2005)	Psychosocial developmental outcomes for children with lesbian or gay parents are comparable to those of children with heterosexual parents. However, they are more aware of homophobia and more appreciative of the family dynamic.
Miller, Kors & Macfie (2017)	Children of gay parents show healthier psychosocial development than those of heterosexual parents with regard to internalising and externalising problems.
Biblarz & Stacey (2010)	Household duties are shared differently between gay, heterosexual and lesbian parents.

Despite the increasing legitimisation of same-gender relationships, and research evidence, heteronormative views about parenting continue to create barriers for same-sex couples hoping to adopt (Scherman, Misca & Tan, 2020). Those wishing to become parents therefore often need to explore other alternatives.

Lesbian couples wanting a family often conceive by donor insemination, meaning the children are raised without a father from the start (Golombock et al., 2003). Fond, Franc and Purper-Ouakil (2012) investigated whether the absence of a father and the sexual orientation of the mother impacted child development. They concluded that there is no evidence of holistic development, identity, behaviour or sexual orientation being any different for the children of lesbian parents than for those of heterosexual parents. Indeed, Golombok et al. (2003) discovered that children have better psychological outcomes as lesbian mothers implemented healthier parenting techniques than fathers in a heterosexual relationship generally do.

For male couples, gestational surrogacy may provide the means to becoming parents (Kim, 2017; Klock & Lindheim, 2020). Embryos are generated *in vitro*, using the biological father's sperm and a donor egg. The embryo is then transferred to a gestational carrier who bears the child. Interestingly, Wells (2011) discovered that, because they are perceived as violating traditional gender roles, gay men are judged more harshly than lesbians.

Case Study – Hannah and Misha

I don't think I've ever immersed myself so deeply in anything as I did in IVF. It becomes an addiction very quickly. It's on your mind 99% of the time. How we got through work, weddings and the rest of our everyday lives, I will never know because it literally consumes everything you've ever known and continue to think you know. We were obsessed with becoming parents and the journey associated with that. We knew early on in our same-sex relationship that the time to consider starting a family would be more about scientific possibilities than romance, but nothing prepared me for the wave of endless emotions associated with it.

Anyone who starts IVF, whether that's as a same-sex couple, a single woman or a heterosexual couple, should prepare to be committed to nothing other than this journey. You cancel plans, you leave early, you do injections in public restrooms and think nothing of it, and you pray, beg and hope for nothing other than a successful round … every single day!

IVF is early morning appointments, bruising, pain, trauma, tracking your cycle, knowing your body, taking all the right things at all the right times. It's anxiety, worry, panic, disappointment, heartache, pain, jealousy and hope. It is the biggest mind game, the worst rollercoaster and the greatest appreciation for science there ever was. It's finding communities of support you never thought about.

No-one warns you for all that you might lose, and equally no-one can prepare you for seeing a tiny heartbeat inside you, for holding your partner's hand, watching your future child on a monitor and knowing that you're one (tiny baby) step closer to the goal after all you've been through. We're roughly £19,000 into this journey, with two cycles of IVF under our belt and yet I'd spend it all over again in a heartbeat!

That's IVF, that's our journey to parenthood and our life-defining, monumental moment.

Final reflection

The received wisdom for many years has been that children do best when raised by their biological parents in a nuclear, heterosexual family. Indeed, research evidence appeared to support the view, but more recent studies have enabled us to investigate which aspects should be attributed to the parenting and which have a deeper underlying cause, such as poverty, discriminatory practice or trauma. What now appears clear is that, as with all parenting, children benefit from warmth and security but become destabilised when surrounded by adversity, hostility and repeated loss.

Key points

- UK children live in many different types of family
- Each type of family brings its own challenges and benefits
- The ability and inclination to nurture and care for the child is of primary importance.

Further reading

Childline - www.childline.org.uk/info-advice/home-families/family-relationships/
    stepfamilies-second-families/

The children's charity Childline provides advice for children moving into a stepfamily or blended family.

Kinship - https://kinship.org.uk

Kinship is the leading kinship care charity in England and Wales. They describe themselves as 'here for all kinship carers – the grandparents and siblings, the aunts, uncles, and family friends who step up to raise children when their parents can't'. They also provide support and resources for professionals.

You can read more about Hannah and Misha's story at @momma.loving on Instagram.

8

THE ADOPTIVE FAMILY
Jenny Boldrin

Overview

This chapter will introduce you to some of the critical debates about adoption. We will outline the possible reasons leading to a child being adopted as well as the potential features of their early life experiences. Consideration will be given to separation and loss as key features of an adopted child's story, while reflecting on the extent to which we understand them as indicators of trauma. The complex and critical notion of identity will be explored for children who may have experienced multiple contexts and experiences of 'family', while pausing to allow us to evaluate the practice of life story work in supporting adopted children to explore their history and make sense of their journey. Finally, we will conclude with a critical overview of adoption breakdown, including consideration of the possible contributing factors to an adoptive placement ending prematurely.

This chapter will…

- Define adoption and explore the reasons why children may enter an adoptive family
- Identify and discuss trauma, including separation and loss as potential features of an adopted child's story
- Discuss identity, belonging and life story work as critical considerations in the adoption narrative
- Identify and discuss the potential factors leading to adoption breakdown.

Key terms

Adopted/adoption; attachment; identity; life story; loss; separation; trauma

Introduction

Our starting point in this chapter is to acknowledge that adoption is complex and often messy. It challenges our definition of family and asks us to confront our preconceptions surrounding the process and emotions which lead to children entering a family unit.

As we will explore through this chapter, while a child entering a family is more traditionally understood through a lens of 'beginnings', adoption must be understood on a far broader and more critical scale. While adopted families undoubtedly 'begin' a new chapter on the child's arrival, the adoption process is also underpinned by endings – the end of relationships, the end of fantasies, the perceived end of an identity – we could go on. As Messina and Brodzinsky (2020) reflect, adoption for a child is not only about gaining a family, but also about losing one. Journeys to adoption for all involved are unique and are often challenging. As such, we will spend time in this chapter exploring the potential realities that adoption presents and introducing you to some important points of reflection when working to support an adopted child and their family.

Defining Adoption

Before we begin, let us pause and consider the facts. 'Adoption' is the term given to the legal process through which a child is placed into the care of adoptive parents. The All-Party Parliamentary Group for Adoption and Permanence (APPGAP) (2019, p. 3) identify that this can occur for one of the following reasons:

1   A child is relinquished by their birth parent(s) and the adoption agency places the child with approved adopters who make an application to the court for an Adoption Order that legally severs the child's relationship with their birth parent(s)
2   A local authority identifies that a child reaches the legal threshold for care proceedings and the care plan for the child is that they should be placed for adoption. On the authorisation of the court, the child is matched and placed with suitable, approved adopters. They later apply to the court for an Adoption Order that legally severs the child's relationship with their birth parent(s)
3   A child is identified for adoption in another country and after due legal process is placed with adopters approved as intercountry adopters with the child.

In 2015 the number of children being adopted annually hit a peak of 5,360. Since that time numbers have been falling with 3,400 reported in 2020 (Department for Education, 2021). These statistics are presented against a backdrop of increased numbers of children in care, a trajectory likely to become more pronounced as a result of the Covid-19 pandemic (Adoption UK, 2020).

Adopted children are often referred to under the umbrella term of 'previously looked after' (PLA), a term which also includes those living under a Special Guardianship Order (SGO) or a Child Arrangement Order.

Why Focus on Adopted Children and Families?

According to Gore Langton and Boy (2017), adopted children are one of the most vulnerable groups in society. Department for Education (2018) statistics suggest that only 40% of PLA children, which includes those adopted from care, achieved the expected levels in reading, writing and maths at the end of Key Stage 2, making them an identified group at risk of poor educational attainment. According to research conducted by Adoption UK (2017), adopted children in Key Stage 1 are also 16 times more likely to receive a fixed period exclusion.

Reasons for such statistics are, of course, complex and nuanced. However, we will endeavour, through this chapter, to explore some of the reasons why an understanding of the needs of adopted children and families is so crucial for the professionals working with them.

Golding (2010) highlights that there has historically been a lack of awareness of the needs of adopted children, suggesting that once a child progresses from the special provision made under the umbrella term of being *looked after* to holding an adopted status they are at risk of becoming invisible. Professionals must acknowledge that an adopted child may still face barriers as a result of their early life experiences, and the presence of an adoption order should not mask their underlying needs (Triseliotis, 2002). As Best (2019, p. 120) reflects, while adoption may signify the end of a child's status as a 'child-in-care', it also triggers the beginning of a new journey, one which requires substantial support for all those involved.

Crucially, these needs are not exclusive to children, with Gore Langton and Boy (2017) reporting that, although there have been positive steps taken in an understanding of the needs of adopted children, support for parents specifically is still patchy. A range of complex motivations may lead people to adopt (Moore, 2020), with it often being the case that adopters' own history may be tinged with trauma from their prior experiences on the road to parenthood. In their survey of adopted parents, Selwyn, Wijedasa and Meakings (2014, p.120) report that 'over three quarters (n = 54) had chosen to adopt because of infertility, pregnancy related health concerns, or following miscarriages'. Support for parents is vital in ensuring the success of the placement and must be delivered through quality post-adoption support services, an area revisited later in the chapter. According to Weistra and Luke (2017), for many adoptive parents it is not uncommon for social stigma to result in promised support for parents from their social network to be withdrawn once problems begin to arise, rendering them isolated in their new reality.

Time to consider

Adoption is often viewed with assumptions, and with those assumptions potentially come feelings. You may feel pity for the adopted child, fear of what their history might

(Continued)

mean, uneasiness about how to plan for them. According to Dahlberg, Moss and Pence (2013), these assumptions and our construction of the child will greatly influence our pedagogical work. Spend a moment reflecting on your own perceptions and assumptions of adoption.

- What assumptions might *you* make about an adopted child?
- How might these assumptions influence *your* professional practice?
- In what ways do *you* feel professional practice may then impact on children's experiences?

Keep a note of these reflections and revisit them regularly as you continue reading this chapter.

The Early Life Experiences of an Adopted Child

Understanding the individual and unique experiences of each child is an essential part of meeting their needs and respecting their position. Children's routes to adoption are varied, although all will spend time in local authority care prior to reaching their final adoptive placement, whether for a matter of days, months or years. Figure 8.1 shows us the primary reasons for children being taken into care in England, as identified by the Department for Education (2021).

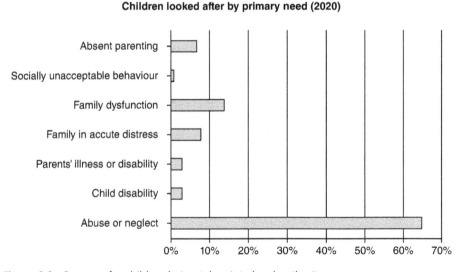

Figure 8.1 Reasons for children being taken into local authority care

The experience of early childhood trauma is a significant feature of the life experiences of children in care, an experience which has the potential to cause far-reaching damage to the developmental regions of the brain associated with managing behaviour, emotional regulation, language, self-concept, attention, relationships, cognition and higher-level thinking (De Young, Kenardy & Cobham, 2011; Ryan, Lane & Powers, 2017; Sufna et al., 2019).

The above undoubtedly suggests that an understanding of trauma and its effects on development is essential in responding to the needs of the adopted child. However, treating adopted children as a homogeneous group based solely on their prior experiences does not do justice to the individual and unique ways in which children's ecological systems have evolved. While we must become more trauma aware in our professional practice, a dominant trauma narrative does not always allow for the personalisation of provision and can lead to the grouping of children under unnecessary labels in response to their history (Gore Langton and Boy, 2017). Applying a label of trauma without the necessary professional reflection will not allow for reflexive practice and may instead lead to an inappropriate response to their needs.

Understanding trauma

Sufna et al. (2019, p. 120) define trauma as the experience of 'an extreme stressor that surpasses one's ability to cope'. This definition is perhaps challenging as it also encompasses one-off experiences of extreme stress, such as involvement in an accident or being bereaved.

The term 'complex trauma' (Ford & Courtois 2009) goes further and attempts to offer a means to distinguish between single-event trauma and the more chronic experiences of individuals who inhabit stress over time, for example, a child living in abusive and/or neglectful environments. Shonkoff and Garner (2012) suggest a conceptual taxonomy of stress to further define the degree of its potential impact. They assert that by viewing stress as positive, tolerable or toxic, we can determine its impact on the physiological development of the individual to a greater extent. Figure 8.2 provides a visual representation of Shonkoff and Garner's model.

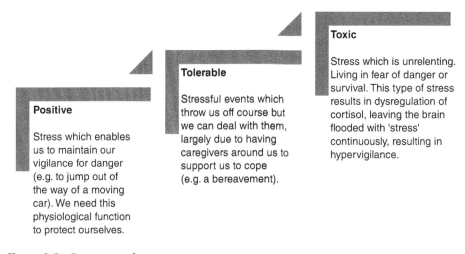

Figure 8.2 Taxonomy of stress

According to Ryan et al. (2017, p. 112), the physical and physiological damage brought about by trauma either prenatally or within the first few years of development will impact 'structure, connectivity and function at higher levels'. The impact of prolonged exposure to toxic levels of stress brought about by the environmental, emotional and psychological experiences in early development can be far-reaching and is, crucially, unique to each child (Perry, 2009).

Separation and loss as trauma

According to D'Amato (2010), adoption begins with loss for all those involved. A birth family loses a child, an adoptive family loses their current reality and the potential fantasy of conventional parenthood, and the child suffers more losses than we can mention … identity, birth family, foster family, to name a few. In her seminal text, *The Primal Wound*, Verrier (1993) questions whether these losses are acknowledged or understood. She claims that 'there is no permission in our society to recognise, in each of life's transitions, the polarities between gain and loss or joy and sorrow' (Verrier, 1993, p. 69). Gore Langton and Boy (2017, p. 22) agree, and assert that a child's move to an adopted status can often be perceived as their 'happy ending' or 'new beginning', with little consideration given to the long-lasting impact of abuse, trauma and loss on development and behaviour. Children transitioning into adoption are often viewed as the lucky ones, when in reality they are simply entering a new stage of what is a life-long journey, dealing with often painful and confusing feelings (Syne, Green & Dyer, 2012).

According to Franke's (2014) explorations of what constitute stressors for a child, feelings of separation and loss can be considered alongside more traditional definitions of trauma in terms of their impact on the child. Franke asserts that stressors may be classed as physical, environmental, emotional or theoretical, all of which may trigger an equal stress response in an individual. This is an important consideration in relation to children who have experienced differing levels of what might be perceived as trauma. It perhaps enables reflection on how the experiences of a child who has witnessed or been subjected to physical or sexual abuse can be comparable to a child who has experienced neglect or a disconnect from birth families.

Table 8.1 Categories of stress, adapted using the ideas of Franke (2014)

Stressor	Examples of potential triggers from a looked after (LA) or previously looked after (PLA) child's life experience
Physical	Physical or sexual abuse, neglect, witnessing domestic violence
Environmental	Neglect, sociological issues within the community, instability within foster placements or adoptive placement, frequent transitions
Emotional	Emotional abuse, fear, separation and attachment loss from birth parents, siblings, extended family, friends, disconnect from culture and a lack of belonging, identity insecurity
Theoretical	Feelings of losing identity, not being wanted by birth parents, lack of belonging, lack of clarity about history

Let us pause and consider Franke's assertions in relation to the experiences of a looked after or previously looked after child (Table 8.1).

Franke's (2014) definition allows for a broader understanding of the taxonomy of stress, encouraging professionals to consider and accept that adopted children who have perhaps not directly experienced abuse can still be subject to life-long feelings of trauma and stress as a result of the psychological impact of their reality.

Case Study – Jessica

Jessica is 7 years old and has recently been adopted. At the age of 4, Jessica was taken into local authority care due to neglect in the family home. She has three siblings, twin sisters who were age 2 when the children were removed and are now 5 years old, and an older brother who was 7 at removal and now age 10. Jessica's brother was placed with maternal grandparents under a Special Guardianship Order (SGO). However, their grandparents did not feel they could also cope with the other children. Jessica and her sisters were placed with a foster family. Since this time, Jessica and her sisters have lived with two further foster families, being moved frequently due to her own challenging behaviour and the complex additional needs of one of her sisters. Throughout this time regular contact arrangements were maintained between Jessica, her sisters, her birth parents and her brother.

It was decided that, as no improvements were being made in the family home, Jessica and her sisters would be placed for adoption. Social workers agreed that the best chance of getting all the sisters adopted would be to separate them and allow Jessica to be adopted alone.

Jessica was matched after eight months and has moved in with her new adoptive family. She has moved schools because her new family live out of the county. Now that her adoption is finalised, she no longer has contact with her birth parents or brother. She currently still sees her sisters while they await adoption placements.

Time to consider

- Can you identify how many different losses Jessica has experienced?
- What impact do you feel this may have on her sense of identity?

This reflection will support you as you navigate into the next section of this chapter.

Identity and Belonging

Laevers (2005) coined the phrase 'fish in water' to describe children who exhibit a deep sense of wellbeing and belonging. Laever's description suggests a feeling of having all your physical and emotional needs met, of knowing you belong, of feeling 'suited to the situation you find yourself in' (O'Conner, 2018, p. 64). A fish out of water cannot survive and therefore cannot thrive in their environment. Knowing you belong is inextricably linked to a clear sense of identity – of who you are and where you 'fit in' to the cultural context in which you exist.

For an adopted child, the experience of one or many transitions between family homes and environments may inevitably lead to identity confusion, conflict and maladjustment. Grotevant et al. (2007) suggest that a dominant Western narrative of kinship arguably places sole emphasis on blood relations in the definition of identity, further compounding an adoptee's perceived marginalisation. According to Cprek et al. (2020), isolation from birth parents, even inadequate ones, has the potential to raise feelings of inadequacy, confusion and a lack of belonging for children on this journey.

Zeleke, Koester and Lock (2018, p. 1428) suggest that the development of identity and wellbeing for adopted children consists of three tasks:

1   Belonging – to identify the place where they are and with whom they belong.
2   Being – to seek and make meaning of their world, neighbourhood and environment.
3   Becoming – to know and understand the rapid and significant changes that occur during childhood.

The above points to an ecological representation of identity, emphasising the significance of protective systems viewed through a socio-cultural lens in understanding children's experiences.

Challenging Boundaries of Identity: Transracial and Same-sex Adoption

For adoptive parents, one complexity perhaps lies in an acceptance that their child inhabits multiple identities – their *story* or *narrative* is multifaceted. Adoption frequently sees children crossing racial, cultural and class divides to integrate in an environment where family homogeneity is absent. Literature commonly depicts childhood as socially and culturally constructed, placing an emphasis on parenting and relationships in providing a child with a framework for development (Zeleke et al., 2018). Where children have experiences of multiple contexts, frameworks may become confused and identities blurred. The development of identity becomes a more complex task in the absence of clear 'biological continuity' (Messina & Brodzinsky, 2020).

In 2014, the Children and Families Act removed the explicit need for local authorities to match children with potential adopters based on race and ethnicity, a move intended to speed up the time spent 'waiting' for ethnic minority children to be matched with a family. Adopters accepting a child placed through transnational or transracial adoption will be required to navigate complex issues of difference and belonging. Tensions may arise as a result of dominant constructions of the family being based on biological similarity (Willing & Fronek, 2014) while needing to accept that their child's culture, language and ethnicity must be nurtured as defining features of their child's identity (Baden & Steward, 2007; Zeleke et al., 2018).

Messina and Brodinsky (2020, p. 518) undertook research to explore the experiences of children adopted by same-sex couples in the formation of identity. Among their findings was a feeling of needing to confront 'a double layer of identity complexity', navigating their adopted status and that of having same-sex parents. Levels of identity, understanding and acceptance were found to be unique, depending on the developmental stage of the child, from origin-based curiosity in early childhood to high degrees of empathy and championing minority-based rights in adolescence. The study concludes that where diversity and difference are features of a life story, there is potential to 'find a way of transforming the life challenges related to their family situation into an element of personal richness' (Messina & Brodzinsky, 2020, p. 520).

The Adoption Triad

The current practice of transparency and openness in adoption practices supports the notion of the child's right to understand their history and the origins of their identity. The symbol of the adoption triad (Figure 8.3) is commonly used to illustrate the ongoing relationship between the child (adoptee), adoptive family and birth family. The symbol exists as a reminder that the presence of both the adoptive and birth families as significant in the child's life is central to their identity and existence.

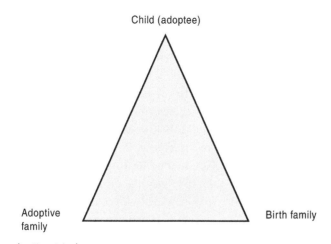

Figure 8.3 The adoption triad

Time to consider

Take a moment now to consider the adoption triad.

- Why do you think maintaining a connection to birth families is important for the child?
- What challenges might this present for an adoptive family?
- And what strategies could be used to support and maintain the triad over time?

Life Story Work

Life story work has become central to the agenda of openness and is now routinely utilised to provide a coherent narrative of a child's life experiences and journey to adoption (Watson, Latter & Bellow, 2015a). Legislation, including the Adoption and Children Act (2002), later updated in the Children and Families Act (2014), places a duty on local authorities to document the history of adopted children in an attempt to prevent knowledge gaps and identity confusion. Guidance requires all adoptive children to be provided with a life story book, which documents details about the child's birth family, placements while in local authority care and transition to their adoptive placement. The book represents both a 'process and a product' (Watson et al., 2015a, p. 90), suggesting that, while providing a physical tool for children, it should also work within a larger narrative of life story work. The production of the book does not signal the end, but the beginning of the conversation, with the story itself being taken forward through the child's life and explored via a range of means and media that meet the child's specific needs.

Life story books, and the ongoing narrative associated with them, are not without their challenges. In a survey of adoptive parents, many reported issues of poor quality, errors and a lack of consideration of appropriate content (Selwyn et al., 2014). Life story work is reportedly often given to inexperienced or student social workers whose training has not prepared them to complete such a sensitive and important task (Moore 2020; Selwyn et al., 2014). Research conducted in partnership with the UK Children's Charity Coram found similar issues, with adoptive parents reporting concerns about the presentation, focus and content of the books (Watson et al., 2015b).

Moore's (2020, p. 5) Theatre of Attachment Model is based on providing children with narrative opportunities to explore their history. The model takes a dramatic, play-based approach to support adoptive parents or foster carers to provide a safe environment to gain 'mastery' over potentially upsetting experiences in their stories. However, the dominance of a behaviour management discourse in adopter training leads Moore (2020) to believe that there is insufficient preparation for adopters to learn how to provide therapeutic support through attachment and play.

Adoption Breakdown

A simple internet search on adoption will soon generate the term 'forever family' as a frequent feature of the adoption narrative. This slightly rose-tinted advert for the adoption journey is ideological and unfortunately is not always based on reality. For many reasons, adoptive placements are sometimes unsuccessful and end in what, for the purposes of this chapter, we will refer to as 'adoption breakdown'. The terminology surrounding adoption breakdown is complex, in part due to the point and conditions at which the child leaves the adoptive family (Palacios et al., 2019). In the context chosen here, we will refer to adoption breakdown as any point at which a child leaves the home after the adoption order has been granted and the adoptive parent(s) is/are no longer legally responsible for them.

Permanency planning is a fundamental principle in child welfare policy and practice. The legal drive to identify permanent arrangements for a child is central to the adoption agenda. According to Brodzinsky and Livingstone-Smith (2019), our understanding of the different aspects of permanence are tied to the way we understand adoption breakdown or instability. Brodzinsky and Livingstone-Smith (2019, p. 185) identify three aspects of permanence, and crucially claim that 'to promote children's long-term well-being and ensure adoptive placement stability, all three components of permanence must be supported and achieved' (see Figure 8.4).

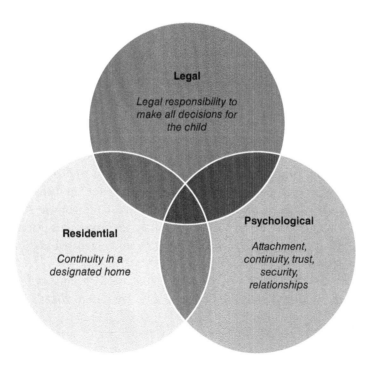

Figure 8.4 The three aspects of child permanence (ideas adapted from Brodzinsky & Livingstone-Smith, 2019, p. 185)

Figure 8.4 depicts the interrelational nature of our understanding of what constitutes permanence for a child. Without consideration being given to each aspect, true permanence is a myth.

Research conducted by Goodwin et al. (2020) groups potential reasons for adoption breakdown into three overarching categories:

- Child factors
- Parental factors
- Systemic factors.

Child factors

The age of the child at adoption is highlighted as a contributing factor to adoption breakdown, with disruption being more likely when a child is placed at an older age (Brodzinsky & Livingstone-Smith, 2019; Goodwin et al., 2020; Selwyn et al., 2014). Potential reasons are identified as: the child having experienced a greater number of adversities, resulting in more challenging behaviour; the frequency with which the child has experienced transition/separation; and the subsequent resistance to attachment. Goodwin et al. (2020) specifically explore the child's age from a developmental perspective, drawing on the work of Piaget (1952) to suggest that the older child may particularly struggle to form bonds with another family as they are beginning the process of individualisation, thus tasked with 'forming long-lasting bonds of attachment with new adoptive parents while simultaneously focused on becoming their own individual' (Goodwin et al., 2020, p. 1).

Parental factors

Parental contributions to breakdown are often attributed to their unrealistic expectations when entering the adoptive relationship. Goodwin et al.'s (2020) findings suggest that the parents' lack of understanding or preparedness for the behaviour brought about by trauma was a key contributing factor to adoption breakdown. There was also reportedly a tendency and desire to rush adoption transition and placement in an attempt to form the *forever* family, thus leading to underprepared and mismanaged transition processes.

The extract below shows us what young people themselves would advise prospective adoptive parents, as identified by the Department for Education (2021).

> To understand what you are taking on. To understand that it's not going to be just like having your own baby, there's probably a little bit more that you need to deal with and maybe a little bit more that you need to prepare yourself for and make sure that you're the type of person that can do that. Because if you're not then you're going to have a hard time and so is the kid. (Selwyn et al., (2014, p. 248)

Systemic factors

Finally, Goodwin et al.'s (2020) findings suggest that a lack of personalised engagement and support from post-adoption services could be considered as being partly responsible for adoption disruption and breakdown. Selwyn et al. (2014, p. 180) report parents feeling frustrated at a lack of services available post-adoption, with 'the majority of adoptive parents (being) dissatisfied with the overall response from their Local Authority', leading to a feeling of being abandoned to navigate unfamiliar territories surrounding children's mental health, specialist educational provision and wider Special Educational Needs and Disability (SEND) support services alone. According to Brodzinsky and Livingstone-Smith (2019, p. 187), systemic factors must also be considered within pre-adoption practices. They highlight the potential for professionals to be tempted to 'stretch' the preferences of adoptive parents, because of a pressure to place children quickly, and thus to place children into a family who are unsuited to the adoptive parents. Conversely, a lack of preparation prior to adoption can also potentially lead to parents stretching themselves as a means to speed up the process, accepting children without consideration of the long-term impact and pressure on their family dynamic (Palacios et al., 2019).

Time to consider

As a final consideration for this chapter, reflect on what lessons you can take away to embed into your professional practice.

- The Children and Social Work Act (2017) places a duty on schools to appoint a member of staff to be responsible for the attainment and needs of PLA children. What would you consider to be the priorities for those appointed people?

Final reflection

In this chapter, we have explored the process of adoption from several perspectives. We have considered the potential reasons for a child entering an adoptive placement and critically explored the notion of childhood trauma which presents as a prevalent feature of the adopted child's story. There is evidence to suggest that experiences of separation and loss, which are universal to all adopted children, must be understood further, with space made to acknowledge that they can represent trauma for the child involved. Ways to support children's identity and belonging are central to their success within adoptive families. Through dynamic and enduring life story work, children must be given opportunities to explore, process and have agency over their story. We must conclude that there is scope to understand the needs of adopted children and families on a much broader scale. As professionals, we must listen without judgement, observe without bias and respond without assumption.

Key points

- Adoption for many does not represent the happily ever after we might presume it does.
- Adopted children and families require wide-reaching and long-term support in order to cope with the evolving challenges brought about by trauma.
- Trauma is multifaced and must be understood on many levels in order to best understand its potential impact on the child.
- Our perception of identity is often inextricably linked to our family ties. For an adopted child that can lead to confusion and an absence of feeling they belong.
- Not all adoptions are successful, and some can result in breakdown. Families must be supported before, during and after the adoption order to minimise the risk of this happening.

Further reading

Adoption UK – www.adoptionuk.org/research

Adoption UK is a charity offering support, advice and guidance to adoptive families. They are also active researchers in adoption-related subjects and publish their research on this dedicated section of their website.

Gore Langton, E., & Boy, K. (2017) *Becoming an Adoption-Friendly School: A Whole School Resource for Supporting Children Who Have Experienced Trauma or Loss*. London: Jessica Kingsley.

For those planning a career in education, this text provides a very useful overview of essential considerations in practice.

Selwyn, J., Wijedasa, D.N., & Meakings, S.J. (2014) *Beyond the Adoption Order: Challenges, Interventions and Disruptions*. London: Department for Education.

This book provides a useful and critical report highlighting the many varied and complex issues surrounding adoption disruption.

9
SIBLINGS
Kay Owen

Overview

Even in adulthood, the mere mention of siblings can provoke intense emotions. Some of us are blessed with brothers or sisters who are our staunchest allies and supporters, others are driven to distraction by their siblings' attitudes and behaviour. The relationship is unusual because, despite not having chosen one another, most people spend much of their childhood with their siblings and have a life-long relationship with them. In this chapter we will consider some of the factors that create happy siblings and investigate the impact siblings have on one another in the early years.

This chapter will…

- Explore the advantages and disadvantages of having siblings
- Consider factors that may influence the nature of the relationship
- Discuss the experience of twins and multiples.

Key terms

Horizontal relationships; multiple birth; siblings

Introduction

'Sibling' is the gender-neutral term for brothers and sisters. Some 80–85% of people have a sibling but, despite its prevalence, every sibling relationship is unique. Some are close and supportive, some are conflictual and aggressive, and others fluctuate between the two. The nature of the relationship is shaped by many factors, including the family's location, the number of children in the family, the age differences between them, their gender, and the dynamic within the household. Generally, the relationship has both positive (Pike & Oliver, 2017) and negative (Tucker et al., 2019) aspects, and can change over the course of the lifespan. Frequent daily interactions over many years means that siblings develop a detailed understanding of one another – which can then be used for support or as ammunition. It comes as no surprise to learn that the heights and depths of emotions experienced with siblings are more intense than they are with either parents or friends (Dunn et al., 1996), and that siblings influence one another in a manner that can last a lifetime.

Sibling relationships are important because:

- they are involuntary yet permanent
- they are pervasive – siblings share spaces and experiences for many years
- they provoke intense positive and negative emotional states
- in many areas of the world, children are more likely to grow up with a sibling than with a father
- children spend more of their free time with siblings than with anyone else (Feinberg, Solmeyer & McHale (2012).

Similar but Different

For generations, humanity has debated the importance of nature and nurture. For siblings, the people who shaped their genetic endowment are usually also the ones who raise them, thus shaping their physical, social and emotional environment. On the face of it, therefore, siblings should be very much alike. However, while we may inherit certain genetic predispositions, they are not set in stone; they merely increase the likelihood we will respond or behave in certain ways and they can be mediated by other characteristics (Liebal & Haun, 2018). The way an individual responds to a situation will also vary according to their age and factors specific to them. Thus, while siblings may share the experience of moving house, the responses and developmental implications will be very different if one is 13 years old and the other 3 years old when the move happens.

Time to consider

Think about your own siblings or a group of siblings you know well.

- In what ways are you/they similar?
- In what ways do you/they differ?
- Can you remember any shared events in which you/they responded differently? Why do you think this was?

As noted in the Introduction, some siblings get on well, while others appear to have nothing in common. Let us consider some contributory factors in order to determine why this might be.

Age Gap

Research considering the optimal age gap between siblings offers no conclusive findings. Siblings who are close in age are usually emotionally closer, but also more competitive. In some instances, this leads to sibling victimisation, especially between brothers (Tucker et al., 2013). Whereas older brothers are inclined to express aggression physically, older sisters are more relationally aggressive, and the sibling who is the victim subsequently replicates this form of aggression towards their peers (Ostrov, Crick & Stauffacher, 2006). Ablow and Measelle's (1993) research suggests that the age of the older sibling is of greater importance than the size of the gap. Five and six year olds felt warmly about their younger siblings, whereas seven and eight year olds reported far less positive relationships. Age gap is therefore probably not a major factor on its own but can become one depending on the gender and age of the elder sibling.

Gender

Research by Buhrmester and Furman (1990) suggests that the warmest sibling relationships are between sisters, while the coolest are between an older brother and younger sister. Interestingly, all those in the study reported greater intimacy and companionship with sisters than with brothers, regardless of gender or age difference. Dyads containing boys are generally more conflictual (Kim et al., 2006). Despite the warmth and closeness, sisters show more aggression and attempts at dominance than are seen among girls with a brother.

Family Dynamic

The relationship with siblings does not exist in isolation, and it would seem that children who report good relationships with their parents also report a good relationship with their siblings (Pike, Coldwell & Dunn, 2006). Furthermore, a positive and happy relationship between parents is reflected in a positive relationship between siblings, whereas tension and ill-will spread throughout the home (McHale, Updegraff & Whiteman, 2012). Thus, harsh and authoritarian parenting is linked to more conflictual sibling relationships (Caffaro, 2020).

Although findings vary, siblings living with a lone parent do not appear to suffer any ill-effects in terms of their relationship with one another, provided there are no additional factors affecting the family. Similarly, the family's socio-economic status or household crowding seem not to be of relevance here.

Temperament

Unsurprisingly, the temperament of each sibling affects the relationship. Very active and highly emotionally children are more likely to have conflictual relationships. The more sociable the individual – particularly sociable older siblings – the more harmonious the relationship (Brody, 1998).

Birth Order

Although the relationship between birth order and personality has been somewhat overstated, a child's place in relation to other children in the family has some impact on how they are treated, their relationships and their personality. Oldest children generally carry the burden of higher parental expectations and of parental inexperience. Subsequent children are usually raised in a more relaxed way. In psychometric testing, first-born children score most highly for conscientiousness, and oldest and youngest children score more highly than middle-borns for extraversion, neuroticism and openness (Cole, 2014). Younger siblings are aware of (particularly academic) comparisons (Davies, 2015). This can fuel feelings of closeness between siblings who possess similar traits or distance and competition.

The Benefits of Siblings

Young children's understanding of how people think, especially their emotions, intentions and beliefs, appears to be supported by interaction with a sibling. Furthermore, studies have shown that children who have not had these opportunities have limited communicative skills (Colvert et al., 2008; Sonuga-Barke et al., 2017; Tarullo et al., 2007). However, we must be careful not to overstate the case here, as many of these studies considered children in very impoverished and isolated circumstances. Other research demonstrates that simply having a sibling does not necessarily confer benefits. There is also a need for quality social interaction between the children (Cole & Mitchell, 2000; Hughes & Ensor, 2005). Where the relationship is warm and cooperative, children benefit in several ways, as set out in Table 9.1.

Table 9.1 Benefits of sibling engagement

Improvements in...	Researchers
Social cognition (primarily false-belief understanding)	Dunn et al., 1991; Perner, Ruffman & Leekam, 1994; Peterson, 2000
Social cognitive development and emotional understanding	Cutting & Dunn, 2010
Social understanding	McAlister & Peterson, 2013
Empathy	Jambon et al., 2018
Social communication	Cutting & Dunn, 2010
Peer acceptance and social competence	Bank et al., 2004
Successful adult relationships	Noland et al., 2004
Good mental health	Waldinger et al., 2007
Gender socialisation	McHale et al., 2001
Academic engagement and attainment	Melby et al., 2008
Language development	Jenkins & Astington, 2003
Boys' cognitive skills, learning skills and self-control benefit from having a sister	Cyron, Schwerdt & Viarengo, 2017

Sibling Relationships and Socio-emotional Development

As Table 9.1 demonstrates, sibling relationships are particularly significant in the area of socio-emotional development, so we will consider this in a little more detail. Social development involves acquiring the necessary knowledge, values and skills to successfully relate to others and participate in society. Emotional development involves learning how to experience, express and interpret a range of emotions and, in doing so, come to understand what it is healthy and appropriate to display publically, and what should be dealt with in private.

Some factors within socio-emotional development are dependent on cognitive maturation. For instance, the child needs to realise that they have control over their own thoughts and behaviour before they can begin to exert that control. However, development is also impacted by the environment and experiences, and by exposure to what other people think and feel. Bandura's (1977) Social Learning Theory suggests that individuals acquire behaviours and beliefs by observation, reinforcement and imitation of salient models, particularly those who are powerful and similar to themselves. Older siblings therefore potentially have a very influential role.

Hartup (1989) suggests that relationships fall into two categories:

- **Vertical relationships** – one person (e.g. a parent) has greater knowledge and power than the other, and so provides support, nurturance and guidance.
- **Horizontal relationships** – the power, status and age are approximately equal (e.g. friends).

Horizontal relationships help children to acquire skills that can only be learned from equals, such as those involving cooperation and competition (Schafer, 2003). The intense, daily interaction young children have with siblings helps to build social understanding and provides rich opportunities to trial and develop strategies. Social failures outside the home can easily destroy friendships for a child, but siblings, even if they are upset, annoyed or offended, will still be there tomorrow. In order to re-establish harmony, one or both parties probably need to practise empathy, negotiation, compromise and/or forgiveness – all useful social skills. The marginal power and knowledge inequalities are also helpful. When Brody et al. (1982) observed children with both their friends and their siblings, they noticed the relationships were equal with friends but older siblings invariably took the role of manager and organiser with younger siblings. How productive this is depends to some extent on the good will of the older sibling, who can use the power inequalities to guide the way towards greater socio-emotional understanding or for their own advantage. Goetting (1986) concludes that, over a lifetime, the sibling bond is one of the most significant sources of emotional support and long-standing companionship and is crucial to a child's positive sense of self-actualisation.

Time to consider

- Warm, cooperative sibling relationships appear to confer a number of benefits. What impact do you think it will have if siblings are conflictual or ambivalent towards one another?
- Is it inevitable that lone children will lose out, or can their absence of siblings be compensated in some way?

Sibling Conflict

Festinger's (1954) classic Social Comparison Theory explains that humans tend to evaluate themselves in comparison to others, particularly those who are similar to themselves and physically proximate. People therefore tend to compare themselves with their siblings, and to compare parental behaviours towards them. Parental Differential Treatment (PDT) in terms of affection, discipline or behaviour is a major cause of antagonism and conflict between siblings (Tucker et al., 2013). Although Western norms advocate equal treatment of offspring, most parents recognise that they treat their children differently, primarily because every child is unique, meaning adjustments in expectations and discipline need to be made.

Disparities in treatment are not problematic if there is an understandable reason (e.g. a sibling requires extra attention due to a disability). However, when there is no apparent need, disfavoured children show higher levels of depression (Shanahan et al., 2008), antisocial or delinquent behaviour (Richmond, Stocker, & Rienks 2005) and substance abuse. PDT has a more negative impact on girls than on boys and on older than on younger children (Tamrouti-Makkink et al., 2004).

As we noted earlier, when tensions and disputes are minor and infrequent, they can play an important role in building children's social and emotional resilience and negotiating skills (Pickering & Sanders, 2017). However, frequent, prolonged or violent attacks can cause considerable physical, emotional and psychological damage, and ongoing sibling conflict is frequently a predictor of future emotional problems (van Berkel et al., 2018). Sibling aggression is the most common form of in-family violence (Straus, 2000), yet it garners relatively little attention. Hoetger et al. (2015) suggest that about 80% of children have been kicked, punched or bitten by their siblings, and Dunn and Munn's (1986) observational research suggests that sibling conflict happens up to eight times per hour. Parents often express dismay and confusion regarding how to calm warring siblings (Pickering & Sanders, 2017). As a result, many simply withdraw and the issues escalate. Ross and Lazinski (2014) propose that involved parenting is crucial if children are to learn to resolve differences and respect differing opinions. However, research indicates that ongoing or high levels of sibling abuse are generally indicative of broader issues around violence within the family, and therefore require investigation (Caffaro, 2020).

Twins and Multiples

Society is fascinated by multiple births and this interest means that its impact on children and their families is frequently scrutinised by both researchers and the public. Studies suggest that whereas dizygotic (non-identical) twins may have a broadly similar experience to any other siblings, monozygotic (identical) twins and those who are part of a larger birth group generally have a very different life experience to singletons (Lewin, 2016).

Impact on parents

Many couples have mixed feelings about having twins (or more). Having multiple children can make couples feel very special, but the additional demands of raising twins can also lead to feelings of having nothing left for each other. Mothers in particular report feeling frustrated that they are unable to give sufficient individual attention to each child and are thus prevented from being the parent they want to be. Many mothers also report feeling overwhelmed and experiencing a 'loss of self', wherein they feel they have no space or time to be anything other than a mother.

Fathers of twins work longer hours, help more at home and are more involved in their children's care than the fathers of singletons. This is probably attributable to the additional financial burden and caring needs twins create. However, where one parent is predominantly the wage-earner while the other is predominantly the carer, resentments can emerge, sometimes coupled with a sense of isolation if the wage-earner feels excluded by the carer's close relationship with the multiple group. In combination, these factors mean that fathers of multiples are more likely to become depressed than fathers of singletons and rates of marital breakdown are higher in families with multiples than those with singletons.

Impact on the family

Nuclear families usually have two distinct groups – the parents and the children. In families with multiples, there is a third group – the twins or triplets. If the multiples always side with one another, they can have a powerful effect on the family dynamic, particularly in single parent families. In such circumstances, the parent can end up feeling alone and isolated. Similarly, being the brother or sister of multiples can be difficult; not only are they excluded from the twins' or triplets' special relationship, but society's interest in multiples frequently results in the twins becoming the focus of attention and the siblings being left out. Even if parents are careful, family, friends and casual contacts can inadvertently reinforce the feeling that the sibling is less important than the multiples, thus damaging the singleton's sense of self-worth. Conversely, jealousy can lead to attention-seeking behaviours and aggression towards multiples. On the whole, boys find it harder to adapt to the existence of multiples among their siblings than girls, but the more siblings there are in the family, the easier it is as the sense of isolation is reduced.

Impact on children

Being part of a twin relationship is a unique phenomenon that has a profound impact on upbringing and development. Twins are together from conception through to young adulthood; they experience significant life events in tandem and spend the majority of their time together. These special environmental conditions, which result from having a life partner from the moment of conception, affect psychological and social development as well as the relationships they form throughout the rest of their lives. This brings benefits in that they can function as one another's transitional objects, providing solace and security.

Twins often lack the usual ego boundaries and, as young children, can struggle to establish where they end and their twin begins. They may therefore feel reprimanded when the twin is told off or cry when their twin cries. This may develop into ego fusion (Stewart, 2000), particularly in identical or monozygotic MZ twins, who may struggle to develop their own, individual identities. This is probably partially attributable to social pressure – twins are often given alliterative or rhyming names to show they are a unit, and others are inclined to resist when twins attempt to separate. During adolescence, when children naturally draw away from their parents in order to establish their unitary identity, twins often struggle to break the bond with one another in the same way. This can create conflict and hesitation or lead to attempts to establish equally powerful bonds with friends or prospective partners. Clearly, it has the potential to make relationships problematic, but research suggests that appropriate parenting can help twins to successfully establish a unitary identity (Bacon, 2019).

Case Study – Three is the magic number by Judith Szenasi, the mother of triplets

I had just started a very exciting job but felt unwell during the autumn with headaches, sickness and tiredness. A colleague suggested that I should do a pregnancy test. The results showed immediately – positive! We shared the happy news with both sets of parents over dinner at our house, while the great storm of November 1987 raged outside. Thinking back, the irony is not lost to me.

An appointment with my GP confirmed the pregnancy but he insisted I must have made a mistake with my dates, as he was convinced I was much further on. My usual flat stomach also started to expand rapidly over the next few weeks. These should have been clues that a multiple birth was a possibility. However, it was not until the first scan at 16 weeks that the monitor showed three little heads. At 33 weeks, our babies were delivered by an elective C-section, boy, girl, boy. The children were a good weight, all over 4 lbs, but boy 1 struggled a little with maintaining his temperature, so they all stayed in the Special Care Baby Unit for about two weeks until they were ready to come home.

It was clear that the girl was developmentally very much ahead of the boys. She walked at 9 months while the boys found their feet at 16 months. As parents, observing the group dynamic was fascinating – they all liked playing together as well as with their peers and were extremely popular and sociable. Growing up, they were all part of the same friendship groups, and the house was always full of children – boys and girls, and later young men and women. As parents of triplets, we notice how supportive they are of each other's needs, and it is wonderful to see how they love spending time together as adults with their partners. They went to different universities and chose different career paths, but always kept in close contact with each other. This year our daughter became a mother in July, and our last-born son became a father in August. I asked them what they thought it was like growing up as a triplet.

Girl: There were so many positives being a triplet. We grew up together, we had the same friendship groups. We never felt alone, and we've always had a laugh together! It was not scary starting school because we always had each other. We are really close and will always have a special bond. We spend a lot of time together as adults with our partners, holidaying together, having family time. All our partners get along and now we are having babies at the same time! I can't actually think of any negatives. We never competed, growing up together was just really fun.

(Continued)

Boy (last born): Growing up, I felt there was no big competition between us. Once myself and my bro were a bit competitive with football but that died out pretty quickly. We always looked out for each other. We were all into different things and hobbies. The relationship between us all is so very special! I think three is a magic number for sibling dynamics. If two of us were annoyed at the other one, it wouldn't last for long as two versus one never felt very fair. I don't really remember arguing, hardly ever, even as teenagers. I always felt a bond where we would all look out for each other. Sometimes I felt a bit like the big brother. The positives of being a triplet are you get to experience the big life events at the same time, and you all grow up together. We always had a great group of friends growing up, as we all hung out together, boys and girls. I can't honestly think of any negatives of being a triplet. It is hard to compare to things when it's all you have ever known, but speaking to friends about their relationships with siblings growing up, they did not have so much fun as we did. Today I feel very lucky to be a triplet.

Boy (first born): Growing up, we were very close and we had the same friends, so we would always be together. That was great but maybe I relied on my brother to make the friends for me. I can't remember us arguing much at all. We weren't competitive. The only example I can remember is football. At a young age we played on separate teams. It was extremely positive for me having siblings that would always look after me and help me out. Perhaps a negative, I guess it hindered my confidence in later life as when we were apart (going to university, for example), it took a while to get used to making my own friends.

As parents, we feel it is a privilege to have brought up triplets and to know that they continue to love and support each other through adulthood.

Time to consider

- Based on the information in this chapter, what would you regard as being the main advantages and disadvantages of having siblings?
- Do you think the advantages and disadvantages of having siblings are different for children who are twins or triplets from singletons?

Final reflection

As we attempt to weigh up why some siblings are best friends and others are sworn enemies, we can find no easy answers. Certainly, some factors seem to increase the chances of harmony or friction, but none of them represent certainties. Every child has their own individual mix of characteristics, and these, together with the individual characteristics of their sibling(s), determine the style, quality and nature of their interactions. Furthermore, this relationship exists within the context of the family environment and the circumstances in which they find themselves. It is the cumulative impact of all these elements that shapes the sibling relationship, rather than a single causal factor. However, where a warm and loving relationship does exist, it provides considerable cognitive, social and emotional benefits for the siblings.

Key points

- Every sibling relationship is unique, but is capable of having a profound impact.
- Whether relations between siblings are harmonious or conflictual depends on a range of intrinsic and extrinsic factors.
- Positive sibling relationships have a positive developmental impact.

Further reading

Howe, N., Della Porta, S., Recchia, H.E., & Ross, H.S. (2016) 'Because if you don't put the top on, it will spill': a longitudinal study of sibling teaching in early childhood. *Developmental Psychology*, 52(11), 1832–1842.

This is an interesting study that considers children's willingness to teach and learn from their siblings, and how this practice changes as the children age.

Sibs – www.sibs.org.uk/

The charity Sibs provides information and support for the siblings of disabled children and young people. You can find more information about them at this website.

10

PARENTING PRETERM NEWBORNS IN HOSPITAL AND DURING CHILDHOOD

Christopher Barnes

Overview

This chapter will discuss the impact that premature birth, low birthweight and/or having a sick newborn has on families. It will consider why these circumstances present such unique challenges and some of the ways in which these challenges can be met. The information covered will include what happens when newborns require neonatal care, the unique circumstances surrounding those born early, and how appropriate support may enhance the developmental outcomes of the child across their lifespan (i.e. cognitively, physically and in their communication). The chapter will specifically focus on those family-based interventions that incorporate parental touch or seek to enhance parenting skills.

This chapter will...

- Consider prematurity and how parenting is characterised during hospitalisation and in the early years
- Consider the impact and outcomes of prematurity across the child's lifespan
- Outline several parent-based interventions that can support and enhance outcomes for children and their families.

Key terms

Hospitalisation; intervention; parenting; prematurity; pre-term; support

Introduction

It is difficult to imagine, unless you have been in the situation yourself, what it is like for parents to have a baby who has been admitted into neonatal or specialist care. The causes may not always be immediately clear but may include premature birth, low birthweight, complications at birth, illness (genetic or acquired) or a need for surgical intervention. Whatever the reason, the changes to the family unit may be wide-ranging, significant and in some cases long-lasting. In this chapter we explore one of the most prolific and multifaceted causes of change, prematurity, and its associated comorbid factors.

Time to consider

Before you read on, take a moment and note down the sorts of things you think might result from being born early (e.g. things that will impact child development or the family).

Prematurity and Newborn Illness

In around 8% (1 in every 13) of live births in the UK, the baby is born early (at less than 37 weeks gestation). This amounts to about 60,000 babies each year (BLISS, 2022). The severity of the prematurity ranges from moderately (32–37 weeks gestation), to very (28–32 weeks gestation), to extremely (less than 28 weeks gestation). It is common for babies who come early to also have a reduced birthweight. Birthweight is classified as low (less than 2.5 kg), very low (less than 1.5 kg) or extremely low (less than 1 kg). When a baby is born both early and of low birthweight, the child is referred to as being preterm. Data from the World Health Organization (WHO, 2022a) indicates that the highest rates of preterm births occur in lower-income countries (with rates between 5–18% globally across all countries). This equates to a global estimate of some 15 million babies and their families being impacted each year by prematurity. The consequences include neonatal morbidity (impacting some 1 million children) with others in some cases facing life-long disability or other health-related complications, such as having an increased risk of blindness and respiratory problems, mental disabilities and cerebral palsy. Research also indicates that children's temperament may be impacted, with an elevated risk for attention-deficit hyperactivity disorder (Cassiano et al., 2020). While not all children and families will experience the most severe types of adversity, they may still face additional challenges to future relationship formation.

Why are babies born prematurely?

The reasons why mothers give birth prematurely are varied and not always clear, but may include intrauterine infection, cervical thinning or length reduction (Iams, 2003), premature rupture of the membranes surrounding the foetus (Kenyon, Boulvain & Neilson, 2003) or multiple births. Social factors, such as living in adverse or deprived circumstances, have been found to have some degree of impact, as have personal factors such as maternal age, hereditary conditions or drug and alcohol misuse (Jewell et al., 2001).

Parenting in a Hospitalised Environment and its Psychological Impact

Whenever I teach the topic of prematurity to my students, I will often ask them to put themselves in the shoes of the parent and say that I want to take them on a journey through the experience itself. There are many things that a parent of a premature baby has to cope with, but the first of these is the surprise and shock of going into premature labour or finding out that (perhaps due to complications) the baby has to be delivered straight away. For many parents, this will be unexpected and will represent a significant change in the planning for and attachment to their baby. The early arrival of their baby may result in emergency transportation to the hospital. The stress encountered will be substantial for all family members and there is evidence from parents' own accounts (Leung, 2004; Manns, 2004) and scientific research (Padden & Glen, 1997) of this. The environment of a neonatal unit is also quite different. It is naturally full of medicalised equipment, but the sounds of the lifesaving equipment and the mix of medical staff and families sharing each other's lives and emotions can be difficult (Redshaw & Harris, 1995), and everything is centred around the babies lying in their cots or incubators. In many circumstances, babies may also be connected by tubes, wires, respirators and intravenous feeds. Things may be difficult too if babies need to be transferred to other more specialised hospitals, or if the mother has been discharged and can no longer stay close by. In combination, it can create a situation that is not only stressful, but also isolates parents from their usual sources of support (Eckerman & Oehler, 1992).

Time to consider

- Did any of the text you have just read surprise you and, if so, what was it?
- How do you think parenting in hospital might impact the formation of new relationships between parent and child?
- Do you think family structures (e.g. single-parent households) or cultural beliefs impact the experience of prematurity at this time, and why?

Developmental Outcomes across the Lifespan: Birth Cohort Studies

There have been many studies that have investigated the implications of prematurity. Some of the research draws attention to the physical, neurodevelopmental or wider psychological impacts of premature birth. In order to understand the outcomes for those born early, it is important to track development over time and, where possible, to follow the same individuals from birth into childhood. The Centre for Longitudinal Studies (CLS; www.cls.ioe.ac.uk/) is an Economic and Social Research Council resource centre that has conducted several of the most important longitudinal follow-up studies. The Centre is responsible for running four exceptional and internationally renowned cohort studies:

- The 1958 National Child Development Study
- The 1970 British Cohort Study
- The Millennium Cohort Study
- Children of the 2020s Study.

These studies are often referred to as birth cohort studies as they attempt to follow a specific group of children with particular characteristics or who are born within a certain timeframe. For example, the 1958 National Child Development Study (NCDS) tracked the lives of 17,000 people born between 3 March and 9 March 1958 in England, Scotland and Wales. Information was collected about these individuals at regular time-points – in 1965, 1969, 1974, 1981, 1991, 1999–2000, 2004, 2008 and 2013. The NCDS was important because it focused on a broad range of factors, including physical and educational development, economic circumstances, employment, family life, health behaviour, wellbeing, social participation and attitudes. Perhaps one of the most interesting findings was the effects of birthweight (BW) and socio-economic status (SES) on future cognitive outcomes when the tracked children were of school age. In 2002 Jefferis, Power, & Hertzman, analysed data from 10,845 children to see whether BW and SES were associated with various cognitive tests when the children were age 7, 11 and 16. The findings suggested that both BW and SES produce independent effects on children's cognitive ability. However, SES produced a much stronger effect in terms of performance in mathematics.

The Millennium Cohort Study (MCS), on the other hand, followed the lives of 19,000 children born in the UK between September 2000 and January 2002. This study aimed to be more representative of the UK population and included a higher number of children from disadvantaged or ethnic minority backgrounds. Data collected ranged across five collection points from 2001 to 2015. Some of the findings suggest that the parents' level of education and family income were the most powerful predictors of cognitive test performance at age 11, that there were significant (but statistically small) differences in cognitive performance between males and females, and that girls were generally more risk-averse than boys (Platt et al., 2014). However, there have also been birth cohort studies including prematurely born babies. These are known as the EPICure studies (www.epicure.ac.uk) and are designed to explore survival and the later health status (e.g. disability) of extremely premature babies (less than 27 weeks gestation).

EPICure 1 (1995) and EPICure 2 (2006)

All 276 maternity units in the UK and the Republic of Ireland (at the time) reported information about the 4,004 registered births that occurred over a 10-month period. Less than a quarter of the newborns were admitted to a neonatal unit (n = 811) with only a third of these babies being discharged home (n = 314). Of those discharged home, a series of studies started when the infant was 1 year old and continued up to age 19. During the early years' period, children had mostly been diagnosed with a developmental or neurological problem or oxygen dependency. However, at age 6, and compared to their peers, children were found to have poorer hand–eye skills and attention, growth did not match their peers but was progressing, but the children were doing reasonably well at school and had normal behaviour patterns (EPICure 1 ref., 1995). The EPICure 2 study was initiated in part because there appeared to be more babies surviving by 2006 as compared to when the 1995 trial began. It was found that the number of babies admitted to neonatal care had risen significantly (44%) from those reported in 1995, and that survival also increased (13%) (EPICure 2 ref., 2006). However, the types of problems experienced by extremely premature babies largely remained unchanged.

What do the EPICure 1 and 2 results mean?

- Birthweight and socio-economic status are highly influential factors in later development. The EPICure studies (2022a and 2022b) suggest that parents' socio-economic status, derived from level of education and family income, is a powerful predictor of cognitive performance in children, and particularly language and executive function in later life (Greenfield & Moorman, 2019). Work by Shahaeian et al. (2018) investigated the longitudinal association between early shared reading and children's later school achievement in more general populations. The data illustrates that children who are often read to by their parents develop better cognitive skills, a finding that is particularly found for low SES families.
- The earlier a baby is born, and particularly for extremely premature babies, the higher the risk of death, long-term disability and poorer motor and cognitive functioning. A recent meta-analysis has suggested that children born pre-term or with a low birthweight generally perform less well in their executive functions – working memory, inhibition and cognitive flexibility – than children born at term. This is important since executive function deficits are associated with poor academic performance at school age (van Houdt et al., 2019). Similarly, Allotey et al. (2018) report test scores that are lower across motor skills, behaviour,

reading, mathematics and spelling at primary school age. Interestingly, these issues continued through to secondary (high) school age (except for mathematics). The findings were also evidenced in a recent meta-analysis (McBryde et al., 2020) that suggests that pre-term birth is associated with academic underperformance in reading and mathematics. Furthermore, there is an increased likelihood that male children born at a lower gestational age will have motor skill deficits or problems with language when of lower birthweight (Hernández, Fernández & Muñoz, 2022).

- The survival of babies born extremely premature increased between 1995 and 2006 but the problems experienced by them have remained largely unchanged. This means that the number of children with significant health and developmentally related problems is now greater.

Parenting Pre-terms and Family Relationships in the Early Years

It is sometimes the case that prematurely born children have different and distinct needs from children born at term. Not only are some infants likely to be poorly, but they may have conditions or delayed development that is with them for some time or indefinitely. Premature babies may be different in terms of their size, weight, appearance (particularly immediately after birth), their pattern of crying as well as their self-regulated behaviours (Levy-Shiff, Sharir & Mogliner, 1989). They may behave differently, being low in alertness, and have fewer periods of wakefulness (Harrison, 1992), be less active and be less responsive to social stimulation (Crnic et al., 1983b; Eckerman et al., 1994). It means that pre-terms are more difficult to bring to an alert state and can easily be over-stimulated (Eckerman et al., 1994; Fearon et al., 2002), making the parents' job of reading their baby's behavioural cues a difficult process, especially when the babies respond in a particularly disorganised and unpredictable way. Failure to interpret the baby's behaviour correctly has been linked to asynchrony in parent–baby interactions and has a long-term impact on the infant's psychological development. It hinders their ability to interact socially and causes psychological difficulties and delays in the long term (Krebs, 1998). Naturally, those professionals who work with premature or sick children and their families have looked for ways to support them and negate the adverse effects where possible.

Family-based Interventions and Outcomes for Children Born Preterm

Research conducted with preterm babies and their families is multi-disciplinary (including Psychologists, Educationalists and those working in areas allied to health). Consequently, research and intervention has focused on four main areas from the postpartum period into the early years, and these are:

- The physical development or early behaviours of the child
- The impact on the cognitive development of the child
- The parent–child relationship
- The impact on parents' psychological functioning.

A few of these interventions are considered below, although many more types and variations exist.

Touch-based interventions during hospitalisation and the postnatal period

The importance of early supplemental touch for hospitalised pre-terms is not a new thing. In the late 1970s and early 1980s, researchers began to consider what the most appropriate forms of stimulation were for prematurely born babies, and the ways that babies could be supported during hospitalisation. Preliminary investigations indicated that some form of stimulation, which was additional to the standard care by medics and parents, could benefit the physiological (e.g. weight gain), immunological (e.g. SIgA – an antibody that has a role in immune function) and behavioural processes of the preterm newborn. As a consequence, many researchers have designed and created sensory nurturing interventions for the prime purpose of enhancing the development of newborns. These types of interventions either stimulated more than one sense (multimodal interventions) or just one sense (unimodal interventions).

Multimodal sensory nurturing interventions

Multimodal interventions use touch (e.g. baby massage), sounds (e.g. infant directed speech), visual (e.g. maintaining eye contact) and vestibular (e.g. rocking) stimulation to enhance the development of newborns. Scientifically speaking, multimodal intervention studies were subject to some critique because they were seen to stimulate too many of the senses at the same time, leading to sensory bombardment (Adamson-Macedo et al., 1994) and making it difficult methodologically to understand which of the senses was accounting for any observed differences. Nevertheless, multimodal interventions designed and delivered by researchers such as White-Traut and colleagues (1997, 2002) have demonstrated benefits to the behavioural state organisation (i.e. how behaviour such as sleep-wake cycles are better regulated) and the progression of feeding, and reduced the length of hospitalisation (Nelson et al., 2001; White-Traut et al., 2002). It is important to note that touch played a particularly integral role (White-Traut et al., 1997).

Unimodal sensory nurturing interventions

The main types of unimodal intervention have focused largely on touch and include techniques that involve (i) simply holding the baby or placing hands on the baby, and

(ii) more actively touching the baby. The first method involves static or passive touch or skin-to-skin contact, such as containment holding – where hands are placed gently on the head and/or torso of the baby (Harrison et al., 1996; Jay, 1982; Tribotti, 1990) and kangaroo care, where the baby is placed onto the bare chest of the mother or father and is undressed to the nappy. The second method involves a more active approach, such as in TAC-TIC (Touching and Caressing-Tender in Caring; Macedo, 1984) that involves gentle, light and systematic stroking of the baby and baby massage (Field, Diego & Hernandez-Reif, 2010) that involves a moderate pressure touch across the babies head, torso and limbs.

Physiological and general outcomes for children of touch-based interventions

When a containment hold was used babies tended to require less supplementary oxygen, demonstrated stability in TcPO2 levels (oxygen saturation in the blood), greater weight gain and reduced periods of hospitalisation. Containment holding has also been used more generally and widely following regular medical procedures, such as the heel prick test when blood samples are taken (Bellieni & Johnston, 2016; Obeidat & Shuriquie, 2015). When kangaroo care is used, the benefits include heart rate regulation, increased oxygen saturation levels, increased weight gain and enhanced sleeping patterns (Furman, Minich & Hack, 2002; Ludington-Hoe et al., 2000; Ohgi et al., 2002; Ruiz-Pelaez, Charpak & Cuervo, 2004). Research on using baby massage reports that, during hospitalisation, the positive outcomes are weight gain, increased bone density and earlier discharge rates (Field, Diego & Hernandez-Reif, 2010). Light and gentle touch, such as that used in TAC-TIC (Macedo, 1984; see also Adamson-Macedo, 1985–86), tends to result in the baby losing less weight during the first week of life, facilitates digestion (Hayes, 1996), bolsters the immune system and increases SIgA concentrations (Hayes et al., 1999). It also leads to earlier discharges from hospital (De Roiste & Bushnell, 1996). The baby progresses to all suck feeds earlier (De Roiste & Bushnell, 1993, 1995, 1996) and displays significantly more comfort behaviours than distress ones (Hayes, 1996).

Familial and psychological outcomes of touch-based interventions

In a recent Cochrane Review, several benefits of kangaroo care/skin-to-skin contact have been reported. These include increased breastfeeding rates and durations, reduced state anxiety, greater parenting confidence and benefits to maternal–infant bonding (Moore, Anderson & Bergman, 2016). In addition, a qualitative study by Anderzén-Carlsson, Lamy and Eriksson (2014) has suggested that the positive benefits to mothers were restorative, in terms of feeling good, relieving emotional suffering, and in finding the use of touch a rewarding and learning experience. Kangaroo care gave mothers a role and improved their self-esteem. They enjoyed getting to know and becoming familiar with how the baby behaved. This familiarity and intimate family time proved to be just as important for the baby in their process of recovery. Baby massage research also indicates benefits to maternal mood (Fujita et al., 2006), mother–infant interaction (Onozawa et al., 2001) and attachment (Gürol & Polat, 2012). Benefits from TAC-TIC indicated that children were more likely to have higher intelligence scores at 7 years of age (Adamson-Macedo et al., 1993), and that it positively impacts maternal self-efficacy, self-esteem and attachment (Barnes & Adamson-Macedo, 2022). Indeed, when women actively use gentle light and systematic touch it increases the opportunity for positive interactions and is likely to enhance their overall confidence in doing things for and with their baby. Therefore, these sorts of positive benefits are important since they improve not only the relationship between mother and child but also enhance family cohesion.

Strategies, skills and training

A recent meta-analysis conducted by Ferreira et al. (2020) investigated whether early interventions that focus on the family improve children's development (e.g. cognitive, motor or language development) in the first three years of life. Data from 12 studies was examined and assessed for the frequency, occurrence and duration of implementation, and the composition of any guidelines or education provided to the parents for delivery to their child. The analysis demonstrated that programmes of early, family-focused intervention did have a positive impact on cognition, but it was not as clear or consistent that either motor/physical or language development was enhanced. Other studies, such as those by Alves et al. (2022), examined the effectiveness of longitudinal psychosocial interventions. The intervention they used was developed to strengthen maternal interactive skills while biological and contextual variables were taken into consideration. The intervention was delivered at six timepoints from birth up to 12 months. Alves et al. (2022) report that the intervention used was most effective for vulnerable groups, particularly for those mothers who had less schooling and whose infants were more impacted by prematurity.

Time to consider

- In what other ways do you think families and children can be supported during hospitalisation and throughout their childhood?
- Is there a role for education and how might a classroom teacher support those who were born early?

Final reflection

In this chapter we have considered how prematurity may affect parenting and family relationships, and how it may impact the development of the child across their lifespan. The information and research presented suggests that parenting a premature baby is complex and, in some instances, it can impact the longer-term development of that child. The children can experience cognitive, motor and language issues, although many will catch up in line with their full-term peers. Nevertheless, there are parent-based interventions that can help support and enhance the development of their child.

Key points

- Prematurely born babies present with a wide range of complex health and developmental needs, which can lead to a broad range of outcomes, depending on their severity.
- Parenting a prematurely born baby can confront families with many challenges during hospitalisation and throughout childhood.
- Longitudinal studies show that prematurity may cause life-long issues in cognition and function. However, with appropriate support and interventions, many issues of delayed development or adversities can be overcome or diminished.

Further reading

Alves, C.R., Gaspardo, C.M., Altafim, E.R., & Linhares, M.B.M. (2022) Effectiveness of a longitudinal psychosocial intervention to strengthen mother–child interactions: the role of biological and contextual moderators. *Children and Youth Services Review*, 133, 106333.

Most studies are only able to provide a snapshot of development at a particular moment in time. This article not only illustrates the importance of studying development over time but also the longer-term consequences of intervention on both parent and child.

Field, T., Diego, M., & Hernandez-Reif, M. (2010) Preterm infant massage therapy research: a review. *Infant Behavior and Development*, 33(2), 115–124.

This article is for anyone who is interested in baby massage and has been written by the foremost experts in the field.

White-Traut, R.C., Schwertz, D., McFarlin, B., & Kogan, J. (2009) Salivary cortisol and behavioral state responses of healthy newborn infants to tactile-only and multisensory interventions. *Journal of Obstetric, Gynecologic, & Neonatal Nursing: Clinical Scholarship for the Care of Women, Childbearing Families, & Newborns*, 38(1), 22–34.

Multi-modal sensory nurturing interventions do not get as much attention within literature in comparison to those that focus on a single sense (such as touch). This article is one of the only ones that directly compares multi- and uni-modal intervention and illustrates some of the differences between them.

11

FAMILY RELATIONSHIPS AND AUTISM

Trevor Cotterill

Overview

Having a child with autism can impact the family, and the people within it, in many ways. This chapter considers some of the issues and challenges for parents and siblings, while also highlighting the positive aspects noted in the research.

This chapter will...

- Review parents' initial reactions to an autism diagnosis
- Review the experiences of siblinghood in relation to autism
- Consider the impact on parents living with an autistic child
- Discuss how families with autistic children may have been impacted by the Covid-19 pandemic.

Key terms

Autism; COVID-19; diagnosis; families; parents; siblinghood

Introduction

There is a substantial body of research investigating how having a child with autism can affect the family. Some of this has focused on the demands that autism can place on a family, while other studies have reflected on the positive consequences. Research informs us that having an autistic child invariably has some impact on family relationships and on individual members within the group. Parents, siblings, grandparents and extended family members are all affected. While there appear to be a few recurrent themes – such as adjusting parental expectations and worrying about sibling relationships (Doheny, 2008) – the degree of challenge may vary depending on the severity of the autism.

Time to consider

Before you read the chapter, consider the following:

- What do you think is the impact on parents when their child receives a diagnosis of autism?
- To what extent do you think having an autistic child affects family relationships?

Parents' Initial Reactions to Diagnosis

Parental views and responses to their child's diagnosis encompass co-existing positive and negative aspects (Meleady et al., 2020). Their emotional responses may involve stress, anger, frustration, sadness, despair and grief, possibly mixed with a sense of acceptance and relief at finally receiving a diagnosis (Kalyva, 2011). While some parents come to terms with the diagnosis (which is referred to as being '*resolved*'), other *unresolved* parents find themselves unable to fully accept it. Several researchers have investigated the underlying reasons for the lack of acceptance and have discovered some notable variations.

On the whole, mothers are more likely to report feeling unresolved and emotionally overwhelmed than fathers (Milshtein et al., 2010), and parents of children with severe symptoms are more likely to struggle with acceptance than those with less severe symptoms (Poslawsky et al., 2014). Understanding the condition and its causes also appear to be an important facet of acceptance. For instance, Milshtein et al. (2010) discovered that unresolved parents were preoccupied with the causes of their child's autism and this made them feel detached and confused. On the other hand, parents who were told their child's autism was genetic found it easier to accept because the diagnosis appeared to be based on facts rather than judgements or self-reports (Reiff et al., 2017). Milshtein et al. (2010) investigated parents' views about their child's autism diagnosis and found that just over half in their sample were unresolved. In contrast, parents who did feel as though they had reached a resolution (a coming to terms) with the diagnosis were much more likely to acknowledge the difficulties during the diagnostic process as well as any positive outcomes since that time. Those who were unable to resolve the diagnosis had more negative perceptions of their child and about the impact of the diagnosis on their family.

Graungaard and Skov (2007) suggest that all parents find the diagnostic process emotionally stressful, and the certainty of the diagnosis is central to parents' experiences. Having received the diagnosis, parents then face an emotionally complex process filled with challenging emotions (Makino et al., 2021). Many parents report a feeling of grief, which Wayment and Brookshire (2018) found to be linked to viewing autism as a loss and unjust. It should be noted, however, that the majority of parents adapted well to the circumstances and the care of their child (Poslawsky et al., 2014). Parents may adjust more easily to the diagnosis if it is framed around positive aspects, if they are supported to understand their child's behaviour, and if they are relieved of guilt and self-blame. Helping them to develop a greater understanding of autism can also lead parents to accessing support.

The Experience of Being a Sibling of an Autistic Child

Being a sibling of someone with autism can have its own set of challenges. Table 11.1 provides details about research on the experience of siblings.

Table 11.1   Research studies on the experiences of siblings of a child with autism

Research	Findings
Corsano et al. (2017)	Typically developing (TD) siblings expressed mixed feelings about their autistic brother. These included feeling a sense of responsibility, concern about their future and concern about friendship difficulties. Most siblings integrated their positive and negative feelings, but some displayed rejection, denial or a sense of persecution.
Laghi et al. (2018)	Younger TD siblings reported more frequent negative behaviours with their siblings than older TD siblings. This was due to the younger children typically spending more time with their siblings.
Jones et al. (2019)	A consideration of how individual characteristics impacted sibling relationships and the emergence of behavioural and emotional difficulties in TD siblings led to the conclusion that: • greater severity of autism can cause depression in TD siblings • a TD sibling's understanding of autism can improve the quality of the sibling relationship.
Tomeny et al. (2017)	Autistic children may demonstrate aggression, self-injurious behaviour, mental health issues, sleep and feeding difficulties. Social support may protect the TD sibling from assuming care of their parent or sibling.
Hooper & Doehler (2012)	One TD sibling frequently assumes a caregiving role, such as providing emotional support, carrying out household tasks or taking care of the individual's physical needs.
Tozer, Atkin and Wenham (2013)	TD siblings who care for their autistic sibling can feel guilty if they decide to move out of the family home, focus on their career or start to have children.
Watson, Hanna and Jones (2021)	Interactions with the autistic sibling can impact self- and personal development, and experiences of coping.

As Table 11.1 shows, typically developing (TD) siblings experience both difficulties and benefits as a result of their relationship with their autistic sibling. On the one hand, they develop greater empathy, understanding and coping abilities, which can make them feel good about themselves. In many instances it can lead to fundraising and steps to improve others' understanding of autism. On the other hand, TD siblings may feel obliged to assume responsibility for household chores or care of their sibling in order to give their parents a break. For instance, Cridland et al. (2016) discovered that the girls in their sample felt they undertook unfair additional caregiving roles and responsibilities and yet received reduced parental attention. Participants in other studies have also spoken of the need to intervene to protect their sibling from bullying or self-harm, which can feel onerous. However, Gorjy, Fielding and Falkmer (2017) found that children's experiences of living with an autistic sibling were neither positive nor negative. Instead, they described their lives as being 'different' from those of their peers.

Many TD siblings describe being proud of their autistic sibling. Costa and da Silva Pereira (2019) found that siblings who have a high degree of knowledge about and understanding of autism feel less embarrassed and are better able to accept the challenges that this difference causes. All participants indicated that:

- they have a solid and close relationship with their siblings
- are more tolerant in the face of existing difficulties in their relationship
- react negatively to the attitudes of others who are less understanding and tolerant
- are proud of their siblings for their progress and accomplishments
- are unconditionally protective of their siblings in all situations.

However, Ward et al. (2016) found negative attributes, including:

- fear of frightening or violent behaviour
- decreased sibling intimacy
- social and emotional difficulties.

Research suggests that the experience of siblings is varied. In some instances, they may feel as though they need to change their own behaviour (e.g. such as having to 'give in' or keep things to themselves to avoid conflict) in order to maintain the social cohesion of the family. Indeed, Angell, Meadan and Stoner (2012) note that children in their study used a variety of both emotion-focused and problem-focused coping strategies. In doing so, the children reported infrequent quarrels and enjoyment of mutual and shared activities. However, there were still times when they felt embarrassed or frustrated with their siblings' aggressive or socially inappropriate behaviour. In some instances, and particularly for the younger participants, they chose to remove themselves from their siblings to defuse potentially conflictual situations.

Nevertheless, there are occasions when a certain event can provoke feelings of anxiety or fears about safety. For example, Benderix and Sivberg (2007) identified feelings of sorrow, particularly when siblings were exposed to frightening behaviour or physical violence, and Ward et al. (2016) discovered that such behaviours often served to reduce sibling intimacy. However, Costa and da Silva Pereira (2019) found that a developed understanding of autism led TD children to be more accepting, less embarrassed and better able to deal with the challenges posed by life with their autistic sibling. This in turn increased their tolerance of any difficulties they might encounter with their sibling, and their intolerance of those who respond negatively to autistic individuals. While they were generally protective of their sibling, TD children frequently spoke of their pride in their siblings' progress and achievements, and of the strength of their relationship. Nevertheless, sisters (of autistics) in Pavlopoulou and Dimitriou's (2020) study indicated that even though they wanted to remain as close to their siblings as possible, they also felt a need to be independent and social outside the family.

The Impact on Parents Caring for an Autistic Child

Having an autistic child in the family can present challenges and makes parenting more demanding. Table 11.2 provides details about research on the experience of parents.

Table 11.2 Research studies on the experiences of parents of a child with autism

Research	Findings
Beurkens, Hobson and Hobson (2013)	Found that the severity of autism affects interactions between child and parent and that parent-reported difficulty in communicating with their children may be related to their child's level of language development.
Clifford and Minnes (2013)	Parents participating in support groups found them beneficial in aiding the development of coping strategies and encouraging them to access emotional and practical support.
Dabrowska and Pisula (2010)	Parents of autistic children are reported to use a range of strategies to cope, with mothers tending to use emotion-oriented and social diversion methods and fathers more problem-avoidance strategies.
Ekas, Lickenbrock & Whitman (2010)	Found that depression and stress in parents was related to negative behaviour displayed by their children (e.g. screaming, sleep problems, meltdowns or aggression).
Ekas et al. (2015)	Investigated and found links between parent reported optimism, benefit finding, social support and relationship satisfaction.
Falk, Norris and Quinn (2014)	Parents of autistic children were at an increased risk of experiencing physical and mental health problems as compared to parents of neurotypical children.
Hartley et al. (2010)	Parents of autistic children are twice as likely to divorce as parents of TD children.

(Continued)

Table 11.2 (Continued)

Research	Findings
Ku, Stinson and MacDonald (2019)	Examined the parenting differences between those with and without an autistic child. They discovered that parents of autistic children had an increased likelihood of displaying more controlling and negative behaviours and less supportive/warm verbal comments.
Lee (2009)	Parents of children with High-Functioning Autism Spectrum Disorder (HFASD) have an increased risk of depression and anxiety, and have less psychological stability, less optimism, lower self-esteem and lower marital adjustment scores. Mothers tended to use various coping mechanisms, such as professional help and family support.
Powers (2000)	The quality of parenting, of those with autistic children, may be impacted in two important ways: (i) they may become overprotective, and/or (ii) feel as though they are neglecting other family members by focusing upon their autistic child.
Totsika et al. (2011)	Mothers of 5-year-olds with autism had no greater instances of psychological problems than the mothers of TD children. However, much greater psychological distress was apparent among the mothers of children who had both autism and an intellectual disability.

Park et al. (2003) define 'family quality of life' (FQOL) as being when a family enjoys time together doing things which are important to them. Kuhlthau et al. (2014) indicate that parental quality of life (QoL) is influenced by having an autistic child, with lower QoL found in caregivers of autistic children compared to the general population. This finding reflects not only the caregiving burden associated with parenting an autistic child, but also the possibility of a knock-on effect for the child themselves. As we noted in Chapter 6, adaptation to the demands of parenting is influenced by the parent's satisfaction with their own relationship, and the extent to which they support one another. Those parents who enjoy strong, supportive relationships with their partners, have been shown to adapt better to these increased demands (García-López, Sarriá and Pozo, 2016)

Potter (2016) identified key themes in his relationship with his autistic son. He learned to appreciate his child's individual qualities, valuing his strong emotional bond with his son, his nurturing role and how it enhanced his own personal development. Similarly, research into the lived experience of female primary caregivers discovered that women with supportive partners reported positively on their role, experiences and relationship with their child (Markoulakis, Fletcher & Bryden, 2012). The provision of social, financial and familial support thus brought benefits for both the mother and the child.

In one interesting study, Timmons, Ekas and Johnson (2017) undertook research with mothers of autistic children. The mothers were divided into two groups. They were asked to write gratitude letters, with one group writing a letter of general gratitude to someone other than their own child and the other group writing a letter of gratitude to their own child (child gratitude). In the general gratitude group, mothers wrote about things such as social support, close personal relationships and other individual positive attributes. However, in the child gratitude group, they wrote about the child's ability to make progress, the child's personality, their inspiration and shared experiences.

The Impact of Covid-19 on Autistic Children and Their Families

In the wake of the Covid-19 pandemic, the world has become a more uncertain environment, which has caused stress and anxiety, especially for autistic individuals and their families. Autistic children may have had difficulty adhering to basic preventative measures, such as mask-wearing, social distancing and hand hygiene. Covid-19 testing methods, especially those that employ nasal swabs, have also likely been difficult to implement given the sensory issues intrinsic to autism (Kalb et al., 2021).

Vasa et al. (2021) suggest that autistic children are at elevated risk of psychiatric problems in response to the Covid-19 pandemic. This risk is due to their high rates of pre-pandemic psychiatric comorbidities and the disruption to routines and access to necessary supports as a result of lockdowns. Their research showed either a worsening of the children's pre-pandemic psychiatric diagnoses and/or the development of new psychiatric symptoms during the pandemic (Vasa et al., 2021). The autistic child's understanding of Covid-19, Covid-19 illness in the family, low family income, and symptoms of depression and anxiety in the parent increased the risk of the child's poor mental health during the pandemic.

A common concern among parents was the absence of socialisation opportunities for their child. Whereas some families attempted to fill this void with virtual socialisation (e.g. video calls and online gaming), other parents lamented that their child would require considerable 'catch up' in developing appropriate social skills following the pandemic. Ahmed et al. (2022) reviewed studies on the impact of Covid-19 carried out in Italy, Turkey, Portugal, Spain and the United Kingdom, with a total of 1,407 participants. The findings showed that behavioural issues in autistic children and adolescents have increased significantly, including emotional problems, aggression and hyperactivity. Responses from most parents indicated that their child experienced negative behavioural changes, including regression in a variety of skill areas, increased or new maladaptive behaviours, and increased mood symptoms.

Positive impacts of the pandemic

Although research findings were primarily negative, some studies did report positive outcomes for both the child and their family. From the child's point of view, the reduction in academic and social demands led to a commensurate reduction in stress, anxiety, self-harm and behavioural issues. Many parents also reported that their work patterns became more flexible during lockdown, enabling them to spend more quality time with their child and to teach them new skills or devise new strategies for learning and leisure. Shepard and Hancock (2020) explored the experiences of 502 parent carers of children with SEND during the time of the Covid-19 pandemic and found that this increased flexibility and freedom from anxiety led to children learning more life skills, such as cooking and gardening. Indeed, most families surveyed by Mumbardó-Adam, Barnet-López and Balboni (2021) said that their children coped better than expected with lockdown, and some felt the experience had helped to increase personal skills such as resilience (Meral, 2022; Parenteau et al., 2020).

In Greece, Papanikolaou et al. (2022) compared the impact of two different social crises – the financial crisis of 2008 and the crisis caused by Covid-19 – on the parenting stress, depressive symptomatology, quality of life and coping strategies of mothers who have autistic children and adolescents. They found that during the first phase of the pandemic crisis, the primary caregivers of autistic people in Greece felt more competent, less restricted and more supported in their role as parents compared to the economic crisis period. There were no opportunities for outdoor leisure activities, but parents had more time to pursue hobbies at home.

Negative impacts of the pandemic

Unfortunately, when asked to describe the early stages of lockdown, the majority of parents said it was challenging, and that the rapidity of social changes (Asbury et al., 2021) made them long for routine, stability and a normal life (Stadheim et al., 2022).

Common concerns included:

- increased sibling conflict
- increased stress (Manning, J., Billian, J. & Matson, J. 2021)
- feeling overwhelmed
- increased parental fatigue
- loss of childcare and therapy resources
- worries about ill health, isolation and money
- damage to psychological wellbeing
- increased behavioural problems (Colizzi et al., 2020).

Panjwani, Bailey and Kelleher (2021) also discovered a substantial shift in eating behaviours among autistic children, with the consumption of meat, seafood, vege-tables and 100% fruit juice significantly decreasing and the consumption of sweets increasing.

Echoing reports of challenges and growth, a mixed-method study of parents of autistic children and developmental disorders in Turkey reported reduced access to educational resources and socialisation opportunities, and increased conflict among family members. The findings showed that parents of autistic children are facing a wide range of challenges, including explaining Covid-19 and safety precautions to their child in a comprehensible way, assisting with e-learning and guiding their child back into social situations and the community (Parenteau et al., 2020).

Time to consider

- What do you think were the positive and negative consequences of the Covid-19 pandemic for autistic children and their families?
- How should schools work with families to support the transition of children back into a curriculum that involves face-to-face teaching?
- What lessons have been learnt from the lockdown experience to support families if another lockdown is ever introduced?

Case Study – James

James is aged 2 and his parents have noticed behaviours that they think might be early indicators of autism. James is always playing the same game by himself, repeatedly lining up his favourite toys in a particular order, and displays unusual behaviour, such as biting, pinching and kicking. He does not respond to his name and does not play with his older brother or his other toys. His parents have decided to see their GP for advice and/or a referral for diagnosis.

Using the information in this chapter, how do you think James's behaviour may impact on family relationships as he grows older?

Final reflection

This chapter has considered the impact that a diagnosis of autism may have on family relationships. It has explored some of the key research and examined the issues and debates affecting the families of autistic children, from initial diagnosis, through family relationships to the impacts of the recent Covid-19 pandemic. There is a mixed picture, with studies citing both positive outcomes and the difficulties that families may face. It is important to appreciate that while research can provide useful information about autism, it is also vital to listen to the lived experience of families, as these can provide rich insights.

Key points

- Receiving the news that a child has been diagnosed with autism can impact parents in a variety of ways, ranging from stress, anger, despair and grief through to relief and acceptance.
- Research into siblinghood has shone a light on the perceptions that family members have about relationships between typically developing (TD) and autistic siblings. Not surprisingly, research has shown that there are reports of positive emotions as well as challenges.
- Having an autistic child in the family can make parenting more demanding and present challenges. However, positive aspects can include family connectedness, closeness, positive meaning-making and spiritual and personal growth.
- The Covid-19 pandemic has impacted the lives of many individuals across the world, including families with autistic members. Research has shown how these families managed throughout the pandemic, revealing some positive outcomes as well as difficulties.

Further reading

Naseef, R. (2012) *Autism in the Family: Caring and Coping Together.* Baltimore, MD: Brookes Publishing.

Robert Naseef is a psychologist and father to an adult son with autism. In this book, he provides both personal and professional reflections and guidance.

Plimley, L., Bowen, M., & Morgan, S.H. (2006) *Autistic Spectrum Disorders in the Early Years.* London: Paul Chapman.

Covering topics such as identification, assessment, teaching and learning, social skills and behaviour, alternative intervention, home-based programs, and transition from preschool to kindergarten, this book provides clear information for all professionals who work with children from birth to five.

Rosenbach, H. (2021) *Family Dynamics: Socioemotional Development in Autistic and Neurotypical Siblings.* [online]. Available at: www.ecsdn.org/wp-content/uploads/2021/12/Helen-Rosenbach-University-of-Derby.pdf (accessed 4 July 2020).

This article provides a detailed and informative account of how autistic and neurotypical siblings can influence one another's social and emotional development.

12

ABUSIVE RELATIONSHIPS WITHIN THE FAMILY

Emma Twigg and Christopher Barnes

Overview

This chapter begins with a brief introduction to abuse within the family and why we should study it. We then go on to define abuse in all of its forms, and follow this with details of its incidence, prevalence and the risk factors associated with it. In the second portion of this chapter, we report on work that has used a social-ecological framework to understand and map out the context in which abuse takes place. Along the way, we invite the reader to sensitively pause for reflection and go deeper into a real-life account of an abusive situation. As we move towards the end of the chapter research is reported to illustrate the importance of psychological intervention and what it tells us about supporting abuse victims and their families.

This chapter will...

- Outline some of the definitions of abuse
- Identify some of the possible risk factors that have been associated with the incidences of abuse
- Consider some potential interventions and therapeutic outcomes.

Key terms

Abuse; risk factors, adverse childhood experiences; impact, outcomes and intervention

---

Introduction

The family is a unit where children and adults should feel the most secure, safe and happy. For many, though, this is not the case. Abuse within the family 'is very common and happens to people from all walks of life: from every social class, race, religion and age group' (Sterne & Poole, 2010, p. xi). The World Health Organization (WHO) (2020) reports that globally:

- '1 out of 2 children … suffer some form of violence each year'
- Of adults who were physically and sexually abused as children:
  - o men are 14 times more likely to perpetrate physical and sexual intimate partner violence
  - o women are 16 times more likely to suffer physical and sexual intimate partner violence.

The impact of any form of abuse can have lasting effects. Individuals who experience abuse will respond very differently depending on a range of factors. One of the most influential studies on the effects of abuse in children associates *adverse childhood experiences* (ACEs) with health and social problems in later life (Felitti et al., 1998). This chapter seeks to provide you with a very brief overview of some of the issues that are associated with child abuse.

Defining Abuse

From a global context the World Health Organization (WHO, 2022) defines child maltreatment as:

> the abuse and neglect that occurs to children under 18 years of age. It includes all types of physical and/or emotional ill-treatment, sexual abuse, neglect, negligence and commercial or other exploitation, which results in actual or potential harm to the child's health, survival, development or dignity in the context of a relationship of responsibility, trust or power.

The United Nations Committee on the Rights of the Child (2007) places a global definition of abuse within General Comment No. 8 (2006) as being:

> The Committee defines 'corporal' or 'physical' punishment as any punishment in which physical force is used and intended to cause some degree of pain or discomfort, however light. Most involves hitting ('smacking', 'slapping', 'spanking') children, with the hand or with an implement – a whip, stick, belt, shoe, wooden spoon, etc. But it can also involve, for example, kicking, shaking or throwing children, scratching, pinching, biting, pulling hair or boxing ears, forcing children to stay in uncomfortable positions, burning, scalding or forced ingestion (for example, washing children's mouths out with soap or forcing them to swallow hot spices). In the view of the Committee, corporal punishment is invariably degrading. In addition, there are other non-physical

forms of punishment that are also cruel and degrading and thus incompatible with the Convention. These include, for example, a punishment which belittles, humiliates, denigrates, scapegoats, threatens, scares or ridicules the child. (United Nations Committee on the Rights of the Child, 2007, p. 4)

The United Nations Convention on the Rights of the Child (UNICEF 2022) states within article 19 that:

Governments must do all they can to ensure that children are protected from all forms of violence, abuse, neglect and bad treatment by their parents or anyone else who looks after them.

What is categorised as abuse, and the way abuse is socially represented differs according to the social and historical context in which it occurs. As Parton (2014) observes, the identification of abuse can be a very politicised activity, reflecting the priorities of the government of the day. Once a government has acknowledged something to be abusive, there is an expectation that steps should be taken to eradicate it and to deal appropriately with perpetrators. The way in which abuse is defined will therefore "impact on policy, practice and research'. Lindon and Webb (2016, p. 18)

The categories of abuse, as defined in England, are set out in the *Working Together to Safeguard Children* document (HM Government, 2018). These are: physical abuse, emotional abuse, sexual abuse, child sexual exploitation, neglect and extremism. Please note, that this chapter applies the definitions applicable to England (Scotland, Wales and Northern Ireland have devolved powers, legislation and policies when it comes to the protection of children. Please see links at the end of the chapter for further information). When considering the different categories of abuse, it is important that everyone working with children understands them and is alert to the possible signs and indicators of each (Twigg, 2018). The categories of abuse, as defined in England, are:

Physical abuse

A form of abuse which can involve hitting, shaking, throwing, poisoning, burning or scalding, drowning, suffocating or otherwise causing physical harm to a child. It can also be caused when a parent or carer fabricates the symptoms of, or deliberately induces, illness in a child. (HM Government, 2018, p. 106)

Sexual abuse

Involves forcing or enticing a child or young person to take part in sexual activities, not necessarily involving a high level of violence, whether or not the child is aware of what is happening. The activities may involve physical contact, including assault by penetration (for example, rape or oral sex) or non-penetrative acts such as masturbation, kissing, rubbing and touching outside of clothing. They may also include non-contact activities, such as involving children in looking at, or in the production of, sexual images, watching sexual activities, encouraging children to behave in sexually inappropriate ways, or grooming a child in preparation for abuse. Sexual abuse can take place online, and technology can be used to facilitate offline abuse. Sexual abuse is not solely perpetrated by adult males. Women can also commit acts of sexual abuse, as can other children (HM Government, 2018, p. 106).

Emotional abuse

The persistent emotional maltreatment of a child such as to cause severe and persistent adverse effects on the child's emotional development. It may involve conveying to a child that they are worthless or unloved, inadequate, or valued only insofar as they meet the needs of another person. It may include not giving the child opportunities to express their views, deliberately silencing them or 'making fun' of what they say or how they communicate. It may feature age or developmentally inappropriate expectations being imposed on children. These may include interactions that are beyond a child's developmental capability, as well as overprotection and limitation of exploration and learning, or preventing the child participating in normal social interaction. It may involve seeing or hearing the ill-treatment of another. It may involve serious bullying (including cyber bullying), causing children frequently to feel frightened or in danger, or the exploitation or corruption of children. Some level of emotional abuse is involved in all types of maltreatment of a child, though it may occur alone (HM Government, 2018, p. 107).

Neglect

The persistent failure to meet a child's basic physical and/or psychological needs, likely to result in the serious impairment of the child's health or development. Neglect may occur during pregnancy as a result of maternal substance abuse. Once a child is born, neglect may involve a parent or carer failing to:

i   provide adequate food, clothing and shelter (including exclusion from home or abandonment)
ii   protect a child from physical and emotional harm or danger
iii ensure adequate supervision (including the use of inadequate caregivers)
iv   ensure access to appropriate medical care or treatment.

It may also include neglect of, or unresponsiveness to, a child's basic emotional needs (HM Government, 2018, p. 108).

Child sexual exploitation

Child sexual exploitation is a form of child sexual abuse. It occurs where an individual or group takes advantage of an imbalance of power to coerce, manipulate or deceive a child or young person under the age of 18 into sexual activity (a) in exchange for something the victim needs or wants, and/or (b) for the financial advantage or increased status of the perpetrator or facilitator.

The victim may have been sexually exploited even if the sexual activity appears consensual. Child sexual exploitation does not always involve physical contact; it can also occur through the use of technology (HM Government, 2018, p. 107).

Extremism

Extremism goes beyond terrorism and includes people who target the vulnerable – including the young – by seeking to sow division between communities on the basis of race, faith or denomination; justify discrimination towards women and girls; persuade others that minorities are inferior; or argue against the primacy of democracy and the rule of law in our society. Extremism is defined in the Counter Extremism Strategy 2015 as the vocal or active opposition to our fundamental values, including the rule of law, individual liberty and the mutual respect and tolerance of different faiths and beliefs. We also regard calls for the death of members of our armed forces as extremist (HM Government, 2018, p. 108).

Abuse may also take the form of 'domestic abuse' or 'intimate partner violence', terms that are used to highlight abusive relationships within the family. Domestic abuse is defined as abuse that can take place between

'family members, teenage relationship abuse and adolescent to parent violence' (HM Government, 2018, p. 110)

According to the WHO (2012),

'Intimate Partner Violence refers to any behaviour within an intimate relationship that causes physical, psychological or sexual harm to those in the relationship'.

These two definitions primarily focus on any person above the age of 16 within the wider family unit.

All of these situations will place considerable stress on the child within the family and in turn place a duty and responsibility on society to ensure the protection of the child.

Time to consider

- Are you familiar with the categories of abuse defined here? If they are different in your context, how do they differ? Why do you think this may be?
- What would you do if you were concerned about a child who was at risk of or suffering from one or more of the categories of abuse described here?

Case Study – Neglect in the family

The serious case review for Child FD17 (Johnston, 2018; National Society for the Prevention of Cruelty to Children) involved neglect but also relates to the serious injury

(Continued)

of a 9-year-old child. The family concerned had relocated from Slovakia and were of Roma heritage. Both mother and father were present as well as six other children of school age. The review identified that the siblings did not always attend medical appointments, were often absent from school, demonstrated challenging behaviour and were left home without parental supervision. In addition to the injury of one of the children, concerns were also raised about the youngest child, where evidence suggested there were signs of neglect. The case review reports that the parents were charged, found guilty and were given suspended sentences. All involved agencies were asked to consider cultural, racial and heritage factors when identifying neglect.

The full case review report for Child FD17 can be accessed at:

National Society for the Prevention of Cruelty to Children (n.d.) Serious case reviews: overview report in respect of: Child FD17. *National Case Review Repository – NSPCC Learning.* Available at: https://learning.nspcc.org.uk/case-reviews/national-case-review-repository.

Read the full case review report, or others you may source from the NSPCC, and consider the following questions:

1 What were the key factors that prevented or slowed recognition of abuse within this family?
2 In reference to this serious case review, how effective was the assessment of the parent's understanding of professional concerns and their ability and willingness to address these?
3 What are the circumstances, factors or major influences likely to impact the occurrence of abuse?
4 Thinking of the environments in which child abuse may occur, such as in a refugee crisis or a mass displacement of people due to war or environmental catastrophe, or in a developing country as opposed to a developed one, how might global events affect the potential for abuse to happen?
5 What might the longer-term impact of abuse be in all its forms and severities?

Incidence and Prevalence

The Office for National Statistics (ONS) reports on the extent and nature of child abuse in England and Wales up to 2019. The ONS (2020a) suggests that most of the instances of child abuse, in all its forms, remain hidden. However, the Crime Survey for England and Wales (CSEW) (2020) estimates that approximately one in five adults over the age of 18 have experienced at least one form of child abuse. This statistic includes emotional, physical and sexual abuse, and whether the person has witnessed domestic violence or abuse. Of those who do experience some form of abuse, around one in four adults abused as a child experienced more than one form of abuse, with slightly more than half of all cases being reported by women.

These are, of course, only estimates and do not necessarily reflect the true nature or scale of abuse involving children in England, or abuse that has a basis within the family environment. Therefore, these figures only relate to adults' past experiences of abuse.

The National Society for the Prevention of Cruelty to Children (NSPCC) regularly report on the incidences of child abuse. Interestingly, it reports that some incidences of abuse are on the rise year on year. This is due in part to the better reporting and recognition of abuse, which has been achieved through increased training of all practitioners working with children and the emphasis that 'everyone is responsible for keeping children safe' (NSPCC, 2022).

Time to consider

Take a moment to reflect on individual differences within the family, such as family structure, age, disability, affluence, religious affiliation, etc., and how they may relate to abuse.

- How might differences within the family play a role in the onset of abuse and the psychological impact it has on the developing child?

Risk Factors for Child Abuse

Since Felitti et al.'s (1998) study on adverse childhood experiences, and publications of serious case reviews following incidences of abuse, emphasis has been placed on the identification of potential risk factors of abuse within families. Together with this, the agenda of *Every Child Matters* (Department for Eduation, 2003), encourages all practitioners working with children and young people to place an increasing emphasis on early intervention (Parton, 2014). This way of working encourages practitioners to become proactive rather than reactive to situations within the family.

In this short chapter, we cannot cover all the risk factors identified from research and serious case reviews, but rather will highlight some of the key types of risk that can potentially lead to abuse. The key types of risk can be categorised into three distinct areas (Hunt 2014);

- Parent, caregiver and family factors
- Child Factors
- Environmental Factors

Parent/caregiver, and family factors

- Drug and alcohol misuse – this has been linked to higher incidences of child physical abuse within families (Goldberg & Blaauw 2019)

- Mental health difficulties – although apparent within lots of families, complex mental health difficulties can be linked to increased incidence of child abuse.
- Domestic abuse/intimate partner violence – child abuse often 'co-occurs' in families where domestic abuse is present (Sousa et al., 2011:113)
- Employment status – lack of financial capabilities places great stress on families which can consequently lead to abuse between partners and children within a family.
- Parents who have experienced abuse themselves are more likely to abuse – this has been termed as the inter-generational transmission of abuse.

Children are most likely to be abused by family members or other individuals with whom they are familiar. Analysis of serious case reviews published in the UK has identified that domestic abuse, mental health difficulties and substance misuse within the family, increase the risk of child abuse. In 2009, Marion Bradon termed this combination the 'toxic trio'. It is interesting to note that recent research on the 'toxic trio' seeks to contest the evidence base for this by stating that previous research on this concept 'is alarmingly weak and lacking in the precision, detail and depth' (Skinner et al., 2021).

Child factors
- Age – infants, and those below school age are at increased risk of abuse. Partially because of their inability to defend themselves, but also as they are not yet in early years provision, they are quite isolated
- Disability – Euser et al., (2016: 83) report that 'worldwide, higher rates of child sexual abuse have been found for the population in general and for children with disabilities'. This is due to their reliance on carers to support them within their daily lives.

Environmental factors
- Socio-economic circumstances – families living in poverty and with little or no access to wider services may find themselves becoming very isolated from their communities. This lack of support can lead to abusive situations within the family due to the pressures that this places on the situation (Peterson, Joseph and Feit 2014)
- Housing instability – this is often linked to or is a consequence of poverty. Instability is a particular issue for those in social housing and can increase the pressures on the family (Marcal 2018).

It is important to note that there is 'no clear type of abuse, abuser or reason' for abuse (Lumsden, 2018, p. 56), which may explain why abuse is such a complex issue. Having some identifiable risk factors will help as a guide, but it is never safe to assume that if families experience these risk factors it is an indication that abuse is happening.

Impacts and Revictimisation

Most of the literature to date has focused only on the symptomology associated with initial abuse experiences. Nevertheless, we know that abuse and victimisation can cause many negative outcomes – psychological, behavioural and neurobiological (De Bellis, Spratt & Hooper, 2011; Putnam, 2003). Therefore, it is unsurprising that many abuse victims experience long-lasting distress, mental health difficulties (such as depression and anxiety), self-destructive behaviour (such as suicidality and self-harm) and may go on to engage in substance and alcohol misuse. It is understandable that abusive experiences will have a varied impact on the child's self-concept, how they interact with others and the way in which they develop into a mature adult, in addition to the sorts of romantic relationships they form.

Pittenger, Huit and Hansen (2016) have attempted to apply Developmental Systems Theory (which was introduced in Chapter 3) to map the current literature and to integrate findings utilising Bronfenbrenner's social-ecological framework (Bronfenbrenner, 1977, 1979). Using theories such as these provides an opportunity to understand the broad context within which abuse occurs, how it impacts a child's development and the interventions that can be employed to prevent or mitigate it. Pittenger et al. (2016) draw attention to specific factors within the family and with the perpetrators to understand the risk of revictimisation and how engagement with helping professionals can mitigate and prevent it. Their categories include: age; race, ethnicity and culture; the frequency and duration of abuse and the severity of abuse; the home environment; influential others; and societal values. We will review the literature using their categorisation as a guide, though this is not intended to be an exhaustive account of all potential contributing factors.

Age has been identified as one of the risk factors for the occurrence of abuse. Indeed, the younger the child at the time of initial victimisation, the higher the likelihood that the child will go on to experience future and multiple such occurrences. In addition, Simmel, Postmus and Lee (2012) examine the effects that disclosing initial abuse experiences has on risk of sexual revictimisation in adulthood. Wallis and Woodworth (2020) show that younger children are more likely to delay disclosing abuse. Their findings revealed that children were at an increased risk of revictimisation if the initial abuse occurred during early childhood (ages 6 to 10 years). Furthermore, the odds of revictimisation almost doubled when the initial victimisation experience happened when the child was below 14 years of age.

Although mixed and inconsistent, there is evidence to suggest that abuse and revictimisation are impacted by **race, ethnicity and culture**. The severity of abuse heightens the risk of psychopathology across racial groups and particularly for intimate partner violence in later life (Dutton et al., 2005; Straus at al., 2009). Similarly, other related research suggests that the highest incidence of child abuse may occur in African American and Hispanic girls (Sedlak et al., 2010), though these findings appear to be inconclusive, and it is unclear why this association might be. Nevertheless, recent research by Atkinson, Fix and Fix (2023) proposes that, whilst there are distinct racial and ethnic differences in rates of reported and substantiated child abuse (in the US), these differences may be explained through two competing models – concentrated risk factors or racial bias:

- **Concentrated risk factors** – a model that proposes children of colour have a greater exposure to certain risk factors (such as greater economic insecurity), and it is more likely that this contributes to higher rates of child maltreatment in these population groups.
- **Racial Bias** – this model instead suggests that in addition to certain risk factors there may be racial biases associated with the way abuse is reported (e.g. the type of language or questions used when screening for abuse). However, due to the complexities surrounding the reporting of abuse it is also possible that any incidence, including those related to race and ethnicity, are not a full or accurate picture and perhaps may never be fully known.

The **frequency and duration of abuse and the severity of abuse** are known to affect repeated victimisation. Using a statistical technique known as path analysis, Arata (2002) found that repeated victimisation was predicted by longer-lasting abuse and the severity of the initial abuse. Furthermore, Waldron et al. (2015) suggest that the frequency of abusive experiences in childhood is related to the increased chance of revictimisation in adulthood. Abuse severity, frequency or family relationship was also likely to increase the chances of delayed disclosure (Wallis & Woodworth, 2020).

The **home environment** has been found to be a critical factor in child abuse and continued victimisation. There is evidence to suggest that children from homes where violence and/or substance abuse are prevalent tend to experience a higher incidence of (unwanted) sexual experiences. This was also found to be the case in children who lived in more deprived neighbourhoods.

Influential others (peers, perpetrators and helping professionals) are the biggest factor in repeat victimisation and can be crucial in recovery. Children and adolescents are more likely to engage in risky behaviours compared to adults (Boyer, 2006), and they are more susceptible to peer influence in making these risky decisions. However, having a parent who more consistently monitors their social interactions is likely to result in reduced (early) sexual activity (Romer et al., 1994; Swenson & Schaeffer, 2018). Where care and attention are lacking there is a higher risk of sexual abuse and exploitation. In addition, research by Matta, Oshima, Jonson-Reid and Seay (2014) suggests that the risk for subsequent revictimisation is heightened when the perpetrator is male and/or the mother's partner (typically the child's non-biological parent). Nevertheless, therapeutic support from helping professionals (such as therapists) can be vital in reducing the risk of repeat victimisation (Mayall & Gold, 1995) though the evidence is inconclusive regarding the efficacy of therapy as a buffer to revictimisation. However, Stith and colleagues (2022), reviewed a range of systemic interventions (such as naturalistic couples therapy) and the subsequent occurence of child maltreatment in situations where there was a history of intimate partner violence. Their findings suggest that there is some evidence that certain types of therapeutic intervention are more effective than others (e.g. family therapy) and may lead to and reduce the re-reporting of further child maltreatment.

The final factor that impacts on abuse and revictimisation are **societal values**. Grauerholz (2000) and Ménard (2003) propose that when communities emphasise more traditional gender roles or hold prejudiced views of sexual assault victims, it may lead to repeat victimisation.

Interventions and Therapeutic Outcomes

Supporting families and survivors of abuse is of course important and likely to be a process that will continue for a prolonged period of time. The effectiveness of any support may depend on multiple factors, not least the severity, frequency and context within which the abuse occurred. There are many types of interventions and therapies available, including psychodynamic therapy, cognitive behavioural therapy (CBT), Eye-Movement Desensitisation and Reprocessing (EMDR) therapy, systemic therapy and person-centred therapy (Caro, Turner & Macdonald, 2019). Below, a brief summary of some of these therapies is provided and several studies are used to highlight how they may help. You should note that in some cases an intervention will involve working with the child only, in other instances a parent may be present or there are times when an entire family may be together. A recent meta-analysis conducted by St-Amand et al. (2022) investigated the importance of involving non-offending caregivers (i.e. typically the biological mother though in this case also included foster carers too) in the therapeutic process and the factors that impact the therapies effectiveness. Their review assessed 18 studies covering 24 types of intervention involving a non-offending caregiver. The studies varied considerably in terms of the intervention characteristics (e.g. number of therapy sessions, theoretical orientation, and the target of the intervention, such as the caregiver and child or caregiver only) and caregiver outcomes (e.g. psychological distress, trauma, stress and parenting practices). Some of the results demonstrate that the age of the child, the type of caregiver and the origin of the abuse are all important factors. For example, children of most ages (the very young or older teenagers) experience significant benefits, and this was also the case when both caregiver and child were involved. However, the findings remain inconclusive when interventions only include the non-offending caregiver. Furthermore, foster caregivers were also less likely to experience the intense emotions associated with child sexual abuse. For example, feeling less ambivalent and feeling lower levels of stress or resentment towards the child's biological parents for failing to protect the child. There is relatively little knowledge about the effectiveness of foster carers and their needs in supporting a childhood victim of abuse. However, interventions seem to be just as beneficial when the source of the abuse was either an intra- or interfamilial perpetrator.

McTavish et al. (2021) conducted a systematic review that looked at the outcomes of psychosocial interventions for child victims of sexual abuse. They found that, due to the broad range of interventions, it was difficult to offer many strong conclusions about the benefits of specific interventions provided only to children. However, they do suggest that CBT with a trauma focus may be useful in symptom reduction when it involves their caregivers. Similarly, Lindstom Johnson et al. (2018) have suggested that when children have been exposed to violence, such as in intimate partner violence, or as the target of violence, there is some evidence that therapeutic interventions (such as trauma informed care) that include the parent may positively impact the child's psychosocial outcomes and enhance parenting practices.

Final reflection

In this chapter we have defined the different types of abuse, discussed rates of occurrence and prevalence, and explored some of the complex and varied risk factors that can predict and prolong child abuse and enable repeated victimisation. Abuse is undoubtedly a complex issue and one which can bring catastrophic and life-changing consequences for children and their families. Research evidence would suggest that the child's age and who the perpetrator is, can impact on vulnerability to abuse and children's ability to disclose. Other factors, such as race and ethnicity are less well understood, and in need of further research. The evidence we presented here seems to suggest that there are some forms of intervention that are more effective than others when aiding an individual's recovery. Nevertheless, with the right sort of support children and their families may recover.

Key points

- Abuse is categorised differently in different contexts, depending on the priorities of a given context or the policies of the government of the day.
- The reporting of incidences of abuse are on the rise, year on year. This is due in part to the increased social awareness of abuse and the enhanced reporting of it.
- There are multiple and complex factors that may impact both the risk of abuse and recovery from abuse. Research suggests that some of these factors include drug and alcohol misuse within the family, the age of the child, and the socio-economic circumstances of the family.
- Interventions can help families and the victims of abuse recover from their experiences. Although the exact nature of what works best is unclear, some interventions have shown that involving non-offending caregivers can have positive benefits.

Further reading

Caro, P., Turner, W., & Macdonald, G. (2019) Comparative effectiveness of interventions for treating the psychological consequences of sexual abuse in children and adolescents. *The Cochrane Database of Systematic Reviews*, 2019(6).

This systematic review provides an analysis of the relative effectiveness of psychosocial therapies to overcome the psychological impact of sexual abuse in children and young people. The review ranks the effectiveness of psychotherapies, discusses dosage requirements and explores a range of factors that impact treatment outcomes.

Crime Survey for England and Wales (CSEW) (2020) Child abuse extent and nature, England and Wales: year ending March 2019. Available at: www.ons.gov.uk/peoplepopulationandcommunity/crimeandjustice/articles/childabuseextentandnatureenglandandwales/yearendingmarch2019 (accessed 17 January 2023)
Lindstrom Johnson, S., Elam, K., Rogers, A.A., & Hilley, C. (2018) A meta-analysis of parenting practices and child psychosocial outcomes in trauma-informed parenting interventions after violence exposure. *Prevention Science*, 19(7), 927–938.

This review discusses the evidence for parenting interventions as a consequence of violence-related trauma and the use of support models of trauma-informed care.

McTavish, J.R., Santesso, N., Amin, A., Reijnders, M., Ali, M.U., Fitzpatrick-Lewis, D., & MacMillan, H.L. (2021) Psychosocial interventions for responding to child sexual abuse: a systematic review. *Child Abuse & Neglect*, 116(Pt 1), 104203. https://doi.org/10.1016/j.chiabu.2019.104203

This review compliments the other further reading suggestions and covers the importance of psychosocial interventions more broadly. The findings from this study also informed the WHO recommendations related to psychosocial interventions for child and adolescent sexual abuse.

National Society for the Prevention of Cruelty to Children (NSPCC) – Serious case reviews can be accessed at the *National Case Review Repository – NSPCC Learning*. Available at: https://learning.nspcc.org.uk/case-reviews/national-case-review-repository.
Scottish Government – Child Protection - www.gov.scot/policies/child-protection/

This link provides details of the child protection procedures in Scotland

Welsh Government – Safeguarding - https://law.gov.wales/safeguarding

This link provides details of the safeguarding procedures in Wales

Northern Ireland – Safeguarding and Child Protection - www.eani.org.uk/school-management/safeguarding-and-child-protection

This link provides details of the safeguarding and child protection procedures in Northern Ireland

St-Amand, A., Servot, S., Pearson, J., & Bussières, È.L. (2021) Effectiveness of interventions offered to non-offending caregivers of sexually abused children: a meta-analysis. *Canadian Psychology/Psychologie Canadienne*, 63(3), 339–356. https://doi. org/10.1037/cap0000296

This meta-analysis offers a discussion of the types of intervention that may aid the non-offending caregiver in child abuse cases.

13

WORKING WITH PARENTS, CARERS AND FAMILIES IN THE EARLY YEARS

Michelle Appleby

Overview

In this chapter, the working relationship between parents, carers, families and practitioners will be explored, often referred to as partnership working. Considerable research has been conducted into the impact partnership with parents can have on the earliest stages of children's education and care, and so this chapter looks at some of the key elements in order to give practitioners a basis for consideration and self-reflection.

This chapter will…

- Explore the principles of partnership working
- Consider the benefits of partnership working
- Investigate potential barriers to successful communication
- Suggest ways to make working with parents and carers constructive in practice.

Key terms

Collaboration; developing early years practice; engagement; partnership; professional reflection

---

Introduction

The adults in a young child's life have an immense impact on their learning and development. On the whole, each of these people will want what is best for the child, and research suggests that cooperation among adults yields the most positive results. However, parents and practitioners sometimes carry assumptions and beliefs about one another that can lead to disharmony or friction. We will therefore consider how practitioners and early years professionals can create a unifying environment for constructive communication to occur. For efficiency's sake, the term 'parents' will be used to allude to all carers and guardians. Similarly, the term 'practitioners' is intended to encompass any professionals working in the early years sector, including (but not limited to) early years teachers, nursery workers, child-minders, teaching assistants and other professional groups. Accepting that parents are often experts on their own children can help guide professional practice and allow everybody's skills and knowledge to be used in order to achieve the best outcomes for children.

What is Partnership Working in the Early Years?

Partnership working is fundamental to early years practice. It is framed by formal requirements in England, contained within the *Statutory Framework of the Early Years Foundation Stage* (Department for Education (DfE), 2017), the *Teachers' Standards* (DfE, 2011), *Teacher Standards (Early Years)* (National College for Teaching & Leadership (NCTL), 2013) and the *Early Years Inspection Framework* (Office for Standards in Education, Children's Services and Skill (OFSTED), 2021). This means that all OFSTED-registered early years providers must observe it. In fact, OFSTED (2011, n.p.) said that:

> Parental engagement can be a powerful lever for raising achievement in schools and there is much research to show the value of schools and parents working together to support pupils' learning. Schools have been encouraged to shift from simply involving parents with the school to enabling them to engage themselves more directly with their children's learning.

Therefore, working in partnership is not optional for practitioners. It is written into policy and is essential to practice. But what does it mean? What does it look like? And how difficult is it to achieve?

What Does Partnership Working Look Like?

'Partnership working' is a general term that is used in early years provision to denote the collaboration with and between stakeholders who have a vested interest in this sector. Partners in this arrangement can vary drastically from day to day. Early years practitioners will work with:

- the local authority
- health and social care agencies

- other schools in the area
- charitable organisations
- local businesses
- each other
- and, perhaps most importantly, the parents and carers at the school.

Because each setting is different and has its own opportunities and challenges, there can never be a single model for partnership in the early years. However, it can be useful to begin with an ideological structure such as Froebelian principles (Froebel Trust, 2022), which stress unity, connectedness, valuing the relationships in a child's life and the need for knowledgeable, nurturing educators. The practical and specific details can then be tailored to the setting, the people and, for instance, whether it is a 'one off', a short-term event or a long-term partnership. Regardless of who is involved and in what capacity, it is important that each party feels empowered to communicate and take action when needed. This necessitates each knowing what their role is and what they have the power to influence. Such fundamentals need to be communicated early (and often) in the working relationship. In the longer term, both parties need to invest time, engage in dialogue and realise that partnership is a two-way process in order to develop trust and a functional relationship.

Why Is It Important and What Are the Benefits of Operating in this Way?

This way of working is mandated by law and has been made statutory because of its inherent value. To be truly successful, there is a need to go well above regulations and requirements and to develop an ethos which puts the needs of the child at the centre of all decision making. One does not have to look far in the literature to find that working with parents and carers has a multitude of benefits for the child.

Time to consider

- Why do you think it is important to establish early positive relationships?
- Can you think of any potential barriers?

Urie Bronfenbrenner's bioecological theory (1977), an often-cited work in early childhood studies, stated that a child's development is affected by everyone in their environment. He divided the environment into five levels, ranging from the immediate surroundings (the Microsystem) of the family and the school, to broad social values, laws and customs, but he put the child at the heart of everything. He said the relationships between the child and those in their environment are '*bi-directional*', meaning that the child can be influenced by others but is capable of changing the people around them too.

Bronfenbrenner's theory (1977) stresses the importance of these social interactions to the child's development. If the child has a strong, nurturing relationship with their carers, then this will have a positive effect on their growth. Similarly, more negative interactions would have a negative effect on the child's development. This theory states that if the people closest to the child, such as their parents and teachers, interact constructively with one another, then the child directly benefits. Indeed, Bronfenbrenner regards this as essential for the child's healthy advancement.

The relationships between those in the Microsystem, such as the interactions between a child's parents and their teachers, forms what he called the Mesosystem, the second level from the child. He highlighted the importance of the interconnectedness of these individuals and the effect and influence that they have on one another and also on the child. Therefore, we cannot underestimate the idea that if there is strong and clear communication between the child's parents and the child's teachers, this is going to have a positive influence on the child in a multitude of ways. Sadly, that development is also likely to suffer if the teachers and parents do not get along.

Parental partnerships can be thought of as bridging two key spheres of children's worlds – the home and the early years setting. Although each environment significantly and independently influences a child, together they interact to offer an even greater influence on the child's development, be it positive or negative. In fact, El Nokali, Bachman and Votruba-Drzal's (2010) study found that parental involvement can be thought of as a product of the interaction between the influences of school and the home settings. For example, if parents are aware of what a teacher is working towards at school, they can provide resources and support for those learning goals at home. Likewise, in terms of social development, parental involvement can aid the development of consistent attitudes and behaviours across home and school.

Partnerships, at their very best, are mutually beneficial (Department for Education, 2019). There is a sense of wellbeing and cohesion for all, which then, in turn, fosters a relationship to draw upon when difficult topics need to be raised, and a sense of being part of a community working towards a common goal. In essence, it is about addressing each party's 'humanness' in relating to their individual needs and situations which is optimal. Working with parents, carers and families places a high value for all stakeholders, including young children, on addressing individual needs, development, achievement and setting the basis for valuing learning and education.

There is evidence to suggest that parental engagement, when focused on the needs of the child, can have a significant effect on a child's learning (Hattie, 2009), with far-reaching implications for the child's educational career. These behaviours can be as simple as attending parents' evenings, volunteering and supporting homework. The foundation of this involvement, or lack thereof, begins in early years settings.

The literature suggests that parental involvement and cooperation have a range of positive effects (see Table 13.1).

Table 13.1 Research studies on the impact of parental involvement and cooperation

Impact of parental involvement and cooperation	Research studies
Positive social and emotional development	Evangelou, Sylva & Kyriacou, 2009; Melhuish et al., 2008; Wheeler, Connor & Goodwin, 2009
Healthy language development	Evangelou et al., 2009; Melhuish et al., 2008; Wheeler et al., 2009
Mathematics proficiency and achievement	Sheldon & Epstein, 2005; Sirvani, 2007
Mathematical concept development	Evangelou et al., 2009; Melhuish et al., 2008; Wheeler et al., 2009
Increased readiness for school	Evangelou et al., 2009; Melhuish et al., 2008; Wheeler et al., 2009
Gains in reading performance	Powell-Smith et al., 2000
Positive performance on academic assessments	Desimone, 1999; Domina, 2005; Jeynes, 2005
Academic success in early years	El Nokali, Bachman & Votruba-Drzal, 2010
Fewer behaviour problems in school	Domina, 2005
Better attendance and class preparation	Simon, 2001
Increased self-belief	Grolnick & Slowiaczek, 1994; Marchant, Paulson & Rothlisberg, 2001
Higher levels of course completion	Simon, 2001
Lower dropout rates	Rumberger, 1995

Indeed, empirical research seems to suggest that children flourish both academically and personally at school if their parents are involved in their education. The reasons for this appear to be allied to both the development of self-esteem and the internalisation of significant values. Hattie (2009) reviewed over 800 previous studies to identify the factors that help children to flourish at school. He concluded that parental encouragement and high aspirations were internalised by children and so helped young learners to develop their own self-concept and ambitions from an early age. Indeed, parents placing a high value on education appears beneficial to children's development (Marchant, Paulson & Rothlisberg, 2001). It seems likely that this helps to shape a young person's level of enthusiasm for learning, good study habits, curiosity, experimentation and enjoyment of reading. All of these begin in early years settings and continue throughout the child's education. Although perhaps unsurprisingly, the earlier these are embedded the greater their effects (Hattie, 2003).

However, it is important to remember that parents can only become fully engaged if they know how to best support their child in those specific circumstances. Essentially, the goal of working together is to benefit the child. That is a profound statement and one which is worth coming back to when, and if, difficulties arise. Some of the potential barriers of partnerships will be explored next.

> ## Time to consider
>
> - How can we inform parents of what to do at home and how to support their child across the two contexts?
> - Are these methods accessible for all?
> - Who might struggle to bridge the gap between school and home?

What Gets in the Way of Partnership Working?

The West Sussex Country Council (2020) cite myriad barriers for teachers engaging effectively with parents, including:

- lack of time for both teachers and parents
- difficulties involving the parents
- lack of training in how to work with parents
- difficult parental behaviours
- parental attitudes and expectations of early years settings.

Let us look at a few barriers in more depth.

Multiple variables

It is important to note that partnership working involves many different variables as the relationships and connections between individuals are unique and often complicated (Daniel, 2015). Because it is so difficult to define what partnership working is, it becomes a challenge to discuss how to do it well. However, it requires all stakeholders to consider the needs of the individual child and of the individual settings in order that these can then be addressed.

Strong and confident leadership is essential and this can only happen when the professionals are confident in their knowledge and practice. If, for instance, an early years practitioner is new to the setting or the sector, a strong mentor is needed to allow conversations and reflections to occur which will eventually build confidence and enable them to meet other challenges and situations.

Lack of communication

Kambouri et al. (2021) discovered that partnership working is not always carried out to the best standard. While it is inevitable, and even desirable, that procedures will vary to some extent from family to family, exactly how the partnership is going to work in this instance needs to be agreed and articulated early in the process. Most problems occur as a result of poor communication and/or differing understandings of what is required from the other side. In other words, individuals' roles and requirements have not been clarified at the outset. Policy does not clearly outline these roles for us, so it is often up to the professionals to interpret and clarify these expectations for parents.

Research by Harper and Pelletier (2010) discovered that English-speaking parents communicate more frequently with early years practitioners than English-language-learning parents. Generally, this is attributable to the lack of a common language or limited confidence regarding the use of English; it does not mean the parents are any less involved or invested in their child's early learning experiences. If poorly navigated, the language barrier reduces opportunities for parental input from the inception of the relationship and may unintentionally lead to parents feeling excluded or misunderstood.

Power differentials

Just as differing language skills may cause a parent to feel alienated from professionals and professional spaces, it is important to acknowledge that a potential power differential exists between teachers and parents (Goodall & Montgomery, 2014; Vincent, 1996). Because the professionals generally have experience and expertise in practice and theory, it may be easy for them to regard themselves as the 'expert'. Often, this is very much needed, but it can be off-putting and place parents in a more passive position. This power differential may also carry over from, for instance, one educational experience to another, and influence how interactions occur throughout the child's schooling (Pieridou, 2013; Ware, 1994). It may potentially leave parents feeling powerless, especially when their holistic knowledge of their child is not requested or valued. If a strong power differential is felt by one member of the partnership, it can lead to intimidation, disengagement and marginalisation.

Assumptions

Practitioners need to be mindful of their assumptions about working partners. People are diverse, and not everyone shares our paradigms or understands the priorities and drivers in early education and care. However, our conscious or unconscious beliefs and biases may also lead us to make assumptions about others we encounter professionally. Just as we do not all share the same worldview, our lives outside work vary drastically. Family composition is varied (see Chapter 7) as are working patterns, health needs, family priorities and prior experience with institutions such as education settings. These may all influence people's ability or willingness to engage and to shape their style and manner of communication.

The barriers that may be encountered when working together are complex and nuanced. The obstacles vary depending on the context and what other players in the partnership bring with them. They are not easily or even consciously acknowledged, but an honest confrontation of these barriers can only serve to enhance the practice of professionals working with young children and, ultimately, the care of the children themselves.

Time to consider

Take a moment to reflect on your own biases or assumptions of others, or perhaps think about which groups may be subject to bias when entering an early years setting.

- How might you make a person or group feel welcome and at ease, even if you do not agree with their attitude or approach?

This is difficult territory to navigate, but certainly worth considering.

How Do We Address the Barriers to Partnership Working?

Unity

Freidrich Froebel, who developed the first Kindergarten in Germany in 1840, emphasised the importance of placing the child at the centre of all decision making. He also stressed the essential nature of working with families and the community in early education and care (Froebel, 1912), creating connectedness and unity.

The concept of unity was central to Froebel's educational theories, materials, methods and early years practice for his whole career (Russell & Aldridge, 2009). He believed in the essential interconnectedness of humans to nature, young to old, school to home, parents and teachers to children, school to community, and so on. He emphasised that for a being to thrive, a harmonious, connected relationship must exist at all levels. Froebel believed that practitioners should point out and express the connections in every activity as he sought to educate young children about the interconnectedness of the world and their place in it (Wolfe, 2002). Froebel also recognised that every child is a unique individual in their own right and a vital part of a family and a community.

Froebel's concepts of 'unity', and the connectedness of all individuals and environments around the child, make this an ecological theory similar to Bronfenbrenner's (1977). Indeed, now that children are spending longer days in early years settings because of parents' need to work, the connections made with practitioners are even more important to ensure healthy development (Elfer et al., 2018; Murray et al., 2018).

In order to feel unified, all parties need to feel empowered and confident to suggest and make changes. It requires all parties to have access to the required information and have a voice when it comes to problem solving. This in turn necessitates that everyone has the skills and resources needed to express their opinions. However, it is likely that working partners will have differing levels of competency and commitment to engage. When these are different, difficulties can occur. In order to achieve partnership working, an ethos of mutual respect is required.

Mutual respect

To work in partnership collaboratively and effectively, practitioners need to approach this relationship with care, balancing professional needs with the perspectives of the partner. One of the best ways to do this is to adopt a non-judgemental mindset and attempt to be approachable to all. This may sound easy, but it is not always so! As clichéd as it sounds, communication is what allows this, and all partnerships, to flourish. Communication should stem from a place of unconditional positive regard (UPR), a term coined by Carl Rogers in his person-centred therapy and an often-used approach in therapeutic contexts. Rogers (1959) said that for a person to develop they need to feel a sense of openness, acceptance (which he called UPR) and a sense that they were being listened to and understood.

You may find someone 'pushes your buttons' or makes you feel defensive or angry. You may want to immediately place blame or dismiss someone. It is important to think about the reasons why you feel this way and then to think if there is a way to adopt a sense of empathy and accept that everyone is on their own journey and doing the best that they can. Perhaps approaching a situation with unconditional positive regard can foster better partnership working.

Achieving this state of UPR requires deep self-examination and self-reflection of unintentional and unconscious bias and a tendency to place blame. It is tough stuff to achieve! It also requires practitioners to deal with what is getting in the way of their own sense of wellbeing to ensure some of their own difficulties are not being carried into the work environment. Talking about how to work through these feelings with co-workers and close friends is crucial to being able to work professionally and supportively. It is part of what it means to be a reflective practitioner in the early years.

Final reflections

Keeping children at the heart of early years practice and working with parents, carers and families is not a straightforward task. It requires making decisions on an individual basis and also working in alignment with professional requirements and policies. It requires empathy, compassion, understanding and forgiveness on the part of all parties. Most professionals working with young children will find themselves needing to work in partnership with parents and with other agencies. However, many professionals have received scant training and find themselves feeling unprepared for the challenges that collaborative working can present. It has been suggested that embracing a judgement-free mindset can perhaps put us on the road to creating a more nurturing and collaborative environment for young children.

Key points

- Partnership working is complicated and if there is a problem, it is not always obvious what is not working.

- Open and honest communication can help get to the root of the issue.
- Power differentials do exist in early years practice. If practitioners are aware of them, they can try to balance these through authentic interactions.
- We all have biases and assumptions, whether we admit them to ourselves or not. Part of being a reflective practitioner is to acknowledge these within ourselves and to work to overcome them.
- Working towards unity and being non-judgemental are helpful goals that enable partnerships with parents to thrive.
- Every partnership relationship is unique, but all need to be underpinned by a sense of mutual respect.
- Within partnership working, the child must always be the primary concern.

Further reading

Hall, M.O. (n.d.) Building relationships between parents and teachers. *TEDxBurnsvilleED*. Available at: www.youtube.com/watch?v=kin2OdchKMQ (accessed 29 March 2022).

Megan Hall talks a lot about schools and teachers but this can easily be related to early years practice too. She emphasises the importance of building connections with parents and families and how some families may struggle with this connection. She discusses how to make all welcome in the setting.

Wilson, T. (2015) *Working with Parents, Carers and Families in the Early Years: The Essential Guide*. London: Routledge.

This book offers an informed and comprehensive framework for working with parents, drawing on the latest evidence and containing practical advice from practitioners and parents to support sound partnership practice.

CONCLUSION
Kay Owen and Christopher Barnes

In the Introduction we posited that no two families are the same due to the differences in composition, circumstances and personnel. Throughout the book, it has become increasingly clear that families also vary according to the characteristics and disposition of those within them. We have discovered that socio-demographics, parental attributes and child characteristics (to name but a few) will affect the dynamic in the family and shape the nature of household interactions. These in turn will shape attitudes towards child rearing and, subsequently, impact how the child develops. While it is tempting to seek out simple causal explanations, the complex, multifaceted nature of both family life and child development means that even children facing similar life events will experience them in very specific and different ways. The first conclusion we can therefore reach, is that there is a need to guard against assumptions and broad generalisations built on stereotypes or generic information.

In a similar way, we must be wary about tying claims about child outcomes too tightly to one specific family format. Certainly, research would seem to indicate that children raised in a stable household by both of their birth parents are more likely to succeed. However, as we have seen, if one parent is abusive or neglectful, the child may do better without them. We also noted that the differences between children raised by opposite-sex and same-sex couples are minimal, as are those between biological and well-established stepfamilies. Thus, provision of a stable and loving home environment would seem to be more important than the genetic links between individuals.

Financial security alone brings no guarantees of a happy childhood. Indeed, long working hours may lead to behaviours which bear many of the hallmarks of neglectful parenting. However, poverty does appear to have wide-ranging adverse effects. There are clear links between financial struggles and mental health issues such as anxiety and depression, and animosity, arguments and relationship breakdown. We have already documented how parental wellbeing and happiness shape children's experiences. It is therefore no surprise that in situations where the family environment is not optimal, and parental relationships are more fragile and transient, children are more likely to experience adverse childhood experiences (ACEs). While some social commentators have picked up on a perceived lack of nurturance and supervision, or blamed parents for their use of inconsistent, erratic or harsh discipline, they often fail to acknowledge the broader contextual factors.

Neverthless, we are probably all aware of individual families who have managed to thrive despite challenging circumstances. Research shows that it is the way parents cope with stressful situations that determines whether stress is transmitted to the children (Moore & Vandivere 2000). In part, this may be attributed to the characteristics noted by Belsky (1984), but it is also often a product of parents' own experiences and upbringing. Thus, patterns of parenting behaviours are often passed from generation to generation.

In conclusion, the evidence presented in this book suggests that children will flourish when they are in warm and nurturing home environments. Indeed, when children feel secure and loved, other aspects of their lives, such as family structure, parents' social class and income, become much less important.

REFERENCES

Ablow, J.C. & Measelle, J.R. (1993). *The Berkeley Puppet Interview: Interviewing and coding systems manuals*. University of Oregon: Department of Psychology.

Abuhammad, S., AlAzzam, M., & AbuFarha, R. (2021) Infant temperament as a predictor of maternal attachment: a Jordanian study. *Nursing Open, 8*(2), 636–645.

Acitelli, L.K., & Antonucci, T.C. (1994) Gender differences in the link between marital support and satisfaction in older couples. *Journal of Personality and Social Psychology, 67*, 688–698. DOI: 10.1037-0022-3514.67.4.688

Action for Children [website]. Available at: www.actionforchildren.org.uk (accessed 26 January 2023).

Adamson-Macedo, E.N. (1985–86) Effects of tactile stimulation on low and very low birthweight infants during the first week of life. *Current Psychological Research and Reviews, 6*, 305–308.

Adamson-Macedo, E.N., Dattani, I., Wilson, A., & De Carvalho, F.A. (1993) A small sample follow-up study. *Journal of Reproductive and Infant Psychology, 11*(3), 165.

Adamson-Macedo, E.N., de Roiste, A., Wilson, A., de Carvalho, F., & Dattani, I. (1994) TAC-TIC therapy with high-risk, ventilated preterms. *Journal of Reproductive and Infant Psychology, 12*(2), 249–252.

Adoption and Children Act (2002). *Adoption and Children Act* [website]. Available at: www.legislation.gov.uk/ukpga/2002/38/contents (accessed 27 April 2021).

Adoption UK (2017) *Adoption UK's Schools and Exclusions Report*. Banbury: Adoption UK.

Adoption UK (2020) Adoption rate down by third since 2015. *Adoption UK* [website]. Available at: www.adoptionuk.org/news/adoption-rate-down-by-third-since-2015 (accessed 28 June 2021).

Aggarwal, J. (2019) How children are affected by divorce. *Psychology Research, 9*(9), 371–376. DOI: 10.17265/2159-5542/2019.09.003

Ahmed, S., Hanif, A., Khaliq, I., Ayub, S., Saboor, S., Shoib, S., … & Mahmood Khan, A. (2022) Psychological impact of the COVID-19 pandemic in children with autism spectrum disorder: a literature review. *International Journal of Developmental Disabilities*, 1–11. https://doi.org/10.1080/20473869.2022.2066248

Ainsworth, M.D., & Bell, S.M. (1970) Attachment, exploration, and separation: illustrated by the behavior of one-year-olds in a strange situation. *Child Development, 41*, 49–67.

Ainsworth, M.D.S., Blehar, M.C., Waters, E., & Wall, S. (1978) *Patterns of Attachment: A Psychological Study of the Strange Situation*. London: Psychology Press.

Allen, B. (2018) Misperceptions of reactive attachment disorder persist: poor methods and unsupported conclusions. *Research in Developmental Disabilities, 77*, 24–29.

Allen, W., & Doherty, W. (1996) The responsibilities of fatherhood as perceived by African American teenage fathers. *Families in Society: The Journal of Contemporary Social Services, 77*, 142–155.

Allotey, J., Zamora, J., Cheong-See, F., Kalidindi, M., Arroyo-Manzano, D., Asztalos, E., … & Thangaratinam, S. (2018) Cognitive, motor, behavioural and academic performances of children born preterm: a meta-analysis and systematic review involving 64,061 children. *BJOG: An International Journal of Obstetrics & Gynaecology*, *125*(1), 16–25.

All-Party Parliamentary Group for Adoption and Permanence (APPGAP) (2019) *Investing in Families: The Adoption Support Fund beyond 2020.* London: APPGAP.

Alves, C.R., Gaspardo, C.M., Altafim, E.R., & Linhares, M.B.M. (2022) Effectiveness of a longitudinal psychosocial intervention to strengthen mother–child interactions: the role of biological and contextual moderators. *Children and Youth Services Review*, *133*, 106333.

Alvis, L., Zhang, N., Sandler, I.N., & Kaplow, J.B. (2022) Developmental manifestations of grief in children and adolescents: caregivers as key grief facilitators. *Journal of Child & Adolescent Trauma*, 1–11. https://doi.org/10.1007/s40653-021-00435-0

Alwin, D.F. (2004) Parenting practices. In J. Scott, J. Treas & M. Richards (eds), *The Blackwell Companion to the Sociology of Families* (pp. 142–157). Oxford: Blackwell Publishing.

Amato, P.R. (2000) The consequences of divorce for adults and children. *Journal of Marriage and Family*, *62*(4), 1269–1287.

Amato, P. R. (2001). Children of divorce in the 1990s: An update of the Amato and Keith (1991) meta-analysis. *Journal of Family Psychology*, *15*(3), 355–370. https://psycnet.apa.org/doi/10.1037/0893-3200.15.3.355

Amato, P.R. (2010) Research on divorce: continuing trends and new developments. *Journal of Marriage and Family*, *72*(3), 650–666.

Amato, P.R., & Afifi, T.D. (2006) Feeling caught between parents: adult children's relations with parents and subjective well-being. *Journal of Marriage and Family*, *68*(1), 222–235.

Amato, P.R., Loomis, L.S., & Booth, A. (1995) Parental divorce, marital conflict, and offspring well-being during early adulthood, *Social Forces*, *73*(3), 895–915, https://doi.org/10.1093/sf/73.3.895

American Psychological Association (2022) *APA Dictionary of Psychology* [website]. Available at: https://dictionary.apa.org/attachment-q-set (accessed 20 January 2022).

Anderson, E. (2009) *Inclusive Masculinities: The Changing Nature of Masculinity.* London: Routledge.

Anderson, M. (1971) *Family Structure in 19th-Century Lancashire.* Cambridge: Cambridge University Press.

Anderson, S.R., Anderson, S.A., Palmer, K.L., Mutchler, M.S., & Baker, L.K. (2010) Defining high conflict. *The American Journal of Family Therapy*, *39*(1), 11–27.

Anderzén-Carlsson, A., Lamy, Z. C., & Eriksson, M. (2014). Parental experiences of providing skin-to-skin care to their newborn infant—Part 1: A qualitative systematic review. *International Journal of Qualitative Studies on Health and Well-being*, *9* (1), 24906.

Angell, M.E., Meadan, H., & Stoner, J.B. (2012) Experiences of siblings of individuals with autism spectrum disorders. *Autism Research and Treatment*, *2012*. https://doi.org/10.1155/2012/949586

Arata, C.M. (2002) Child sexual abuse and sexual revictimization. *Clinical psychology: Science and Practice*, *9*(2), 135.

Arnold, C. (1998) Children and stepfamilies: a snapshot. *Centre for Law and Social Policy* [website]. Available at: www.clasp.org (accessed 20 January 2022).

Asbury, K., Fox, L., Deniz, E., Code, A., & Toseeb, U. (2021) How is COVID-19 affecting the mental health of children with special educational needs and disabilities and their families? *Journal of Autism and Developmental Disorders*, *51*(5), 1772–1780.

Atkinson, K. D., Fix, S. T., & Fix, R. L. (2023). Racial Disparities in Child Physical and Sexual Abuse Substantiations: Associations with Childs' and Accused Individuals' Race. *Journal of Child and Family Studies*, *32*(1), 44–56.

Ayuso, L. et al. (2020) The effects of COVID-19 confinement on the Spanish family: adaptation or change? *Journal of Comparative Family Studies*, *51*(3/4), 274–287.

Babycentre (1997) About us. *Babycentre* [website]. Available at: www.babycentre.co.uk/e1001100/about-babycentre (accessed 16 June 2021).

Bacon K. (2019) 5 Contexts of Twinship: Discourses and Generation. In: Frankel S., McNamee S. (eds) *Contextualizing Childhoods*. Palgrave Macmillan, Cham. https://doi.org/10.1007/978-3-319-94926-0_8

Baden, A. L., & Steward, R. J. (2007). The cultural-racial identity model: A theoretical framework for studying transracial adoptees. In R. A. Javier, A. L. Baden, F. A. Biafora, & A. Camacho-Gingerich (Eds.), *Handbook of Adoption: Implications for Researchers, Practitioners, and Families* (pp. 90–112). Sage Publications, Inc. https://doi.org/10.4135/9781412976633.n7https://doi.org/10.4135/9781412976633.n7

Baldwin, S., Malone, M., Sandall, J., & Bick, D. (2018) Mental health and wellbeing during the transition to fatherhood: a systematic review of first-time fathers' experiences. *JBI Database of Systematic Reviews and Implementation Reports*, *16*(11), 2118.

Baldwin, S., Malone, M., Sandall, J., & Bick, D. (2019) A qualitative exploratory study of UK first-time fathers' experiences, mental health and wellbeing needs during their transition to fatherhood. *BMJ Open*, *9*(9), e030792. doi:10.1136/bmjopen-2019-030792

Bank et al., 2004 Bank, L., Patterson, G.R., Reid, J.B. (1996). Negative sibling interaction patterns as predictors of later adjustment problems in adolescent and young adult males. In Brody, G.H. (Ed.) *Sibling relationships: Their causes and consequences* (pp.197–229). Norwood, NJ: Ablex.

Bandura, A. (1977) Self-efficacy: toward a unifying theory of behavioural change. *Psychological Review*, *84*, 191–215.

Bandura, A. (1989) Regulation of cognitive processes through perceived self-efficacy. *Developmental Psychology*, *25*, 729–735.

Bandura, A. (1997) *Self-Efficacy: The Exercise of Control*. New York: W.H. Freeman and Company.

Bandura, A. (2006) Toward a psychology of human agency. *Perspectives on Psychological Science*, *1*(2), 164–180.

Bandura, A., Ross, D., & Ross, S.A. (1963) Imitation of film-mediated aggressive models. *The Journal of Abnormal and Social Psychology*, *66*(1), 3.

Barnes, C., & Adamson-Macedo, E.N. (2007) Perceived maternal parenting self-efficacy (PMP S-E) tool: development and validation with mothers of hospitalized preterm neonates. *Journal of Advanced Nursing*, *60*(5), 550–560.

Barnes, C., & Adamson-Macedo, E.N. (2022) Understanding the impact of newborn touch upon mothers of hospitalized preterm neonates. *Journal of Human Growth and Development, 32*(2), 294–301.

Barnes, C., Harvey, C., Holland, F., & Wall, S. (2021) Development and testing of the Nature Connectedness Parental Self-Efficacy (NCPSE) scale. *Urban Forestry & Urban Greening, 65,* 127343.

Bates, J. E., & Pettit, G. S. (2007). Temperament, Parenting, and Socialization. In J. E. Grusec & P. D. Hastings (Eds.), *Handbook of Socialization: Theory and Research* (pp. 153–177). The Guilford Press.

Baumrind, D. (1971) Current patterns of parental authority. *Developmental Psychology, 4*(1, part 2), 1.

Baumrind D. (1991) The Influence of Parenting Style on Adolescent Competence and Substance Use. *The Journal of Early Adolescence 11* (1), 56–95 https://doi.org/10.1177/0272431691111004

Bayat, M. (2007) Evidence of resilience in families of children with autism. *Journal of Intellectual Disability Research, 51*(9), 702–714.

Beaupre Gillespie, B., & Schwartz Temple, H. (2011) *Good Enough is the New Perfect.* Winnipeg, Canada: Harlequin.

Bellieni, C.V., & Johnston, C.C. (2016) Analgesia, nil or placebo to babies, in trials that test new analgesic treatments for procedural pain. *Acta Paediatrica, 105*(2), 129–136.

Belsky, J. (1984) The determinants of parenting: a process model. *Child Development, 55*(1), 83–96. http://dx.doi.org/10.2307/1129836

Belsky, J., Conger, R., & Capaldi, D.M. (2009) The intergenerational transmission of parenting: introduction to the special section. *Developmental Psychology, 45*(5), 1201–1204. http://dx.doi.org/10.1037/a0016245

Belsky, J., & Jaffee, S.R. (2006) The multiple determinants of parenting. In D. Cicchetti & D.J. Cohen (eds), *Developmental Psychopathology: Risk, Disorder, and Adaptation* (2nd edn, pp. 38–85). Hoboken, NJ: John Wiley & Sons.

Belsky, J., Jaffee, S.R., Sligo, J., Woodward, L., & Silva, P.A. (2005) Intergenerational transmission of warm-sensitive-stimulating parenting: a prospective study of mothers and fathers of 3-year-olds. *Child Development, 76*(2), 384–396.

Benderix, Y., & Sivberg, B. (2007) Siblings' experiences of having a brother or sister with autism and mental retardation: a case study of 14 siblings from five families. *Journal of Pediatric Nursing, 22*(5), 410–418.

Berger, P., & Kellner, H. (1964) Marriage and the construction of reality: an exercise in the microsociology of knowledge. *Diogene, 12*(46), 1–24.

Bernstein, R., Keltner, D., & Laurent, H. (2012) Parental divorce and romantic attachment in young adulthood: Important role of problematic beliefs, *Marriage & Family Review, 48*:8, 711-731. DOI: 10.1080/01494929.2012.700910

Best, R.K. (2019) *Exploring the Educational Experiences of Children and Young People Adopted from Care: Using the Voices of Children and Parents to Inform Practice.* PhD thesis. Institute of Education, *University College London* [website]. Available at: https://discovery.ucl.ac.uk/10081067 (accessed 27 April 2021).

Beurkens, N.M., Hobson, J.A., & Hobson, R.P. (2013) Autism severity and qualities of parent–child relations. *Journal of Autism and Developmental Disorders, 43*(1), 168–178.

Biblarz, T.J., Carroll, M., & Burke N. (2014) Same-sex families. In J. Treas, J. Scott & M. Richards (eds), *The Blackwell Companion to the Sociology of Families*. Oxford: Blackwell Publishing.

Biblarz, T.J., & Stacey, J. (2010) How does the gender of parents matter? *Journal of Marriage and Family 72*(1), 3–22.

Bick, J., Zhu, T., Stamoulis, C., Fox, N.A., Zeanah, C., & Nelson, C.A. (2015) A randomized clinical trial of foster care as an intervention for early institutionalization: long-term improvements in white matter microstructure. *JAMA Pediatrics, 169*(3), 211.

Binet, A., & Simon, T. (1948). The development of the Binet-Simon Scale, 1905–1908. In W. Dennis (Ed.), *Readings in the History of Psychology* (pp. 412–424). Appleton-Century-Crofts. https://doi.org/10.1037/11304-047

Blackburn, C., & Harvey, M. (2019) 'We weren't prepared for this': parents' experiences of information and support following the premature birth of their infant. *Infants & Young Children, 32*(3), 172–185.

BLISS (2022) *BLISS: For babies born premature or sick* [website]. Available at: www.bliss.org.uk (accessed 27 April 2021).

Bomber, L. (2007) *Inside I'm hurting. Practical strategies for supporting children with attachment difficulties in school*. London, Worth Publishing.

Booth, A., & Amato, P.R. (2001) Parental pre-divorce relations and offspring post-divorce well-being. *Journal of Marriage and Family, 63*(1), 197–212.

Bornstein, M.H., & Lamb, M.E. (eds) (2017) *Developmental Science: An Advanced Textbook*. London: Psychology Press.

Bowers, B.F., & Myers, B.J. (1999) Grandmothers providing care for grandchildren: consequences of various levels of caregiving. *Family Relations, 48*(3), 303–311.

Bowlby, J. (1969) *Attachment and Loss, Vol. 1: Attachment*. New York: Basic Books.

Bowlby, J. (1973) *Attachment and Loss: Vol. II: Separation, Anxiety and Anger*. London: The Hogarth Press and the Institute of Psycho-Analysis.

Bowlby, J. (1980). By ethology out of psycho-analysis: An experiment in interbreeding. *Animal Behaviour, 28*(3), 649–656. https://doi.org/10.1016/S0003-3472(80)80125-4

Bowlby, J., May, D.S., & Solomon, M. (1989) *Attachment Theory*. Los Angeles, CA: Lifespan Learning Institute.

Boyer, T.W. (2006) The development of risk-taking: a multi-perspective review. *Developmental Review, 26*(3), 291–345.

Brand, C., Howcroft, G., & Hoelson, C.N. (2017) The voice of the child in parental divorce: implications for clinical practice and mental health practitioners. *Journal of Child and Adolescent Mental Health 29*(2), 169–178. https://doi.org/10.2989/17280583.2017.1345746

Brandon, M. (2009). Child fatality or serious injury through maltreatment: Making sense of outcomes. *Children and Youth Services Review, 31*(10), 1107–1112.

Brandtstädter, J. (2006) *Action Perspectives on Human Development*. Hoboken, NJ: John Wiley & Sons.

Bretherton, I. (1985). Attachment theory: Retrospect and prospect. *Monographs of the Society for Research in Child Development, 50*(1-2), 3–35. https://doi.org/10.2307/3333824

Brody, G.H. (1998). Sibling relationship quality: Its causes and consequences. *Annual Review of Psychology, 49*, 1–24.

Brody, G., Stoneman, Z., & MacKinnon, C. (1982). Role asymmetries in interactions among school-aged children, their younger siblings, and their friends. *Child Development, 53*(5), 1364–1370. DOI: 10.2307/1129027

Brodzinsky, D., & Livingstone-Smith, S. (2019) Commentary: understanding research, policy, and practice issues in adoption instability. *Research on Social Work Practice, 29*(2), 185–194.

Bronfenbrenner, U. (1977) Toward an experimental ecology of human development. *American Psychologist, 32*(7), 513.

Bronfenbrenner, U. (1979) *The Ecology of Human Development: Experiments by Nature and Design*. Cambridge, MA: Harvard University Press.

Brown, S., Cohon, D., & Wheeler, R. (2002) African American extended families and kinship care: how relevant is the foster care model for kinship care? *Children and Youth Services Review, 24*(1–2), 55–78.

Buhrmester, D. & Furman, W. (1990). Perceptions of sibling relationships during middle childhood and adolescence. *Child Development, 61*, 1387–1398.

Burke, P. (2004) *Brothers and Sisters of Disabled Children*. London: Jessica Kingsley.

Burman, E. (2008) *Deconstructing Developmental Psychology* (2nd edn). London: Routledge.

Burton, L.M. (1992) Black grandparents rearing children of drug-addicted parents: stressors, outcomes, and social service needs. *The Gerontologist, 32*(6), 744–751.

Busby, N., & Weldon-Johns, M. (2019) Fathers as carers in UK law and policy: Dominant ideologies and lived experience. *Journal of Social Welfare and Family Law, 41*(3), 280–301.

Cadman, T., Diamond, P.R., & Fearon, P. (2018) Reassessing the validity of the attachment Q-sort: an updated meta-analysis. *Infant and Child Development, 27*(1), e2034.

Caffaro J. (2020) Sibling abuse of other children. In: Geffner R., White J.W., Hamberger L.K., Rosenbaum A., Vaughan-Eden V., Vieth V.I. (eds) *Handbook of Interpersonal Violence and Abuse Across the Lifespan*. Springer, Cham. https://doi.org/10.1007/978-3-319-62122-7_11-1

Cairns, R.B. & Cairns, B.D. (2007). The making of developmental psychology. *Handbook of Child Psychology* (eds W. Damon, R.M. Lerner and R.M. Lerner). https://doi-org.ezproxy.derby.ac.uk/10.1002/9780470147658.chpsy0103

Campbell, M., Thomson, H., Fenton, C., & Gibson, M. (2016) Lone parents, health, wellbeing and welfare to work: a systematic review of qualitative studies. *BMC Public Health, 16*(1), 1–10.

Canzi, E., Molgora, S., Fenaroli, V., Rosnati, R., Saita, E., & Ranieri, S. (2019) 'Your stress is my stress': a dyadic study on adoptive and biological first-time parents. *Couple and Family Psychology: Research and Practice, 8*(4), 197.

Capaldi, D.M., Pears, K.C., Patterson, G.R., & Owen, L.D. (2003) Continuity of parenting practices across generations in an at-risk sample: a prospective comparison of direct and mediated associations. *Journal of Abnormal Child Psychology, 31*(2), 127–142.

Caputo, V. (2007) She's from a good family': performing childhood and motherhood in a Canadian private school setting. *Childhood, 14*(2), 173–192.

Carlson, E.A., Hostinar, C.E., Mliner, S.B., & Gunnar, M.R. (2014) The emergence of attachment following early social deprivation. *Development and Psychopathology, 26*(2), 479–489.

Caro, P., Turner, W., & Macdonald, G. (2019) Comparative effectiveness of interventions for treating the psychological consequences of sexual abuse in children and adolescents. *The Cochrane Database of Systematic Reviews, 2019*(6).

Cartwright, C., Farnsworth, V., & Mobley, V. (2009) Relationships with step-parents in the life stories of young adults after divorce. *Family Matters, 82*, 30–37.

Cartwright, P. (2014) Step-parenting. In A. Hayes & D. Higgins (eds), *Families, Policy and the Law: Selected Essays*. Melbourne, Vic.: Australian Institute of Family Studies.

Cassiano, R.G., Provenzi, L., Linhares, M.B.M., Gaspardo, C.M., & Montirosso, R. (2020) Does preterm birth affect child temperament? A meta-analytic study. *Infant Behavior and Development, 58*, 101417.

Cassidy, J., & Shaver, P. (2008) *Handbook of Attachment: Theory, Practice and Clinical Applications*. New York: Guilford Press.

Centre for Law and Social Policy (2022) *Centre for Law and Social Policy* [website]. Available at: www.clasp.org (accessed 20 January 2022).

Chaiklin, S. (2003) Analysis of learning and instruction. *Vygotsky's Educational Theory in Cultural Context, 39*.

Chang, L., Schwartz, D., Dodge, K.A., & McBride-Chang, C. (2003) Harsh parenting in relation to child emotion regulation and aggression. *Journal of Family Psychology, 17*(4), 598–606. http://dx.doi.org/10.1037/0893-3200.17.4.598

Chao, R.K. (1994) Beyond parental control and authoritarian parenting style: understanding Chinese parenting through the cultural notion of training. *Child Development, 65*(4), 1111–1119.

Cheah, C.S.L., Li, J., Zhou, N., Yamamoto, Y., & Leung, C.Y.Y. (2015) Understanding Chinese immigrant and European American mothers' expressions of warmth. *Developmental Psychology, 51*(12), 1802–1811.

Childcare Act (2006). *Childcare Act* [website]. Available at: www.legislation.gov.uk/ukpga/2006/21/enacted (accessed 3 August 2021).

Children and Families Act (2014). *Children and Families Act* [website]. Available at: www.legislation.gov.uk/ukpga/2014/6/contents/enacted (accessed 27 April 2021).

Children and Social Work Act (2017). *Children and Social Work Act* [website]. Available at: www.legislation.gov.uk/ukpga/2017/16/section/5/enacted (accessed 28 June 2021).

Children's Commissioner (2022) Family Review. Family and its protective effect, Part 1. *Children's Commissioner* [website]. Available at: www.childrenscommissioner.gov.uk/resource/family-and-its-protective-effect-part-1-of-the-independent-family-review (accessed 28 June 2021).

Christiansen, S. L., & Palkovitz, R. (2001). Why the 'good provider' role still matters: Providing as a form of paternal involvement. *Journal of Family Issues, 22*(1), 84–106.

Chuang, S.S., Glozman, J., Green, D.S., & Rasmi, S. (2018) Parenting and family relationships in Chinese families: a critical ecological approach. *Journal of Family Theory and Review, 10*(2), 367–383.

Clarke-Stewart, K.A., Vandell, D.L., McCartney, K., Owen, M.T., & Booth, C. (2000) Effects of parental separation and divorce on very young children. *Journal of Family Psychology, 14*(2), 304–326.

Clements, C.M., Bennett, V.E., Hungerford, A., Clauss, K., & Wait, S.K. (2019) Psychopathology and coping in survivors of intimate partner violence: associations with race and abuse severity. *Journal of Aggression, Maltreatment & Trauma, 28*(2), 205–221.

Clifford, T., Minnes, P. (2013) Logging on: evaluating an online support group for parents of children with autism spectrum disorders. *Journal of Autism and Developmental Disorders 43*, 1662–1675

Cohen, G.J. (2002) Helping children and families deal with divorce and separation. *Pediatrics, 110*(5), 1019–1023.

Cole, E. (2014) *Birth Order. An examination of its relationship with the Big Five personality theory and Trait Emotional Intelligence* https://discovery.ucl.ac.uk/id/eprint/1428439/

Cole, K., & Mitchell, P. (2000) Siblings in the development of executive control and a theory of mind. *British Journal of Developmental Psychology, 18*, 279–295

Coleman L., & Glenn, F. (2010) The varied impact of couple relationship breakdown on children: Implications for practice and policy. *Children and Society 24*(3), 238–249 https://doi.org/10.1111/j.1099-0860.2009.00289

Coleman, P.K., & Karraker, K.H. (1997) Self-efficacy and parenting quality: findings and future applications. *Development Review, 18*, 47–85. http://dx.doi.org/10.1006/drev.1997.0448

Colizzi, M., Sironi, E., Antonini, F., Ciceri, M.L., Bovo, C., & Zoccante, L. (2020) Psychosocial and behavioral impact of COVID-19 in autism spectrum disorder: an online parent survey. *Brain Sciences, 10*(6), 341.

Colvert, E., Rutter, M., Kreppner, J., Beckett, C., Castle, J., Groothues, C., Hawkins, A., Stevens, S., Songuga-Barke, E.J.S. (2008) Do theory of mind and executive function deficits underlie the adverse outcomes associated with profound early deprivation? Findings from the English and Romanian adoptees study. *Journal of Abnormal Child Psychology, 36*, 1057-1068.

Cook, D.A., & Williams, T. (2015) Expanding intersectionality: fictive kinship networks as supports for the educational aspirations of Black women. *The Western Journal of Black Studies, 39*(2), 157.

Cooke, J.E., Deneault, A.A., Devereux, C., Eirich, R., Fearon, R.P., & Madigan, S. (2022) Parental sensitivity and child behavioral problems: a meta-analytic review. *Child Development, 93*(5), 1231–1248.

Cooklin, A.R., Giallo, R., & Rose, N. (2012) Parental fatigue and parenting practices during early childhood: an Australian community survey. *Child: Care, Health and Development, 38*(5), 654–664.

Cooper, S.M., Ross, L., Dues, A., Golden, A.R., & Burnett, M. (2019) Intergenerational factors, fatherhood beliefs, and African American fathers' involvement: building the case for a mediated pathway. *Journal of Family Issues, 40*(15), 2047–2075.

Corby, B. (2006) *Child Abuse: Towards a Knowledge Base* (3rd edn). Maidenhead: Open University Press.

Corby, B., Shemmings, D., & Wilkins, D. (2012) *Child Abuse: An Evidence Base for Confident Practice* (4th edn). Maidenhead: Open University Press.

Corsano, P., Musetti, A., Guidotti, L., & Capelli F. (2017) Typically developing adolescents' experience of growing up with a brother with an autism spectrum disorder. *Journal of Intellectual & Developmental Disabilities, 42*(2), 151–161.

Costa, T.M., & da Silva Pereira, A.P. (2019) The child with autism spectrum disorder: the perceptions of siblings. *Support for Learning*, 34(2), 193–210.

Coster, W. (2016) *Baptism and Spiritual Kinship in Early Modern England*. London: Routledge.

Cox, C.B. (2000) *To Grandmother's House We Go and Stay: Perspectives on Custodial Grandparents*. New York: Springer.

Cprek, S.E., Williamson, L.H., McDaniel, H., Brase, R., & Williams, C.M. (2020) Adverse childhood experiences (ACEs) and risk of childhood delays in children ages 1–5. *Child and Adolescent Social Work Journal*, 37(1), 15– 24.

Craig, L., Powell, A., & Smyth, C. (2014) Towards intensive parenting? Changes in the composition and determinants of mothers' and fathers' time with children 1992–2006. *British Journal of Sociology*, 65(3), 555–579.

Cridland, E.K., Jones, S.C., Stoyles, G., Caputi, P., & Magee, C.A. (2016) Families living with autism spectrum disorder: roles and responsibilities of adolescent sisters. *Focus on Autism & Other Developmental Disabilities*, 31(3), 196–207.

Crime Survey for England and Wales (CSEW) (2020) Child abuse extent and nature, England and Wales: year ending March 2019. Available at: www.ons.gov.uk/ peoplepopulationandcommunity/crimeandjustice/articles/ childabuseextent andnatureenglandandwales/yearendingmarch2019 (accessed 17 January 2023).

Crnic, K.A., Greenberg, M.T., Ragozin, A.S., Robinson, N.M., & Basham, R.B. (1983a) Effects of stress and social support on mothers and premature and full-term infants. *Child Development*, 54(1), 209–217.

Crnic, K.A., Ragozin, A.S., Greenberg, M.T., Robinson, N.M., & Basham, R.B. (1983b) Social interaction and developmental competence of preterm and full-term infants during the first year of life. *Child Development*, 54, 119–1210.

Crouter, A.C., & Booth, A. (eds) (2003) *Children's Influence on Family Dynamics: The Neglected Side of Family Relationships*. London: Routledge.

Cui, M., & Conger, R.D. (2008) Parenting behavior as mediator and moderator of the association between marital problems and adolescent maladjustment. *Journal of Research on Adolescence*, 18(2), 261–284.

Cutting, A.L., & Dunn, J. (2010) Conversations with siblings and friends: Links between relationship quality and social understanding. *Developmental Psychology* 24 (1), 73–87

Cyron, L., Schwerdt, G., & Viarengo, M. (2017) The effect of opposite sex siblings on cognitive and noncognitive skills in early childhood, *Applied Economics Letters*, 24:19, 1369-1373, DOI: 10.1080/13504851.2017.1279263

Dabrowska, A., & Pisula, E. (2010) Parenting stress and coping styles in mothers and fathers of preschool children with autism and Down syndrome. *Journal of Intellectual Disability Research* 54(3), 266–280

Dahlberg, G., Moss, P., & Pence, P. (2013) *Beyond Quality in Early Childhood Education and Care: Languages of Evaluation*. London: Routledge.

D'Amato, B. (2010) Adoption: perspectives and fantasy. *Modern Psychoanalysis*, 35(1), 53–67.

Daniel, B. (2015) Why have we made neglect so complicated? Taking a fresh look at noticing and helping the neglected child. *Child Abuse Review*, 24, 82–94.

Daniels, E., Arden-Close, E., & Mayers, A. (2020) Be quiet and man up: a qualitative questionnaire study into fathers who witnessed their partner's birth trauma. *BMC Pregnancy and Childbirth*, 20(1), 1–12.

Davies, K. (2015) 'Siblings, Stories and the Self: The Sociological Significance of Young People's Sibling Relationships.' *Sociology.* *49* (4), p. 679–695. doi: 10.1177/0038514551091

Davis, A. (2012) *Modern Motherhood: women, family and England* 1945-2000. Manchester: University Press.

Davison, K.K., Kitos, N., Aftosmes-Tobio, A., Ash, T., Agaronov, A., Sepulveda, M., & Haines, J. (2018) The forgotten parent: fathers' representation in family interventions to prevent childhood obesity. *Preventive Medicine, 111,* 170–176.

Dearing, E. (2004) The developmental implications of restrictive and supportive parenting across neighbourhoods and ethnicities: exceptions are the rules. *Journal of Applied Developmental Psychology, 25,* 555–575.

De Bellis, M.D., Spratt, E.G., & Hooper, S.R. (2011) Neurodevelopmental biology associated with childhood sexual abuse. *Journal of Child Sexual Abuse, 20*(5), 548–587.

Delaney, M. (2017) *Attachment for Teachers: An Essential Handbook for Trainees and NQTs.* London, Worth Publishing

De Roiste, A., & Bushnell, I.W.R. (1993) Tactile stimulation and preterm infant performance on an instrumental conditioning task. *Journal of Reproductive and Infant Psychology, 11,* 155–163.

De Roiste, A., & Bushnell, I.W.R. (1995) The immediate gastric effects of a tactile stimulation programme on premature infants. *Journal of Reproductive and Infant Psychology, 13,* 57–62.

De Roiste, A., & Bushnell, I.W.R. (1996) Tactile stimulation: short- and long-term benefits for premature infants. *Journal of Reproductive and Infant Psychology, 11,* 155–163.

De Young, A., Kenardy, J., & Cobham, V. (2011) Trauma in early childhood: a neglected population. *Clinical Child and Family Psychology Review, 14*(3), 231–250.

Deković, M., & Janssens, J.M. (1992) Parents' child-rearing style and child's sociometric status. *Developmental Psychology, 28*(5), 925.

Demby, K.P., Riggs, S.A., & Kaminski, P.L. (2017) Attachment and family processes in children's psychological adjustment in middle childhood. *Family Process, 56*(1), 234–249.

Department for Education (DfE) (2003) *Every Child Matters.* London: Department for Education.

Department for Education Teachers' Standards (2011) *Department for Education* [website]. Available at: www.gov.uk/government/publications/teachers-standards (accessed 3 December 2021).

Department for Education Statutory Framework for the Early Years Foundation Stage (2017). *Department for Education* [website]. Available at: www.gov.uk/government/publications/early-years-foundation-stage-framework--2 (accessed 14 August 2021).

Department for Education Promoting the Education of Looked After Children and Previously Looked After Children: Statutory Guidance for Local Authorities (2018). *Department for Education* [website]. Available at: www.gov.uk/government/publications/promoting-the-education-of-looked-after-children (accessed 14 August 2021).

Department for Education Guidance Partnership Models Guide (2019). *Department for Education* [website]. Available at: www.gov.uk/government/publications/setting-up-school-partnerships/partnership-models-guide (accessed 14 August 2021).

Department for Education Children Looked After in England including Adoptions (2021). *Department for Education* [website]. Available at: https://explore-education-statistics.service.gov.uk/find-statistics/children-looked-after-in-england-including-adoptions/2020#releaseHeadlines-tables (accessed 27 April 2021).

Department for Education and Skills Care Matters: Time for Change (2007). Department for Education and Skills [website]. Available at: www.gov.uk/government/publications/care-matters-time-for-change (accessed 27 April 2021).

Dermott, E., & Pomati, M. (2016) The parenting and economising practices of lone parents: policy and evidence. *Critical Social Policy*, *36*(1), 62–81. https://doi.org/10.1177/0261018315602198

Desimone, L. (1999) Linking parent involvement with student achievement: Do race and income matter? *The Journal of Educational Research*, *93*(1), 11–30.

Desjardins, J., Zelenski, J.M., & Coplan, R.J. (2008) An investigation of maternal personality, parenting styles, and subjective well-being. *Personality and Individual Differences*, *44*(3), 587–597.

Diener, E., Gohm, C.L., Suh, E., & Oishi, S. (2000) Similarity of the relations between marital status and subjective well-being across cultures. *Journal of Cross-Cultural Psychology*, *31*, 419–436. DOI: 10.1177/0022022100031004001

Doheny, K. (2008) *Autism and Family Relationships* [website]. Available at: www.webmd.com/brain/autism/features/autism-and-family-relationships (accessed 10 March 2022).

Doinita, N.E., & Maria, N.D. (2015) Attachment and parenting styles. International Conference Education and Psychology Challenges – Teachers for the Knowledge Society. EPC-TKS 2015 (3rd edn). *Procedia – Social and Behavioral Sciences*, *203*(2015), 199–204.

Domina, T. (2005) Leveling the home advantage: assessing the effectiveness of parental involvement in elementary school. *Sociology of Education*, *78*(3), 233–249.

Donaldson, M. (2006) *Children's Minds*. London, Harper Perennial.

Dorval, A., Lamothe, J., Hélie, S., & Poirier, M.A. (2020) Different profiles, different needs: an exploration and analysis of characteristics of children in kinship care and their parents. *Children and Youth Services Review*, *108*, 104531.

Doss, B.D., & Rhoades, G.K. (2017) The transition to parenthood: impact on couples' romantic relationships. *Current Opinion in Psychology*, *13*, 25–28.

Douglas, S.J., & Michaels, M.M. (2005) *The Mommy Myth: The Idealization of Motherhood and How It Has Undermined All Women*. New York: Free Press.

Dowling, E., & Barnes, G.G. (2020) *Working with Children and Parents through Separation and Divorce: The Changing Lives of Children*. London: Bloomsbury.

du Bois-Reymond, M., Bucher, P., & Kruger, H.-H. (1993) Modern family as everyday negotiation: continuities and discontinuities in parent–child relationships. *Childhood*, *1*(2), 87–99.

Dunedin Multidisciplinary Health and Development Study. *Dunedin Study* [website]. Available at: dunedinstudy.otago.ac.nz (accessed 27 April 2021).

Dunn, J. (1996). Siblings: The first society. In N. Vanzetti & S. Duck (Eds.), *A lifetime of relationships* (pp. 105–124). Thomson Brooks/Cole Publishing Co.

Dunn, J., Brown J., Slomkowki, C., Tesla, C., & Youngblade, L. (1991) Young children's understanding of other people's feelings and beliefs: Individual differences and their antecedents. *Child Development, 62*, 1352–1366

Dunn, J., Creps, C. & Brown, J. (1996). Children's family relationships between two and five: Developmental changes and individual differences. *Social Development, 5*, 230–250.

Dunn, J., & Munn, P. (1986). Siblings and the development of prosocial behaviour. *International Journal of Behavioural Development, 9*, 265–284 DOI: 10.1177/016502548600900301

Dunn, J., O'Connor, T.G., & Levy, I. (2002) Out of the picture: a study of family drawings by children from step-, single-parent, and non-step families. *Journal of Clinical Child and Adolescent Psychology, 31*(4), 505–512.

Dunning, M.J., & Giallo, R. (2012) Fatigue, parenting stress, self-efficacy and satisfaction in mothers of infants and young children. *Journal of Reproductive and Infant Psychology, 30*(2), 145–159.

Durrant, J., Rose-Krasnor, L., & Broberg, A.G. (2003) Physical punishment and maternal beliefs in Sweden and Canada. *Journal of Comparative Family Studies, 34*(4), 585–604.

Dutton, M.A., Kaltman, S., Goodman, L.A., Weinfurt, K., & Vankos, N. (2005) Patterns of intimate partner violence: correlates and outcomes. *Violence and Victims, 20*(5), 483–497.

Dykens, E.M., Lambert, W. Trajectories of diurnal cortisol in mothers of children with autism and other developmental disabilities: relations to health and mental health. *Journal of Autism and Developmental Disorders 43*, 2426–2434. https://doi.org/10.1007/s10803-013-1791-1

Ebrahimi, L., Amiri, M., Mohamadlou, M., & Rezapur, R. (2017) Attachment styles, parenting styles, and depression. *International Journal of Mental Health and Addiction, 15*(5), 1064–1068.

Eckerman, C.O., & Oehler, J.M. (1992) Very-low birthweight newborns and parents as early social partners. In S.L. Friedman & M.D. Sigman (eds), *The Psychological Development of Low Birthweight Children*. New York: Ablex Publishing.

Eckerman, C.O., Oehler, J.M., Medvin, M.B., & Hannan, T.E. (1994) Premature newborns as social partners before term age. *Infant Behavior and Development, 17*(1), 55–70.

Edwards, B., Gray, M., & Hunter, B. (2009) A sunburnt country: the economic and financial impact of drought on rural and regional families in Australia in an era of climate change. *Australian Journal of Labour Economics, 12*(1), 109–131.

Edwards, O.W., & Daire, A.P. (2006) School-age children raised by their grandparents: problems and solutions. *Journal of Instructional Psychology, 33*(2), 113–119.

Ekas, N., & Whitman, T.L. (2010) Autism symptom topography and maternal socioemotional functioning. *American Journal on Intellectual and Developmental Disabilities, 115*(3), 234–249.

Ekas, N.V., Lickenbrock, D.M. & Whitman, T.L. Optimism, social support, and well-being in mothers of children with autism spectrum disorder. *Journal of Autism and Developmental Disorders 40*, 1274–1284 (2010). https://doi.org/10.1007/s10803-010-0986-y

Ekas, N. V., Timmons, L., Pruitt, M., Ghilain, C., & Alessandri, M. (2015). The power of positivity: Predictors of relationship satisfaction for parents of children with autism spectrum disorder. *Journal of Autism and Developmental Disorders, 45*, 1997–2007.

Eklund, L., & Lundqvist, A. (2021) Children's rights and gender equality in Swedish parenting support: policy and practice. *Journal of Family Studies*, *27*(1), 32–47.

El Nokali, N.E., Bachman, H.J., & Votruba-Drzal, E. (2010) Parent involvement and children's academic and social development in elementary school. *Child Development*, *81*(3), 988–1005.

Elfer, P., Greenfield, S., Robson, S., Wilson, D., & Zachariou, A. (2018) Love, satisfaction and exhaustion in the nursery: methodological issues in evaluating the impact of work discussion groups in the nursery. *Early Child Development and Care*, *188*(7), 892–904.

Emery, R.E., & Forehand, R. (1996) Parental divorce and children's well-being: a focus on resilience. In R.J. Haggerty, L.R. Sherrod, N. Garmezy & M. Rutter (eds), *Stress, Risk, and Resilience in Children and Adolescents*. Cambridge: Cambridge University Press.

EPICure (2022a) *EPICure 1995* [website]. Available at: www.ucl.ac.uk/womens-health/research/neonatology/epicure/epicure-1995 (accessed 19 January 2023).

EPICure (2022b) *EPICure 2* [website]. Available at: www.ucl.ac.uk/womens-health/epicure-2 (accessed 19 January 2023).

Erikson, E. H. (1950). Growth and crises of the 'healthy personality.' In M. J. E. Senn (Ed.), *Symposium on the healthy personality* (pp. 91–146). Josiah Macy, Jr. Foundation.

Eun, B. (2010) From learning to development: a sociocultural approach to instruction. *Cambridge Journal of Education*, *40*(4), 401–418.

Eurostat (2020) *European Union Labour Force Survey (EU LFS)* [website]. Available at: https://ec.europa.eu/eurostat/web/microdata/european-union-labour-force-survey (accessed 14 December 2021).

Euser, S., Alink, L. R., Tharner, A., van IJzendoorn, M. H., & Bakermans-Kranenburg, M. J. (2016). The prevalence of child sexual abuse in out-of-home care: Increased risk for children with a mild intellectual disability. *Journal of Applied Research in Intellectual Disabilities, 29*(1), 83–92.

Evangelou, M., Sylva, K., & Kyriacou, M. (2009) *Early Years Learning and Development Literature Review* [website]. Available at: https://foundationyears.org.uk/wp-content/uploads/2012/08/DCSF-RR1761.pdf (accessed 3 December 2021).

Evangelou, M., Sylva, K., Kyriacou, M., Wild, M., & Glenny, G. (2009). *Early Years Learning and Development*. Department for Children, Schools and families. Research report DCSGF-RR176.

Evans, N., Jenkins, S., & Pereira, I. (2009) Families in Britain: the impact of changing family structures and what the public think. *Policy Exchange* [website]. Available at: https://policyexchange.org.uk/publication/families-in-britain-the-impact-of-changing-family-structures/ (accessed 29 July 2021).

Falk, N.H., Norris, K., & Quinn, M.G. (2014) The factors predicting stress, anxiety, and depression in the parents of children with autism. *Journal of Autism and Developmental Disorders*, *44*(12), 3185–3203.

Fan, J., & Zhang, L.F. (2014) The role of perceived parenting styles in thinking styles. *Learning and Individual Differences*, *32*, 204–211.

Fang, Y., Boelens, M., Windhorst, D.A., Raat, H., & van Grieken, A. (2021) Factors associated with parenting self-efficacy: a systematic review. *Journal of Advanced Nursing*, *77*(6), 2641–2661.

Farmer, E., & Moyers, S. (2008) *Kinship Care: Fostering Effective Family and Friend Placements*. London: Jessica Kingsley.

Farrant, B.M., Devine, T.A.J., Maybery, M.T., & Fletcher, J. (2012) Empathy, perspective taking and prosocial behavior: the importance of parenting practice. *Infant and Child Development*, *21*(2), 175–188. https://doi.org/10.1002/icd.740

Farrant, B. (2014). Mal adaptive Parenting and Child Emotional Symptoms in the Early School Years: Findings from the Longitudinal Study of Australian Children. *Australasian Journal of Early Childhood*, *39*(2), 118–125. https://doi.org/10.1177/183693911403900215

Fauk, N.K., Mwakinyali, S.E., Putra, S., & Mwanri, L. (2017) The socio-economic impacts of AIDS on families caring for AIDS-orphaned children in Mbeya rural district, Tanzania. *International Journal of Human Rights in Healthcare*, *10*(2), 132–145.

Fearon, I., Hains, S.M.J., Muir, D.W., & Kisilevsky, B.S. (2002) Development of tactile responses in human preterm and fullterm infants from 30 to 40 weeks postconceptional age. *Infancy*, *3*(1), 31–51.

Feinberg, Solmeyer & McHale (2012). The Third Rail of Family Systems: Sibling Relationships, Mental & Behavioural Health and Preventative Intervention in Childhood and Adolescence. *Clinical Child and Family Psychological Review*, *15*, 43–57

Felitti, V.J., Anda, R.F., Nordenberg, D., Williamson, D.F., Spitz, A.M., Edwards, V., & Marks, J.S. (1998) Relationship of childhood abuse and household dysfunction to many of the leading causes of death in adults: the Adverse Childhood Experiences (ACE) study. *American Journal of Preventive Medicine*, *14*(4), 245–258.

Ferreira, R.D.C., Alves, C.R.L., Guimarães, M.A.P., Menezes, K.K.P.D., & Magalhães, L.D.C. (2020) Effects of early interventions focused on the family in the development of children born preterm and/or at social risk: a meta-analysis. *Jornal de Pediatria*, *96*, 20–38.

Festinger, L. (1954) A theory of social comparison processes. *Human Relations*, *7* (2), 117–140

Field, T., Diego, M., & Hernandez-Reif, M. (2010) Preterm infant massage therapy research: a review. *Infant Behavior and Development*, *33*(2), 115–124.

Fond, G., Franc, N., & Purper-Ouakil, D. (2012) Homosexual parenthood and child development: present data. *L'encephale*, *38*(1), 10–15.

Ford, J.D., & Courtois, C.A. (2009) *Treating Complex Traumatic Stress Disorders: An Evidence-Based Guide*. New York: Guilford Press.

Foster, R., Longton, C., & Roberts, J. (2003) *Mums on Babies, Trade Secrets from the Real Experts*. London: Cassell Illustrated.

Franke, H. (2014) Toxic stress: effects, prevention and treatment. *Children*, *1*(3), 390–402. DOI: 10.3390/children1030390

Freud, S. (1917) Mourning and melancholia. *The Standard Edition of the Complete Psychological Works of Sigmund Freud*, Vol. *14* (1914–1916), pp. 237–258.

Freud, S. (1923) The ego and the id. *The Standard Edition of the Complete Psychological Works of Sigmund Freud*, Vol. *19*, pp. 29–77.

Freud, S. (1930) Civilization and its discontents. *The Standard Edition of the Complete Psychological Works of Sigmund Freud*, Vol. *21*, pp. 59–145.

Froebel, F. (1912) *Froebel's Chief Writings on Education*. Trans. S.S.F. Fletcher & J. Welton. London: Edward Arnold.

Froebel Trust (2022) Froebelian principles. *Froebel Trust* [website]. Available at: www. froebel.org.uk (accessed 11 March 2022).

Fujita, M., Endoh, Y., Saimon, N., & Yamaguchi, S. (2006) Effect of massaging babies on mothers: pilot study on the changes in mood states and salivary cortisol level. *Complementary Therapies in Clinical Practice, 12*(3), 181–185.

Fuller-Thomson, E., & Minkler, L. (2000) America's grandparent carers: who are they? In B. Hayslip & R. Goldberg-Glen (eds), *Grandparents Raising Grandchildren*. New York: Springer.

Furedi, F. (2001) *Paranoid Parenting*. Harmondsworth: Penguin.

Furedi, F. (2008) *Paranoid Parenting: Why Ignoring the Experts May Be Best for Your Child*. London: Continuum.

Furman, L., Minich, N., & Hack, M. (2002) Correlates of lactation in mothers of very low birth weight infants. *Pediatrics, 109*(4), 7.

García-López, C., Sarriá, E., & Pozo, P. (2016) Parental self-efficacy and positive contributions regarding autism spectrum condition: an actor–partner interdependence model. *Journal of Autism and Developmental Disorders, 46*(7), 2385–2398.

Geen, R. (2004) The evolution of kinship care policy and practice: the future of children. *Children, Families and Foster Care, 14*(1), 130–149. https://doi.org/10.2307/1602758

Gerlach, J., Fößel, J.M., Vierhaus, M., Sann, A., Eickhorst, A., Zimmermann, P., & Spangler, G. (2022) Family risk and early attachment development: the differential role of parental sensitivity. *Infant Mental Health Journal, 43*(2), 340–356.

Ghani, F.B.A., bt Roeswardi, S.I., & bt Abd Aziz, A. (2014) Parenting styles and their relation to teenagers' personality profile in single mother families: a case study. *Procedia-Social and Behavioral Sciences, 114*, 766–770.

Giddens, A. (1993) Dare to care, conserve and repair. *New Statesman & Society, 6*(276), 18–24

Gingerbread (2022) *Gingerbread* [website]. Available at: www.gingerbread.org.uk (accessed 7 January 2022).

Godfrey-Smith, P. (2001). On the status and explanatory structure of developmental systems theory. *Cycles of contingency: Developmental systems and evolution*, 283–297.

Goetting, A. (1986) The developmental tasks of siblingship over the life cycle. *Journal of Marriage and the Family, 48* (4), 703–714

Goldberg, A. E., & Blaauw, E. (2019). Parental substance use disorder and child abuse: risk factors for child maltreatment? *Psychiatry, Psychology and Law, 26*(6), 959–969.

Golding, K. S. (2008). *Nurturing attachments: Supporting children who are fostered or adopted*. London: Jessica Kingsley.

Golding, K.S. (2010) Multi-agency and specialist working to meet the mental health needs of children in care and adopted. *Clinical Child Psychology and Psychiatry, 15*(4), 573–587.

Golombok, S., Perry, B., Burston, A., Murray, C., Mooney-Somers, J., Stevens, M., & Golding, J. (2003) Children with lesbian parents: a community study. *Developmental Psychology, 39*(1), 20–33.

Goodall, J., & Montgomery, C. (2014) Parental involvement to parental engagement: a continuum. *Educational Review, 66*(4), 399–410.

Goodman, S.H., & Garber, J. (2017) Evidence-based interventions for depressed mothers and their young children. *Child Development, 88*(2), 368–377

Goodwin, B., Madden, E., Singletary, J., & Scales, T.L. (2020) Adoption workers' perspectives on adoption adjustment and the honeymoon period. *Children and Youth Services Review, 119*, Art. 105513.

Gordo, L., Oliver-Roig, A., Martínez-Pampliega, A., Elejalde, L. I., Fernández-Alcantara, M., & Richart-Martínez, M. (2018) Parental perception of child vulnerability and parental competence: the role of postnatal depression and parental stress in fathers and mothers. *PLoS One, 13*(8), e0202894. https://doi.org/10.1371/journal. pone.0202894

Gore Langton, E., & Boy, K. (2017) *Becoming an Adoption-Friendly School: A Whole School Resource for Supporting Children Who Have Experienced Trauma or Loss.* London: Jessica Kingsley.

Gorjy, R.S., Fielding, A., & Falkmer, M. (2017) 'It's better than it used to be': perspectives of adolescent siblings of children with an autism spectrum condition. *Child & Family Social Work, 22*(4), 1488–1496.

Gottlieb, G. (1996) Developmental psychobiological theory. In R.B. Cairns, G.H. Elder, Jr, & E.J. Costello (eds), *Developmental Science* (pp. 63–77). Cambridge: Cambridge University Press.

Gov.uk (2010) Lone parent households with dependent children. *Gov.uk* [website]. Available at: www.data.gov.uk/dataset/36b44e58-22f7-4f5c-83d5-d08009e3e00c/lone-parent-households-with-dependent-children (accessed 7 January 2022).

Grandparents Plus (2020) State of the Nation report. *Grandparents Plus* [website]. Available at: www.grandparentsplus.org.uk/wp-content/uploads/annual-surevy-report-2020.pdf (accessed 7 January 2022).

Grauerholz, L. (2000) An ecological approach to understanding sexual revictimization: linking personal, interpersonal, and sociocultural factors and processes. *Child Maltreatment, 5*(1), 5–17.

Graungaard, A.H., & Skov, L. (2007) Why do we need a diagnosis? A qualitative study of parents' experiences, coping and needs, when the newborn child is severely disabled. *Child: Care, Health and Development, 33*(3), 296–307.

Greenfield, E.A., & Moorman, S.M. (2019) Childhood socioeconomic status and later life cognition: evidence from the Wisconsin Longitudinal Study. *Journal of Aging and Health, 31*(9), 1589–1615.

Greenough, W.T., Black, J.E., & Wallace, C.S. (2002) Experience and brain development. In M.H. Johnson, Y. Munakata & R.O. Gilmore (eds), *Brain Development and Cognition: A Reader* (pp. 186–216). Oxford: Blackwell Publishing.

Griffiths, P.E., & Tabery, J. (2013) Developmental systems theory: what does it explain, and how does it explain it. *Advances in Child Development and Behavior, 44*, 65–94.

Grolnick, W.S., & Slowiaczek, M.L. (1994) Parents' involvement in children's schooling: a multidimensional conceptualization and motivational model. *Child Development, 65*(1), 237–252.

Grotevant, H., Dunbar, N., Kohler, J., & LashEsau, A. (2007) Adoptive identity: how contexts within and beyond the family shape developmental pathways. In R.A. Javier, A.L. Baden, F.A. Biafora, & A. Camacho-Gingerich (eds), *Handbook of Adoption: Implications for Researchers, Practitioners and Families* (pp. 77–89). Thousand Oaks, CA: Sage.

Gunnar, M.R., & Reid, B.M. (2019) Early deprivation revisited: contemporary studies of the impact on young children of institutional care. *Annual Review of Developmental Psychology*, 1, 93–118.

Gürol, A., & Polat, S. (2012) The effects of baby massage on attachment between mother and their infants. *Asian Nursing Research*, 6(1), 35–41.

Guyon-Harris, K.L., Humphreys, K.L., Fox, N.A., Nelson, C.A., & Zeanah, C.H. (2018) Course of disinhibited social engagement disorder from early childhood to early adolescence. *Journal of the American Academy of Child & Adolescent Psychiatry*, 57(5), 329–335.

Guyon-Harris, K.L., Humphreys, K.L., Miron, D., Gleason, M.M., Nelson, C.A., Fox, N.A., & Zeanah, C.H. (2019a) Disinhibited social engagement disorder in early childhood predicts reduced competence in early adolescence. *Journal of Abnormal Child Psychology*, 47(10), 1735–1745.

Guyon-Harris, K.L., Humphreys, K.L., Degnan, K., Fox, N.A., Nelson, C.A., & Zeanah, C.H. (2019b) A prospective longitudinal study of reactive attachment disorder following early institutional care: considering variable- and person-centered approaches. *Attachment & Human Development*, 21(2), 95–110.

Habib, C. (2012) The transition to fatherhood: a literature review exploring paternal involvement with identity theory. *Journal of Family Studies*, 18(2–3), 103–120.

Hakoyama, M. (2020). Fathering styles: Qualities children expect in their fathers. *Marriage & Family Review*, 56(5), 391–424.

Hamilton, P. (2021) *Black Mothers and Attachment Parenting: A Black Feminist Analysis of Intensive Mothering in Britain and Canada*. Bristol, UK: Bristol University Press.

Hardyment, C. (2007) *Dream Babies: Childcare Advice from John Locke to Gina Ford*. London: Frances Lincoln Publishers.

Harlow, H. F. (1958). The nature of love. *American Psychologist*, 13(12), 673.

Harper, S.N., & Pelletier, J. (2010) Parent involvement in early childhood: a comparison of English language learners and English first language families. *International Journal of Early Years Education*, 18(2), 123–141.

Harré, R., & Gillet, G. (1994) Emotion words and emotional acts. In R. Harré & G. Gillet, *The Discursive Mind* (pp. 144–166). Thousand Oaks, CA: Sage.

Harris, J.R. (1998) *The Nurture Assumption: Why Children Turn Out the Way They Do*. New York: Free Press.

Harris, J., Germain, J., Maxwell, C., & Mackay, S. (2020) The ethical implications of collecting data from online health communities. *SAGE Research Methods Cases: Medicine and Health*. London: Sage.

Harrison, L.L. (1992) Effects of tactile stimulation programmes for premature infants: review of the literature. *Maternal Child Nursing Journal*, 14, 69–90.

Harrison, L.L., Olivet, L., Cunningham, K., Bodin, M.B., & Hicks, C. (1996) Effects of gentle human touch on preterm infants: pilot study results. *Neonatal Network*, 15(2), 35–42.

Hart, C.M., Bush-Evans, R.D., Hepper, E.G., & Hickman, H.M. (2017) The children of narcissus: insights into narcissists' parenting styles. *Personality and Individual Differences*, 117, 249–254.

Hart, C.H., Newell, L.D., & Olsen, S.F. (2003) Parenting skills and social-communicative competence in childhood. In J.O. Greene & B.R. Burleson (eds), *Handbook of*

Communication and Social Interaction Skills (pp. 753–797). Mahwah, NJ: Lawrence Erlbaum Associates.

Hartley, S.L., Barker, E.T., Seltzer, M.M., Floyd, F., Greenberg, J., &d Orsmond, G. (2010) The relative risk and timing of divorce in families of children with an autism spectrum disorder. *Journal of Family Psychology, 24*(4), 449–457.

Hartup, W. W. (1989). Social relationships and their developmental significance. *American Psychologist, 44*(2), 120–126. https://doi.org/10.1037/0003-066X.44.2.120

Harwin, J., Alrouh, B., Golding, L., McQuarrie, T., Broadhurst, K., & Cusworth, L. (2019) *The Contribution of Supervision Orders and Special Guardianship to Children's Lives and Family Justice*. Final Report (March 2019). Lancaster, UK: Centre for Child and Family Justice Research, Lancaster University.

Hashemi, L., & Homayuni, H. (2017) Emotional divorce: child's well-being. *Journal of Divorce & Remarriage, 58*(8), 631–644. DOI: 10.1080/10502556.2016.1160483

Hattie, J.A.C. (2003) Teachers make a difference: what is the research evidence? Paper presented at the Building Teacher Quality: *What Does the Research Tell Us?* ACEReSearch Conference, Melbourne, Australia [website]. Available at: http://research.acer.edu.au/research_conference_2003/4 (accessed 7 January 2022).

Hattie, J.A.C. (2009) *Visible Learning: A Synthesis of over 800 Meta-analyses Relating to Achievement*. London: Routledge.

Hayes, J.A., Adamson-Macedo, E.N., Perera, S., & Anderson, J. (1999) Detection of secretory immunoglobulin A (SIgA) in saliva of ventilated and non-ventilated preterm neonates. *Neuroendocrinology Letters, 20*(1), 109–113.

Hayes, S.A., & Watson, S.L. (2013) The impact of parenting stress: a meta-analysis of studies comparing the experience of parenting stress in parents of children with and without autism spectrum disorder. *Journal of Autism and Developmental Disorders, 43*(3), 629–642.

Hayes, J.A. (1996) TAC-TIC: A non pharmacological approach to the alleviation of neonatal pain. Unpublished doctoral dissertation, University of Wolverhampton, Wolverhampton: UK

Hays, S. (1996) *The Cultural Contradictions of Motherhood*. London and New Haven, CT: Yale University Press.

Hayslip, B., Wang, C.D.C., Sun, Q., & Zhu, W. (2019) Grandparents as the primary care providers for their grandchildren: a cross-cultural comparison of Chinese and US samples. *International Journal of Aging and Human Development, 89*(4), 331–355.

Henderson, A., Harmon, S., & Houser, J. (2010) A new state of surveillance: applying Michael Foucault to modern motherhood. *Surveillance and Society, 7*(3/4), 231–247.

Henderson, A., Harmon, S., & Newman, H. (2015) The price mothers pay, even when they are not buying it: mental health consequences of idealized motherhood. *Sex Roles, 74*, 512–526.

Henwood, K., & Procter, J. (2003) The 'good father': reading men's accounts of paternal involvement during the transition to first-time fatherhood. *British Journal of Social Psychology, 42*(3), 337–355.

Hernández, A.L., Fernández, M.L., & Muñoz, E.P. (2022) Executive functions, child development and social functioning in premature preschoolers: a multi-method approach. *Cognitive Development, 62*, Art. 101173.

Herrero, M., Martínez-Pampliega, A., & Alvarez, I. (2020) Family communication, adaptation to divorce and children's maladjustment: the moderating role of coparenting. *Journal of Family Communication, 20*(2), 114–128. DOI: 10.1080/15267431.2020.1723592

Hetherington, E.M. (1999) Should we stay together for the sake of the children? In E.M. Hetherington (ed) *Coping with Divorce, Single Parenting and Remarriage*. New York and London: Psychology Press.

Hill, M. (2005) Children's boundaries within and beyond families. In L. McKie, S. Cunningham Burley & J. Campling (eds), *Families in Society: Boundaries and Relationships*. Bristol: Policy Press.

HM Government (2018) *Working Together to Safeguard Children*. London: HMSO.

Ho, I.T., & Hau, K.-T. (2008) Academic achievement in the Chinese context: the role of goals, strategies, and effort. *International Journal of Psychology, 43*(5), 892–897.

Hodel, A.S., Hunt, R.H., Cowell, R.A., Van Den Heuvel, S.E., Gunnar, M.R., & Thomas, K.M. (2015) Duration of early adversity and structural brain development in post-institutionalized adolescents. *NeuroImage, 105*, 112–119.

Hoetger, L.A., Hazen, K.P. & Brank, E.M. (2015) All in the family: a retrospective study comparing sibling bullying and peer bullying. *Journal of Family Violence 30*, 103–111 https://doi.org/10.1007/s10896-014-9651-0

Hofstede, G. (1980) Culture and organizations. *International Studies of Management & Organization, 10*(4), 15–41. https://doi.org/10.1080/00208825.1980.11656300

Hofstede, G. (1983) National cultures in four dimensions: a research-based theory of cultural differences among nations. *International Studies of Management & Organization, 13*(1–2), 46–74. http://dx.doi.org/10.1080/00208825.1983.11656358

Hoghughi, M., & Speight, A.N.P. (1998) Good enough parenting for all children: a strategy for a healthier society. *Archives of Disease in Childhood, 78*(4), 293–296.

Hooper, L. M., & Doehler, K. (2012). Assessing family caregiving: A comparison of three retrospective parentification measures. *Journal of Marital and Family Therapy, 38*(4), 653–666.

Horowitz, F.D. (1992) John B. Watson's legacy: learning and environment. *Developmental Psychology, 28*(3), 360.

Hrdy, S.B. (2000) *Mother Nature: Maternal instincts and how they shape the human species*. New York, Ballantine Books.

Hughes, C., & Ensor, R. (2005) Executive function and theory of mind in 2 year olds: A family affair? *Developmental Neuropsychology, 28*, 645–668.

Hughes, K., Bellis, M.A., Hardcastle, K.A., Sethi, D., Butchart, A., Mikton, C., Jones, L., & Dunne, M.P. (2017) The effect of multiple adverse childhood experiences on health: a systematic review and meta-analysis. *Lancet Public Health, 2*(8), e356–e366. https://doi.org/10.1016/S2468-2667(17)30118-4

Hughes, M., & Cossar, J. (2016) The relationship between maternal childhood emotional abuse/neglect and parenting outcomes: a systematic review. *Child Abuse Review, 25*(1), 31–45.

Hunt, J. (2018) Grandparents as substitute parents in the UK. *Journal of the Academy of Social Sciences, 13*(2), 175–186.

Hunt, K. (2014) Safeguarding children – the need for vigilance. *Practice Nurse, 44*(6), 18–22.

Iams, J.D. (2003) Prediction and early detection of preterm labor. *Obstetric Gynaecology*, *101*, 402–412.

Isaeva, O.M., & Volkova, E.N. (2016) Early psycho-social intervention program WHO/ICDP as an effective optimization method for child–parental relationships. *Procedia-Social and Behavioral Sciences*, *233*, 423–427.

Jambon, M., Madigan, S., Plamondon, A., Daniel, E., & Jenkins, J.M. (2018) The development of empathetic concern in siblings: A reciprocal influence model. *Child Development*, *90*(5), 1598–1613

Janssens, A.A.P.O. (1993) *Family and Social Change: The Household as a Process in an Industrializing Community*. Cambridge: Cambridge University Press

Jay, S.S. (1982) The effects of gentle human touch on mechanically ventilated very-short gestation infants. *Maternal-Child Nursing Journal*, *11*(4), 199–256.

Jedwab, M., Xu, Y., & Shaw, T.V. (2020) Kinship care first? Factors associated with placement moves in out-of-home care. *Child and Youth Services Review*, *115*, Art. 105104. https://psycnet.apa.org/doi/10.1016/j.childyouth.2020.105104

Jefferis, B. J., Power, C., & Hertzman, C. (2002). Birth weight, childhood socioeconomic environment, and cognitive development in the 1958 British birth cohort study. *Bmj*, *325*(7359), 305.

Jenkins, J.M., & Astington, J.W. (2003) Cognitive factors and family structures associated with theory of mind development in young children. *Developmental Psychology*, *32*, 70–78.

Jensen, J.K., Ammari, T., & Bjørn, P. (2019) Into Scandinavia: when online fatherhood reflects societal infrastructures. *Proceedings of the ACM on Human–Computer Interaction*, *3*(GROUP), 1–21.

Jensen, T.M., Shafer, K., & Larson, J.H. (2018) (Step) Parenting attitudes and expectations: implications for stepfamily functioning and clinical intervention. *Families in Society: The Journal of Contemporary Social Services*, *95*(3), 213–220.

Jewell, V.C., Northrop-Clewes, C.A., Tubman, R., & Thurnham, D.I. (2001) Nutritional factors and visual function in premature infants. *The Proceedings of the Nutritional Society*, *60*(2), 171–178.

Jeynes, W.H. (2005) A meta-analysis of the relation of parental involvement to urban elementary school student academic achievement. *Urban Education*, *40*(3), 237–269.

Johansson, T. (2011) THE CONUNDRUM OF FATHERHOOD: theoretical explorations. *International Journal of Sociology of the Family*, *37*(2), 227–242.

Johnston, Glenys and Derby City Safeguarding Children Board (2018) *Serious case review overview report in respect of: Child FD17*. Derby: Derby City Safeguarding Children Board.

Johnston, D.D., & Swanson, D.D. (2003) Invisible mothers: a content analysis of motherhood ideologies and myths in magazines. *Sex Roles*, *49*(1/2), 21–33.

Jones, E.A., Fiani, T., Stewart, J.L, Sheikh, R., Neil, N., & Fienup, D.M. (2019) When one sibling has autism: adjustment and sibling relationship. *Journal of Child and Family Studies 28*, 1272–1282. https://doi.org/10.1007/s10826-019-01374-z

Jones, T.L., & Prinz, R.J. (2005) Potential roles of parental self-efficacy in parent and child adjustment: a review. *Clinical Psychology Review*, *25*(3), 341–363.

Jover, M., Colomer, J., Carot, J.M., Larsson, C., Bobes, M.T., Ivorra, J.L., Martín-Brufau, R., & Sanjuan, J. (2014) Maternal anxiety following delivery, early infant temperament and mother's confidence in caregiving. *The Spanish Journal of Psychology*, *17*, E95. https://doi.org/10.1017/sjp.2014.87

Kalb, L.G., Badillo-Goicoechea, E., Holingue, C., Riehm, K.E., Thrul, J., Stuart, E.A., Smail, E.J., Law, K., White-Lehman, C., & Fallin, D. (2021) Psychological distress among caregivers raising a child with autism spectrum disorder during the COVID-19 pandemic. *Autism Research*, *14*(10), 2183–2188.

Kalmijn, M. (2015) Father-child relations after divorce in four European countries: patterns and determinants. *Comparative Population Studies*. *40*, (3). DOI: https://doi.org/10.12765/CPoS-2015-10.

Kalyva, E. (2011) *Autism: Educational and Therapeutic Approaches*. London, Sage.

Kambouri, M., Wilson, T., Pieridou, M., Quinn, S., & Liu, J. (2021) Making partnerships work: proposing a model to support parent–practitioner partnerships in the early years. *Early Childhood Education Journal*, *50*, 639–661.

Kamp Dush, C.M., & Amato, P.R. (2005) Consequences of relationship status and quality for subjective well-being. *Journal of Social and Personal Relationships*, *22*, 607–627. DOI: 10.1177/0265407505056438

Kamp Dush, C.M., Taylor, M.G., & Kroeger, R.A. (2008) Marital happiness and psychological wellbeing across the life course. *Family Relations*, *57*(2), 211–226. DOI: 10.1111/j.1741-3729.2008.00495

Kamperman, A.M., Kooiman, C.G., Lorenzini, N., Aleknaviciute, J., Allen, J.G., & Fonagy, P. (2020) Using the attachment network Q-sort for profiling one's attachment style with different attachment-figures. *PLoS One*, *15*(9), e0237576.

Kashdan, T.B., Biswas-Diener, R., & King, L.A. (2008) Reconsidering happiness: the costs of distinguishing between hedonics and eudaimonia. *The Journal of Positive Psychology*, *3*(4), 219–233. DOI: 10.1080/17439760802303044

Kaufmann, D., Gesten, E., Lucia, R. C. S., Salcedo, O., Rendina-Gobioff, G., & Gadd, R. (2000). The relationship between parenting style and children's adjustment: The parents' perspective. *Journal of Child and Family studies*, *9*(2), 231–245.

Kelly, J.B. (2000) Children's adjustment in conflicted marriage and divorce: A decade review of research. *Journal of the American Academy of Child and Adolescent Psychiatry* 39(8), 963-973 https://doi.org/10.1097/00004583-200008000-00007

Kelly, J.B., & Emery, R.E. (2003) Children's adjustment following divorce: risk and resilience perspectives. *Family Relations*, *52*(4), 352–362.

Kenyon, S., Boulvain, M., & Neilson, J. (2003) Antibiotics for premature rupture of membranes. *Cochrane Database of Systematic Reviews*, *2*, CD001058.

Kerrick, M., & Henry, R.L. (2016) 'Totally in love': evidence of a master narrative for how new mothers should feel about their babies. *Sex Roles*, *76*(1), 1–16.

Kim, H.H. (2017) Family building by same-sex male couples via gestational surrogacy. Seminars in Reproductive Medicine, *35*(5), 408–414. DOI: 10.1055/s-0037-1607333

Kim, J.-Y., McHale, S., Osgood, D.W., & Crouter, A.C. (2006) Longitudinal course and family correlates of sibling relationships from childhood through adolescence. *Child Development*, *77* (6), 1746–1761

King, K.A., Vidourek, R.A., & Merianos, A.L. (2016) Authoritarian parenting and youth depression: results from a national study. *Journal of Prevention & Intervention in the Community*, *44*(2), 130–139.

King, L.A., Heintzelman, S.J., & Ward, S.J. (2016) Beyond the search for meaning: a contemporary science of the experience of meaning in life. *Current Directions in Psychological Science*, *25*(4), 211–216. doi:10.1177/0963721416656354

King, L.A., Hicks, J.A., Krull, J.L., & Del Gaiso, A.K. (2006) Positive affect and the experience of meaning in life. *Journal of Personality and Social Psychology*, *90*, 179–196. DOI: 10.1037/0022-3514.90.1.179

Klock, S.C., & Lindheim, S.R. (2020) Gestational surrogacy: medical psychosocial and legal considerations. *Fertility and Sterility*, *113*(5), 889–891. https://doi.org/10.1016/j.fertnstert.2020.03.016

Knibb, R.C., Barnes, C., & Stalker, C. (2016) Parental self-efficacy in managing food allergy and mental health predicts food allergy-related quality of life. *Pediatric Allergy and Immunology*, *27*(5), 459–464.

Kohl, P. L., Jonson-Reid, M., & Drake, B. (2011). Maternal mental illness and the safety and stability of maltreated children. *Child Abuse & Neglect*, *35*(5), 309–318. https://doi.org/10.1016/j.chiabu.2011.01.006

Kooraneh, A. E., & Amirsardari, L. (2015). Predicting early maladaptive schemas using Baumrind's parenting styles. *Iranian Journal of Psychiatry and Behavioral Sciences*, *9*(2).

Koster, J. (2018) Family ties: the multilevel effects of households and kinship on the networks of individuals. *Royal Society Open Science*, *5*(4). https://doi.org/10.1098/rsos.172159

Koster, T., Poortman, A.-R., Van der Lippe, T., & Kleingard, P. (2020) Parenting in postdivorce families: the influence of residence, repartnering and gender. *Journal of Marriage and Family*, *83*(2), 498–515. https://doi.org/10.1111/jomf.12740

Krebs, T. L. (1998). Clinical pathway for enhanced parent and preterm infant interaction through parent education. *The Journal of Perinatal & Neonatal Nursing*, *12*(2), 38-49.

Ku, B., Stinson, J.D., & MacDonald, M. (2019) Parental behavior comparisons between parents of children with autism spectrum disorder and parents of children without autism spectrum disorder: a meta-analysis. *Journal of Child and Family Studies*, *28*(6), 1445–1460.

Kuhlthau, K., Payakachat, N., Delahaye, J., Hurson, J., Pyne, J.M., Kovacs, E., & Tilford, J.M. (2014) Quality of life for parents of children with autism spectrum disorders. *Research in Autism Spectrum Disorders*, *8*(10), 1339–1350.

Laevers, F. (ed.) (2005) *Well-being and Involvement in Care: A Process-orientated Self-evaluation Instrument for Care Settings*. Leuven: Kind & Gezin. Kindengezin [website]. Available at: www.kindengezin.be/img/sics-ziko-manual.pdf (accessed 27 April 2021).

Laghi, F., Lonigro, A., Pallini, S., Bechini, A., Gradilone, A., Marziano, G., & Baiocco, R. (2018) Sibling relationships and family functioning in siblings of early adolescents, adolescents and young adults with autism spectrum disorder. *Journal of Child and Family Studies 27*, 793–801 (2018). https://doi.org/10.1007/s10826-017-0921-3

Lang, K., Bovenschen, I., Gabler, S., Zimmermann, J., Nowacki, K., Kliewer, J., & Spangler, G. (2016) Foster children's attachment security in the first year after placement: a longitudinal study of predictors. *Early Childhood Research Quarterly*, *36*, 269–280.

Langlois, J.H., Kalakanis, L., Rubenstein, A.J., Larson, A., Hallam, M., & Smoot, M. (2000) Maxims or myths of beauty? A meta-analytic and theoretical review. *Psychological Bulletin*, *126*(3), 390.

Laslett, P. & Wall, R. (1972) England. *In Household and Family in Past Times*. Cambridge, Cambridge University Press.

Larsson, J., Nyborg, L., & Psouni, E. (2022) The role of family function and triadic interaction on preterm child development: a systematic review. *Children*, *9*(11). https://doi.org/10.3390/children9111695

Laws, R., Walsh, A.D., Hesketh, K.D., Downing, K.L., Kuswara, K., & Campbell, K.J. (2019) Differences between mothers and fathers of young children in their use of the internet to support healthy family lifestyle behaviors: cross-sectional study. *Journal of Medical Internet Research*, *21*(1), e11454.

Leach, L.S., Bennetts, S.K., Giallo, R., & Cooklin, A.R. (2019) Recruiting fathers for parenting research using online advertising campaigns: evidence from an Australian study. *Child: Care, Health and Development*, *45*(6), 871–876.

Lee, E., Bristow, J., Faircloth, C., & Macvarish, J. (2014) *Parenting Culture Studies*. London: Palgrave Macmillan.

Lee, J. Y. (2009) The relationship between parenting knowledge and parenting style of mothers with infants: the mediating effect of parenting efficacy. *Journal of Korean Home Economics Association*, *47*(5), 35–48.

Lee, K. (2009). *Predictors of Depression in Children with High-functioning Autism Spectrum Disorders: The relationship Between Self-perceived Social Competence, Intellectual Ability, and Depressive Symptomology*. State University of New York at Buffalo.

Lee, Y., & Hofferth, S.L. (2017) Gender differences in single parents' living arrangements and child care time. *Journal of Child and Family Studies*, *26*(12), 3439–3451 https://doi.org/10.1007/s10826-017-0850-1

Leiferman, J.A., Farewell, C.V., Jewell, J., Lacy, R., Walls, J., Harnke, B., & Paulson, J.F. (2021) Anxiety among fathers during the prenatal and postpartum period: a meta-analysis. *Journal of Psychosomatic Obstetrics & Gynecology*, *42*(2), 152–161.

Lerner, R.M., & Kauffman, M.B. (1985) The concept of development in contextualism. *Developmental Review*, *5*(4), 309–333.

Lerner, R.M., Rothbaum, F., Boulos, S., & Castellino, D.R. (2002) Developmental systems perspective on parenting. *Handbook of Parenting*, *2*, 315–344.

Lerner, R.M., Wang, J., Chase, P.A., Gutierrez, A.S., Harris, E.M., Rubin, R.O., & Yalin, C. (2014) Using relational developmental systems theory to link program goals, activities, and outcomes: the sample case of the 4-H Study of Positive Youth Development. *New Directions for Youth Development*, *2014*(144), 17–30.

Letablier, M. T., & Wall, K. (2017) Changing lone parenthood patterns: new challenges for policy and research. In L. Bernardi & D. Mortelmans (eds), *Lone Parenthood in the Life Course*. Cham, Switzerland: Springer International.

Leung, C. (2004) Born too soon. In E.N. Adamson-Macedo (ed.), *Expanding Frontiers of Neonatology: Special Issue of Neuroendocrinology Letters*, *25*(1), 133–136.

Levy-Shiff, R., Sharir, H., & Mogliner, M.B. (1989) Mother– and father–preterm infant relationship in the hospital preterm nursery. *Child Development*, *60*, 93–102.

Lewin, V. (2016) *The Twin Enigma: An exploration of our enduring fascination with twins*. London, Routledge

Li, A., Wang, S., & Liu, X. (2020) Parent involvement in schools as ecological assets, prosocial behaviors and problem behaviors among Chinese middle school students: mediating role of positive coping. *Current Psychology*, 1–9.

Liebal, K., & Haun, D.B.M. (2018) Why cross-cultural psychology is incomplete without comparative and developmental perspectives. *Journal of Cross-Cultural Psychology*, *49*(5), 751–763 https://doi.org/10.1177/0022022117738085

Lin, C.H. (2018) The relationships between child well-being, caregiving stress and social engagement among informal and formal kinship care families. *Children and Youth Services Review*, *93*, 203–216. https://doi.org/10.1016/j.childyputh.2018.07.016

Lindon, J., & Webb, J. (2016) *Safeguarding and Child Protection* (5th edn). London: Hodder Education.

Lindstrom Johnson, S., Elam, K., Rogers, A.A., & Hilley, C. (2018) A meta-analysis of parenting practices and child psychosocial outcomes in trauma-informed parenting interventions after violence exposure. *Prevention Science*, *19*(7), 927–938.

Liu, J., Xiao, B., & Hipson, W.E. (2018) Self-regulation, learning problems, and maternal authoritarian parenting in Chinese children: a developmental cascades model. *Journal Child Family Studies*, *27*, 4060–4070.

Liu, L., & Wang, M. (2015) Parenting stress and harsh discipline in China: the moderating roles of marital satisfaction and parent. *Gender, Child Abuse & Neglect*, *43*, 73–82.

Lorber, M.F., O'Leary, S.G., & Kendziora, K.T. (2003) Mothers' overreactive discipline and their encoding and appraisals of toddler behavior. *Journal of Abnormal Child Psychology*, *31*(5), 485–494.

Lorenz, K. (1935). Der Kumpan in der Umwelt des Vogels. Der Artgenosse als auslösendes Moment sozialer Verhaltungsweisen. *Journal für Ornithologie*. Beiblatt. (Leipzig).

Lorenz, K. (1973) *Motivation of Human and Animal Behavior: An Ethological View*. New York: Van Nostrand Reinhold.

Lucas, R.E. (2005) Time does not heal all wounds: a longitudinal study of reaction and adaptation to divorce. *Psychological Science*, *16*(12), 945–950. DOI: 10.1111/j.1467-9280.2005.01642

Ludington-Hoe, S.M., Nguyen, N., Swinth, J.Y., & Satyshur, R.D. (2000) Kangaroo care compared to incubators in maintaining body warmth in preterm infants. *Biological Research for Nursing*, *2*(1), 60–73.

Lumsden, E. (2018) *Child Protection in the Early Years: A Practical Guide*. London: Jessica Kingsley.

Luster, T., Rhoades, K., & Haas, B. (1989) The relation between parental values and parenting behavior: a test of the Kohn hypothesis. *Journal of Marriage and the Family*, *51*(1), 139–147.

Lykes, V.A., & Kemmelmeier, M. (2014) What predicts loneliness? Cultural difference between individualistic and collectivistic societies in Europe. *Journal of Cross-Cultural Psychology*, *45*(3), 468–490. https://doi.org/10.1177/0022022113509881

Maccoby, E.E., & Martin, J.A. (1983) Socialization in the context of the family: parent–child interaction. In P.H. Mussen (series ed.) & E.M. Hetherington (vol. ed.), *Handbook of Child Psychology*. Vol. *IV*: *Socialization, Personality and Social Development* (4th edn, pp. 1–101). New York: Wiley.

Macedo, E.N. (1984) The effects of early tactile stimulation on low birth weight infants: a 2-year follow-up. Unpublished doctoral thesis, Bedford College, London.

Main, M. (1977) Analysis of a peculiar form of reunion behaviour seen in some daycare children. In R. Webb (ed.), *Social Development in Childhood.* Baltimore, MD: Johns Hopkins University Press.

Main, M., Kaplan, N., & Cassidy, J. (1985). Security in infancy, childhood, and adulthood: A move to the level of representation. *Monographs of the Society for Research in Child Development, 50,* 66–104. DOI: 10.2307/3333827

Main, M., & Solomon, J. (1986) Discovery of an insecure-disorganized/disoriented attachment pattern. In T.B. Brazelton & M.W. Yogman (eds), *Affective Development in Infancy* (pp. 95–124). New York: Ablex Publishing.

Main, M., & Solomon, J. (1990) Procedures for identifying infants as disorganized/ disoriented during the Ainsworth Strange Situation. *Attachment in the Preschool Years: Theory, Research, and Intervention, 1,* 121–160.

Makino, A., Hartman, L., King, G., Wong, P.Y., & Penner, M. (2021) Parent experiences of autism spectrum disorder diagnosis: a scoping review. *Review Journal of Autism and Developmental Disorders, 8*(3), 267–284.

Malone, P.A. (2010) Childhood and adolescence growing up in the shadow of divorce. In E.C. Pomeroy & R.B. Garcia (eds), *Children and Loss: A Practical Handbook for Professionals.* Oxford: Oxford University Press.

Manning, J., Billian, J. & Matson, J. (2021) Perceptions of Families of Individuals with Autism Spectrum Disorder during the COVID-19 Crisis. *Journal of Autism and Developmental Disorders 51,* 2920–2928. https://doi.org/10.1007/s10803-020-04760-5

Manning, W.D., Fettro, N.M., & Lamidi, E. (2014) Child well-being in same-sex parent families: review of research prepared for American Sociological Association Amicus Brief. *Population Research and Policy Review, 33,* 485–502. https://doi.org/10.1007/ s11113-014-9329-6

Manning, W.D., & Smock, P.J. (2000) 'Swapping' families: serial parenting and economic support for children. *Journal of Marriage and Family, 62*(1), 111–122. https://doi.org/1 0.1111/j.1741-3737.2000.00111

Manns, S.V. (2004) Life after the NNU: the long-term effects on mothers' lives, managing a child at home with bronchopulmonary dysplasia and on home oxygen. In E.N. Adamson-Macedo (ed.), *Expanding Frontiers of Neonatology: Special Issue of Neuroendocrinology Letters, 25*(1), 127–132.

Marcal, K. E. (2018). The impact of housing instability on child maltreatment: A causal investigation. *Journal of Family Social Work, 21*(4-5), 331–347.

Marchant, G., Paulson, S., & Rothlisberg, B. (2001) Relations of middle school students' perceptions of family and school contexts with academic achievement. *Psychology in the Schools, 38,* 505–519.

Margolis, R., & Myrskyla, M. (2015) Parental well-being surrounding first birth as a determinant of further parity progression. *Demography, 52,* 1147–1166. DOI: 10.1007/ s13524-015-0413-2

Marino, S. (2020) *Comparatico* (godparenthood) as an emblematic form of social capital among Australian families originating from rural Calabria living in Adelaide, South Australia. *Social Anthropology/Anthropologie Sociale, 28*(1), 136–152.

Markoulakis, R., Fletcher, P., & Bryden, P. (2012) Seeing the glass half full: benefits to the lived experiences of female primary caregivers of children with autism. *Clinical Nurse Specialist, 26*(1), 48–56.

Martela, F., & Steger, M.F. (2016) The three meanings of meaning in life: distinguishing coherence, purpose, and significance. *The Journal of Positive Psychology, 11,* 531–545. DOI: 10.1080/17439760.2015.1137623

Matejević, M., Todorović, J., & Jovanović, D. (2015) Traditional and contemporary in assessments of family relationships of students of the university of Niš. In T. Petrović-Trifunović, S. Milutinović Bojanić, & G. Pudar Draško (eds), *MIND THE GAP(S): Family, Socialization and Gender* (p. 185). Belgrade: Institute for Philosophy and Social Theory.

Mathambo, V., & Gibbs A. (2009) Extended family childcare arrangements in a context of AIDS: collapse or adaptation? *AIDS Care, 21*(1), 22–27.

Matta Oshima, K.M., Jonson-Reid, M., & Seay, K.D. (2014) The influence of childhood sexual abuse on adolescent outcomes: the roles of gender, poverty, and revictimization. *Journal of Child Sexual Abuse, 23*(4), 367–386.

Mayall, A., & Gold, S.R. (1995) Definitional issues and mediating variables in the sexual revictimization of women sexually abused as children. *Journal of Interpersonal Violence, 10*(1), 26–42.

McBryde, M., Fitzallen, G.C., Liley, H.G., Taylor, H.G., & Bora, S. (2020) Academic outcomes of school-aged children born preterm: a systematic review and meta-analysis. *JAMA Network Open, 3*(4), e202027.

McAlister, A.R., & Peterson, C.C. (2013) Siblings, theory of mind, and executive function in children aged 3-6 years: New longitudinal evidence. *Child Development, 84,* 1442–14.

McCabe, J.E. (2014) Maternal personality and psychopathology as determinants of parenting behavior: a quantitative integration of two parenting literatures. *Psychological Bulletin, 140*(3), 722.

McCurdy, K. (2005) The influence of support and stress on maternal attitudes. *Child Abuse & Neglect, 29*(3), 251–268.

McDaniel, B.T., Coyne, S.M., & Holmes, E.K. (2011) New mothers and media use: associations between blogging, social networking and maternal well-being. *Maternal Child Health, 16*(1), 1509–1517.

McElwain, N.L., & Booth-LaForce, C. (2006) Maternal sensitivity to infant distress and nondistress as predictors of infant–mother attachment security. *Journal of Family Psychology, 20*(2), 247.

McHale, J. P., & Fivaz-Depeursinge, E. (2010). Principles of effective co-parenting and its assessment in infancy and early childhood. *Parenthood and Mental Health: A Bridge Between Infant and Adult Psychiatry,* 357–371.

McHale, S.M., Updegraff, K.A., Helms-Erikson, H., & Crouter, A.C. (2001) Sibling influences on gender development in middle childhood and early adolescence: a longitudinal study. *Developmental Psychology, 37,* 115–25.

McHale, S. M., Updegraff, K. A., & Whiteman, S. D. (2012). Sibling relationships and influences in childhood and adolescence. *Journal of Marriage and Family, 74*(5), 913–930.

McKie, L., & Cunningham-Burley, S. (eds) (2005) *Families in Society: Boundaries and Relationships.* Bristol: Policy Press.

McLanahan, S., & Sandefur, G.D. (2009) *Growing Up with a Single Parent: What Hurts, What Helps.* Cambridge, MA: Harvard University Press.

McTavish, J.R., Santesso, N., Amin, A., Reijnders, M., Ali, M.U., Fitzpatrick-Lewis, D., & MacMillan, H.L. (2021) Psychosocial interventions for responding to child sexual abuse: a systematic review. *Child Abuse & Neglect*, *116*(Pt 1), 104203. https://doi.org/10.1016/j.chiabu.2019.104203

Mehrinejad, S.A., Rajabimoghadam, S., & Tarsafi, M. (2015) The relationship between parenting styles and creativity and the predictability of creativity by parenting styles. *Procedia-social and Behavioral Sciences*, *205*, 56–60.

Meleady, J., Clyne, C., Braham, J., & Carr, A. (2020) Positive contributions among parents of children on the autism spectrum: a systematic review. *Research in Autism Spectrum Disorders*, *78*. https://doi.org/10.1016/j.rasd.2020.101635

Melby J.N, Conger R.D, Fang S.A, Wickrama K.A, Conger K.J. (2008). Adolescent family experiences and educational attainment during early adulthood. *Developmental Psychology*, *44*(6) 1519-36.

Melhuish, E.C., Sylva, K., Sammons, P., Siraj-Blatchford, I., Taggart, B., Phan, M.B., & Malin, A. (2008) Preschool influences on mathematics achievement. *Science*, *321*(5893), 1161–1162.

Ménard, K.S. (2003) *Sexual Victimization Reporting: The Effects of Individual and County Factors on Victims' Decision to Report to the Police*. State College, PA: Pennsylvania State University.

Mence, M., Hawes, D.J., Wedgwood, L., Morgan, S., Barnett, B., Kohlhoff, J., et al. (2014) Emotional flooding and hostile discipline in the families of toddlers with disruptive behavior problems. *Journal of Family Psychology*, *28*(1), 12.

Meral, B.F. (2022) Parental views of families of children with autism spectrum disorder and developmental disorders during the COVID-19 pandemic. *Journal of Autism and Developmental Disorders*, *52*(4), 1712–1724.

Mesman, J., Oster, H., & Camras, L. (2012) Parental sensitivity to infant distress: what do discrete negative emotions have to do with it? *Attachment & Human Development*, *14*(4), 337–348.

Messina, R., & Brodzinsky, D. (2020) Children adopted by same sex couples: identity related issues from preschool years to late adolescence. *Journal of Family Psychology*, *34*(5), 509–522.

Metsäpelto, R.L., & Pulkkinen, L. (2005) The moderating effect of extraversion on the relation between self-reported and observed parenting. *Journal of Applied Developmental Psychology*, *26*(4), 371–384.

Miller, A., & Sassler, S. (2012) The construction of gender in cohabiting relationships. *Qualitative Sociology*, *35*(4), 427–446.

Miller, B.G., Kors, S., & Macfie, J. (2017) No differences? Meta-analytic comparisons of psychological adjustment in children of gay fathers and heterosexual parents. *Psychology of Sexual Orientation and Gender Diversity*, *4*(1), 14–22. https://doi.org/10.1037/sgd0000203

Miller, N.B., Cowan, P.A., Cowan, C.P., Hetherington, E.M., & Clingempeel, W.G. (1993) Externalizing in preschoolers and early adolescents: a cross-study replication of a family model. *Developmental Psychology*, *29*(1), 3.

Miller, T. (2010) 'It's a triangle that's difficult to square': men's intentions and practices around caring, work and first-time fatherhood. *Fathering*, *8*(3), 362.

Milshtein, S., Yirmiya, N., & Oppenheim, D. (2010) Resolution of the Diagnosis among parents of children with autism spectrum disorder: associations with child and parent characteristics. *Journal of Autism and Developmental Disorders 40*, 89–99

Mirande, A. (2012) The Muxes of Juchitán: a preliminary look at transgender identity and acceptance. *California Western International Law Journal*, *42*, 509. Corpus ID 141520818.

Moore, E.R., Bergman, N., Anderson, G.C., & Medley, N. (2016) Early skin-to-skin contact for mothers and their healthy newborn infants. *Cochrane Database of Systematic Reviews*, (11).

Moore, J. (2020) *Narrative and Dramatic Approaches to Children's Life Story with Foster, Adoptive and Kinship Families: Using the 'Theatre of Attachment' Model*. London: Routledge.

Moore, K. A., & Vandivere, S. (2000). *Stressful family lives: Child and parent well-being*. www.academia.edu/51616905/Stressful_family_lives_Child_and_parent_well_being (accessed 3 May 2023).

Morrill, M.I., Hines, D.A., Mahmood, S., & Cordova, J.V. (2010) Pathways between marriage and parenting for wives and husbands: the role of coparenting. *Family Process*, *49*(1), 59–73.

Morris, A.S., Houltberg, B.J., Criss, M.M., & Bosler, C.D. (2017) Family context and psychopathology: the mediating role of children's emotion regulation. In L.C. Centifanti & D.M. Williams (eds), *The Wiley Handbook of Developmental Psychopathology* (pp. 365–389). New York: Wiley-Blackwell.

Morrow, V. (1998) My animals and other family: children's perspectives on their relationships with companion animals. *Anthrozoos*, *11*(4), 218–226.

Mosek, A., & Adler, L. (2001) The self-concept of adolescent girls in non-relative versus kin foster care. *International Social Work*, *44*(2), 149–162. https://doi.org/10.1177/002087280104400202

Mousavi, S.E., Low, W.Y., & Hashim, A.H. (2016) Perceived parenting styles and cultural influences in adolescent's anxiety: a cross-cultural comparison. *Journal of Child and Family Studies*, *25*, 2102–2110.

Müller, U., & Racine, T.P. (2010) The development of representation and concepts. In W.F. Overton & R.M. Lerner (eds), *The Handbook of Life-span Development*. Vol. *1: Cognition, Biology, and Methods* (pp. 346–390). New York: John Wiley. https://doi.org/10.1002/9780470880166.hlsd001011

Mumbardó-Adam, C., Barnet-López, S., & Balboni, G. (2021) How have youth with autism spectrum disorder managed quarantine derived from COVID-19 pandemic? An approach to families' perspectives. *Research in Developmental Disabilities*, *110*, 103860. https://doi.org/10.1016/j.ridd.2021.103860

Mumsnet (2000) About us. *Mumsnet* [website]. Available at: www.mumsnet.com/info/about-us (accessed 16 June 2021).

Murphy, S.E., Jacobvitz, D.B., & Hazen, N.L. (2016) What's so bad about competitive co-parenting? Family level predictors of children's externalising symptoms. *Journal of Child and Family Studies*, *25*(5), 1684–1690. https://doi.org/10.1007/s10826-015-0321-5

Murray, J., Teszenyi, E., Nagy Varga, A., Pálfi, S., Tajiyeva, M., & Iskakova, A. (2018) Parent–practitioner partnerships in early childhood provision in England, Hungary and Kazakhstan: similarities and differences in discourses. *Early Child Development and Care*, *188*(5), 594–612.

National College for Teaching & Leadership (NCTL) (2013) *Teacher' Standards (Early Years): From September 2013* [website]. Available at: https://assets.publishing.service. gov.uk/government/uploads/system/uploads/attachment_data/file/211646/Early_ Years_Teachers__Standards.pdf (accessed 3 December 2021).

National Society for the Prevention of Cruelty to Children (NSPCC) (n.d.) Serious case reviews: overview report in respect of: Child FD17. *National Case Review Repository – NSPCC Learning* [website]. Available at: https://learning.nspcc.org.uk/case-reviews/ national-case-review-repository (accessed 3 December 2021).

National Society for the Prevention of Cruelty to Children (NSPCC) (2022) Half a million children suffer abuse in the UK every year. *NSPCC* [website], 21 April. Available at: www.nspcc.org.uk/about-us/news-opinion/2022/childhood-day (accessed 29 April 2022).

Nelson, M.N., White-Traut, R.C., Vasan, U., Silvestri, J.M., Comiskey, E., & Meeledy-Rey, P. (2001) One-year outcome of auditory-tactile-visual-vestibular intervention in the neonatal intensive care unit: effects of severe prematurity and central nervous system injury. *Journal of Child Neurology*, *16*(7), 493–498.

Nelson-Coffey, S.K. (2018) Married…with children: the science of well-being in marriage and family life. In E. Diener, S. Oishi & L. Tay (eds), *Handbook of Well-being*. Salt Lake City, UT: DEF Publishers.

Netmums (2000) About us. *Netmums* [website]. Available at: www.netmums.com/info/ about-us (accessed 16 June 2021).

Noland, V. J., Liller, K. D., McDermott, R.J., Coulter, M.L., Seraphine, A. E. (2004) Is adolescent sibling violence a precursor to college dating violence? *American Journal of Health Behavior*, *28* (1) S13-S23(11)

Obeidat, H. M., & Shuriquie, M. A. (2015) Effect of breast-feeding and maternal holding in relieving painful responses in full-term neonates. *The Journal of Perinatal & Neonatal Nursing*, *29*(3), 248–254.

O'Conner, A. (2018) *Understanding Transitions in the Early Years: Supporting Change through Attachment and Resilience* (2nd edn). London: Routledge.

O'Connor, T.G., & Scott, S. (2007) *Parenting and Outcomes for Children*. York: Joseph Rowntree Foundation.

Office for National Statistics (ONS) (2019) Families. *ONS – People, Population and Community* [website]. Available at: www.ons.gov.uk/peoplepopulationandcommunity/ birthsdeathsandmarriages/families (accessed 15 April 2021).

Office for National Statistics (ONS) (2020a) Child abuse extent and nature, England and Wales: year ending March 2019. *ONS – People, Population and Community* [website]. Available at: www.ons.gov.uk/peoplepopulationandcommunity/crimeandjustice/articles/ childabuseextentandnatureenglandandwales/yearendingmarch2019 (accessed 5 May 2022).

Office for National Statistics (ONS) (2020b) Divorce. *ONS – People, Population and Community* [website]. Available at: www.ons.gov.uk/peoplepopulationandcommunity/ birthsdeathsandmarriages/divorce (accessed 7 January 2022).

Office for National Statistics (ONS) (2021) Families. *ONS – People, Population and Community* [website]. Available at: www.ons.gov.uk/peoplepopulationandcommunity/births deaths andmarriages/families (accessed 15 January 2023).

Office for National Statistics (ONS) (2022) Families and households. *ONS – People, Population and Community* [website]. Available at: www.ons.gov.uk/peoplepopulationandcommunity/birthsdeathsandmarriages/families (accessed 15 August 2022).

Office for Standards in Education, Children's Services and Skills (OFSTED) (2011) *OFSTED Schools and Parents* [website]. Available at: https://assets.publishing.service.gov.uk/government/uploads/system/uploads/attachment_data/file/413696/Schools_and_parents.pdf (accessed 11 March 2022).

Office for Standards in Education, Children's Services and Skills (OFSTED) (2021) OFSTED *Early Years Inspection Framework* [website]. Available at: www.gov.uk/government/publications/early-years-inspection-handbook-eif (accessed 3 December 2021).

Ohgi, S., Fukunda, M., Morruchi, H., Kusumoto, T., Akiyama, T., & Nugent, J.K. (2002) Comparison of kangaroo care and standard care: behavioural organization, development, and temperament in healthy low-birth-weight infants through 1 year. *Journal of Perinatology, 22*, 374–379.

Onozawa, K., Glover, V., Adams, D., Modi, N., & Kumar, R.C. (2001) Infant massage improves mother–infant interaction for mothers with postnatal depression. *Journal of Affective Disorders, 63*(1–3), 201–207.

Ostrov, J.M., Crick, N.R., & Stauffacher, K. (2006) Relational aggression in sibling and peer relationships during early childhood, *Journal of Applied Developmental Psychology, 27* (3), 241–253, ISSN 0193-3973, https://doi.org/10.1016/j.appdev.2006.02.005.

Overton, W.F. (1973) On the assumptive base of the nature-nurture controversy: additive versus interactive conceptions. *Human Development, 16*(1–2), 74–89.

Overton, W.F. (1998). Relational-developmental theory: A psychological perspective. *International Studies on Childhood and Adolescence, 5*, 315–335.

Overton, W.F. (2006) Developmental psychology: philosophy, concepts, methodology. In R.M. Lerner & W. Damon (eds), *Handbook of Child Psychology: Theoretical Models of Human Development* (pp. 18–88). New York: Wiley & Sons.

Overton, W.F. (2013). A new paradigm for developmental science: Relationism and relational-developmental systems. *Applied Developmental Science, 17*(2), 94–107.

Oyserman, D., Radin, N., & Saltz, E. (1994) Predictors of nurturant parenting in teen mothers living in three generational families. *Child Psychiatry and Human Development, 24*, 215–230.

Padden, T., & Glenn, S. (1997) Maternal experiences of preterm birth and neonatal intensive care. *Journal of Reproductive and Infant Psychology, 15*, 121–139.

Palacios, J., Rolock, N., Selwyn, J., & Barbosa-Ducharne, M. (2019) Adoption breakdown: concept, research, and implications. *Research on Social Work Practice, 29*(2), 130–142.

Panjwani, A.A., Bailey, R.L., & Kelleher, B.L. (2021) COVID-19 and behaviors in children with autism spectrum disorder: disparities by income and food security status. *Research in Developmental Disabilities, 115*, 104002. https://doi.org/10.1016/j.ridd.2021.104002

Papanikolaou, K., Ntre, V., Gertsou, I.-M., Tagkouli, E., Tzavara, C., Pehlivanidis, A., & Kolaitis, G. (2022) Parenting children with autism spectrum disorder during crises: differential responses between the financial and the COVID-19 pandemic crisis. *Journal of Clinical Medicine, 11*(5), 1264.

Parenteau, C.I., Bent, S., Hossain, B., Chen, Y., Widjaja, F., Breard, M., & Hendren, R.L. (2020) COVID-19 related challenges and advice from parents of children with autism spectrum disorder. *SciMedicine Journal, 2*, 73–82.

Park, J., Hoffman, L., Marquis, J., Turnbull, A. P., Poston, D., Mannan, H., Wang, M. & Nelson, L. L. (2003). Toward assessing family outcomes of service delivery: Validation of a family quality of life survey. *Journal of Intellectual Disability Research, 47*(4-5), 367–384.

Park, Y.D. (2003) The effects of vagus nerve stimulation therapy on patients with intractable seizures and either Landu-Kleffner syndrome or autism. *Epilepsy and Behavior 4*(3), 286–290.

Parke, R.D. (2000) Father involvement: a developmental psychological perspective. *Marriage and Family Review, 29*(2–3), 43–58.

Parton, N. (2014) *The Politics of Child Protection: Contemporary Developments and Future Directions.* Basingstoke: Palgrave Macmillan.

Pavlov, I. P. (1960). *Conditioned reflexes: An investigation of the physiological activity of the cerebral cortex.* (G. V. Anrep, Trans.). New York: Dover. (Original work published 1927).

Pavlopoulou, G., & Dimitriou, D. (2020) In their own words, in their own photos: adolescent females' siblinghood experiences, needs and perspectives growing up with a preverbal autistic brother or sister. *Research in Developmental Disabilities, 97*, 103556.

Pedersen, S. (2016) The good, the bad and the 'good enough' mother on the UK parenting forum Mumsnet. *Women's Studies International Forum, 59*, 32–38.

Pellerin, L.A. (2005) Applying Baumrind's parenting typology to high schools: toward a middle-range theory of authoritative socialization. *Social Science Research, 34*(2), 283–303.

Petersen, A. C., Joseph, J., Feit, M., & National Research Council. (2014). Consequences of child abuse and neglect. In *New Directions in Child Abuse and Neglect Research.* National Academies Press (US).

Perner, J., Ruffman, S.R., & Leekam, S.R. (1994) Theory of mind is contagious: You catch it from your sibs. *Child Development, 65*, 1228–1238.

Perry, B.D. (2009) Examining child maltreatment through a neurodevelopmental lens: clinical applications of the neurosequential model of therapeutics (NMT). *Journal of Trauma and Loss, 14*, 1–16.

Peterson, C.C. (2000) Kindred spirits: Influences of sibling perspectives on theory of mind. *Cognitive Development, 19*, 253-273

Phares, V., Lopez, E., Fields, S., Kamboukos, D., & Duhig, A.M. (2005) Are fathers involved in pediatric psychology research and treatment? *Journal of Pediatric Psychology, 30*(8), 631–643.

Phoenix, A., Woollett, A., & Lloyd, E. (1991) *Motherhood: Meaning, Practices and Ideologies.* London: Sage.

Piaget, J. (1952) *The Origins of Intelligence in Children.* Trans. M. Cook. New York: W.W. Norton.

Piaget, J. (1972) Intellectual evolution from adolescence to adulthood. *Human Development, 15*(1), 1–12.

Piaget, J., & Inhelder, B. (1956) *The Child's Concept of Space*. London: Routledge & Kegan Paul.

Pickering, J. A., & Sanders, M. R. (2017). Integrating parents' views on sibling relationships to tailor an evidence-based parenting intervention for sibling conflict. *Family Process, 56*(1), 105–125. https://doi.org/10.1111/famp.12173

Pieridou, M. (2013) *Special and inclusive education in Cyprus: case study of a school unit with regards to the implementation of the 113(I)/99 law in educational practice*. PhD thesis, University of Cyprus, Nicosia, Cyprus.

Pike, A., Coldwell, J. & Dunn, J. (2006). *Family relationships in middle childhood*. York: York Publishing Services/Joseph Rowntree Foundation.

Pike, A., & Oliver, B. R. (2017). Child behavior and sibling relationship quality: A cross-lagged analysis. *Journal of Family Psychology, 31*(2), 250–255. https://doi.org/10.1037/fam0000248

Pittenger, S.L., Huit, T.Z., & Hansen, D.J. (2016) Applying ecological systems theory to sexual revictimization of youth: a review with implications for research and practice. *Aggression and Violent Behavior, 26*, 35–45.

Platt, L., Smith, K., Parsons, S., Connelly, R., Joshi, H., Rosenberg, R., … & Mostafa, T. (2014). *Millennium Cohort Study: initial findings from the Age 11 survey*. Centre for Longitudinal Studies, Institute of Education.

Porter, C.L., & Hsu, H. (2003) First-time mothers' perceptions of efficacy during the transition to motherhood: links to infant temperament. *Journal of Family Psychology, 17*, 54–64.

Poslawsky, I.E., Naber, F., Van Daalen, E., & Van Engeland, H. (2014) Parental reaction to early diagnosis of their children's autism spectrum disorder: an exploratory study. *Child Psychiatry & Human Development, 45*(3), 294–305.

Potter, C.A. (2016) 'I accept my son for who he is – he has incredible character and personality': fathers' positive experiences of parenting children with autism. *Disability & Society, 31*(7), 948–965.

Powell, S., & Smith, K. (eds) (2018) *An Introduction to Early Childhood Studies*. London: Sage.

Powell-Smith, K.A., Shinn, M.R., Stoner, G., & Good, R.H. III (2000) Parent tutoring in reading using literature and curriculum materials: impact on student reading achievement. *School Psychology Review, 29*(1), 5–27.

Powers, M.D. (2000) Children with autism and their families. In M.D. Powers (ed.), *Children with Autism: A Parents' Guide* (pp. 119–153). Bethesda, MD: Woodbine House.

Prinzie, P., Stams, G.J.J.M., Deković, M., Reijntjes, A.H.A., & Belsky, J. (2009) The relations between parents' Big Five personality factors and parenting: a meta-analytic review. *Journal of Personality and Social Psychology, 97*(2), 351–362. http://dx.doi.org/10.1037/a0015823

Pritchett, R., Pritchett, J., Marshall, E., Davidson, C., & Minnis, H. (2013) Reactive attachment disorder in the general population: a hidden ESSENCE disorder. *The Scientific World Journal*, 2013, 18 April. https://doi.org/10.1155/2013/818157

Public Health England (2021). Statistical commentary: children living with parents in emotional distress, March 2021 update - GOV.UK (www.gov.uk)

Putnam, F.W. (2003) Ten-year research update review: child sexual abuse. *Journal of the American Academy of Child & Adolescent Psychiatry, 42*(3), 269–278.

Putnick, D.L., Bornstein, M.H., & Lansford, J.E. (2012) Agreement in mother and father acceptance-rejection, warmth and hostility/rejection/neglect of children across nine countries. *Cross-Cultural Research, 46*(3), 191–223.

Reczek, C. (2020) Sexual- and gender-minority families: a 2010–2020 decade in review. *Journal of Marriage and Family, 82*(1), 300–332.

Redshaw, M., & Harris, A. (1995) Maternal perceptions of neonatal care. *Acta Paediatrica, 84*, 593–598.

Reiff, M., Bugos, E., Giarelli, E. et al. (2017) 'Set in Stone' or 'Ray of Hope': Parents' beliefs about cause and prognosis after genomic testing of children diagnosed with ASD. *Journal of Autism and Developmental Disorders 47*, 1453–1463. https://doi.org/10.1007/s10803-017-3067-7

Relationship Foundation (2018) *Relationship Foundation* [website]. Available at: www.therelationshipfoundation.org (accessed 19 January 2022).

Richmond, M. K., Stocker, C. M., & Rienks, S. L. (2005). Longitudinal associations between sibling relationship quality, parental differential treatment, and children's adjustment. *Journal of Family Psychology, 19*(4), 550–559. https://doi.org/10.1037/0893-3200.19.4.550

Risser, H.J., Messinger, A.M., Fry, D.A., Davidson, L.L., & Schewe, P.A. (2013) Do maternal and paternal mental illness and substance abuse predict treatment ooutcomes for children exposed to violence? *Child Care in Practice 19*(3), 221–236.

Robertson, J., & Robertson, J. (1989) *Separation and the Very Young*. London: Free Association Press.

Rogers, C. (1959) A theory of therapy, personality and interpersonal relationships as developed in the client-centered framework. In S. Koch (ed.), *Psychology: A Study of a Science*. Vol. *3: Formulations of the Person and the Social Context*. New York: McGraw-Hill.

Romer, D., Black, M., Ricardo, I., Feigelman, S., Kaljee, L., Galbraith, J., ... & Stanton, B. (1994) Social influences on the sexual behavior of youth at risk for HIV exposure. *American Journal of Public Health, 84*(6), 977–985.

Roos, L.L., Wall-Wieler, E., & Lee, J.B. (2019) Poverty and early childhood outcomes. *Pediatrics 143*(6), https://doi.org/10.1542/peds.2018-3426

Ross, H.S., & Lazinski, M.J. (2014) Parent mediation empowers sibling conflict resolution. *Early Education and Development 25*(2), 259–275.

Rowe, S.M., & Wertsch, J.V. (2002) Vygotsky's model of cognitive development. In U. Goswami (ed.), *The Blackwell Handbook of Childhood Cognitive Development* (pp. 538–554). Oxford: Blackwell Publishing.

Roy, K.M., & Dyson, O. (2010) Making daddies into fathers: community-based fatherhood programs and the construction of masculinities for low-income African American men. *American Journal of Community Psychology, 45*, 139–154.

Rudy, D., & Grusec, J.E. (2006) Authoritarian parenting in individualist and collectivist groups: associations with maternal emotion and cognition and children's self-esteem. *Journal of Family Psychology, 20*(1), 68.

Ruiz-Pelaez, G., Charpak, N., & Cuervo, L. (2004) Kangaroo mother care: an example to follow from developing countries. *British Medical Journal, 329*, 1179–1182.

Rumberger, R.W. (1995) Dropping out of middle school: a multilevel analysis of students and schools. *American Educational Research Journal, 32*(3), 583–625.

Russell, K.A., & Aldridge, J. (2009) Play, unity and symbols: parallels in the works of Froebel and Jung. *Journal of Psychology and Counselling, 1*(1), 1–4.

Russo, D.A., Stochl, J., Hodgekins, J., Iglesias-González, M., Chipps, P., Painter, M., Jones, P.B., & Perez, J. (2018) Attachment styles and clinical correlates in people at ultra high risk for psychosis. *British Journal of Psychology, 109*(1), 45–62.

Rutter, M. (1972) *Maternal Deprivation Reassessed.* Harmondsworth, Penguin Education.

Rutter, M. (1979). Maternal deprivation, 1972–1978: New findings, new concepts, new approaches. *Child Development,* 283–305.

Ryan, K., Lane, S., & Powers, D. (2017) A multidisciplinary model for treating complex trauma in early childhood. *International Journal of Play Therapy, 26*(2), 111–123.

Sanders, M.R., & Turner, K.M.T. (2018) The importance of parenting in influencing the lives of children. In M.R. Sanders & A. Morawska (eds), *Handbook of Parenting and Child Development across the Lifespan* (pp. 3–26). Cham, Switzerland: Springer International. https://doi.org/10.1007/978-3-319-94598-9_1

Saphire-Bernstein, S., & Taylor, S. E. (2013) Close relationships and happiness. In S.A. David, I. Boniwell & A. Conley Ayers (eds), *The Oxford Handbook of Happiness* (pp. 821–833). Oxford: Oxford University Press.

Sarwar, S. (2016) Influence of parenting style on children's behaviour. *Journal of Education and Educational Development, 3*(2).

Schafer, R. (2003). *Introducing Child Psychology.* Oxford: Blackwell.

Scherman, R., Misca, G., & Tan, T.X. (2020) The perceptions of New Zealand lawyers and social workers about children being adopted by gay couples and lesbian couples. *Frontiers in Psychology, 11,* 520703. DOI: 10.3389/fpsyg.2020.520703

Schiffrin, H.H., Godfrey, H., Liss, M., & Erchull, M.J. (2015) Intensive parenting: does it have the desired impact on child outcomes? *Journal of Child and Family Studies, 24*(8), 2322–2331.

Scourfield, J., & Evans, R. (2014) Why might men be more at risk of suicide after a relationship breakdown? Sociological Insights. *American Journal of Men's Health* [online], 26 August. https://doi.org/10.1177/1557988314546395

Seccombe, W. (1995) *A Millennium of Family Change: Feudalism to Capitalism in Northwestern Europe.* London: Verso.

Sedlak, A.J., Mettenburg, J., Basena, M., Petta, I., McPherson, K., Greene, A., & Li, S. (2010). *Fourth National Incidence Study of Child Abuse and Neglect* (NIS-4): Report to Congress. Washington, DC: U.S. Department of Health and Human Services, Administration for Children and Families.

Seim, A.R., Jozefiak, T., Wichstrøm, L., Lydersen, S., & Kayed, N.S. (2020) Reactive attachment disorder and disinhibited social engagement disorder in adolescence: co-occurring psychopathology and psychosocial problems. *European Child & Adolescent Psychiatry,* online first, *13* November, 1–14.

Selwyn, J., Wijedasa, D.N., & Meakings, S.J. (2014) *Beyond the Adoption Order: Challenges, Interventions and Disruptions.* London: Department for Education.

Shahaeian, A., Wang, C., Tucker-Drob, E., Geiger, V., Bus, A.G., & Harrison, L.J. (2018) Early shared reading, socioeconomic status, and children's cognitive and school competencies: six years of longitudinal evidence. *Scientific Studies of Reading, 22*(6), 485–502.

Shanahan, L., McHale, S., Crouter, A.C., & Osgood, D.W. (2008) Linkages between parents' differential treatment, youth depressive symptoms, and sibling relationships.

Journal of Marriage and Family, 70 (2), 480-494 https://doi.org/10.1111/j. 1741-3737.2008.00495

Shaver, P.R., Collins, N., & Clark, C.L. (1996) Attachment styles and internal working models of self and relationship partners. In G.O. Fletcher & J. Fitness (eds), *Knowledge Structures in Close Relationships: A Social Psychological Approach*. Mahwah, NJ: Lawrence Erlbaum Associates.

Shaw, D.S., Criss, M.M., Schonberg, M.A., & Beck, J.E. (2004) The development of family hierarchies and their relation to children's conduct problems. *Development and Psychopathology, 16*(3), 483–500.

Sheldon, S.B., & Epstein, J.L. (2005) Involvement counts: family and community partnerships and mathematics achievement. *The Journal of Educational Research, 98*(4), 196–206.

Shepard, J., & Hancock, C.L. (2020) *Education and Covid-19: Perspectives from Parent Carers of Children with SEND* [website]. Available at: https://amazesussex.org.uk/wp-content/uploads/2020/09/Brief-Report_Education-and-Covid-19_-Perspectives-from-parent-carers-of-children-with-SEND-FINAL.pdf (accessed 4 April 2022).

Sherifali, D., & Ciliska, D. (2006) Parenting children with diabetes and Belsky's determinants of parenting model: literature review. *Journal of Advanced Nursing, 55*(5), 636–642.

Shields-Zeeman, L., & Smit, F. (2022) The impact of income on mental health. *The Lancet 7*(6), DOI: https://doi.org/10.1016/S2468-2667(22)00094-9

Shirani, F., & Henwood, K. (2011) Continuity and change in a qualitative longitudinal study of fatherhood: relevance without responsibility. *International Journal of Social Research Methodology, 14*(1). DOI: 10.1080/13645571003690876

Shirani, F., Henwood, K., & Coltart, C. (2012) Meeting the challenges of intensive parenting culture: gender, risk management and the moral parent. *Sociology, 46*(1), 25–40.

Shonkoff, J., & Garner, A. (2012) The Lifelong Effects of Early Childhood Adversity and Toxic Stress. *Pediatrics 129*(1), e232-e246 https://doi.org/10.1542/peds.2011-2663

Shulman, S. (2005) Parental divorce and young adult children's romantic relationships: Resolution of the divorce experience. *Social Work Diagnosis in Contemporary Practice*, 68.

Shulman, S., Scharf, M., Lumer, D., & Maurer, O. (2001) Parental divorce and young adult children's romantic relationships: resolution of the divorce experience. *American Journal of Orthopsychiatry, 71*(4), 473–478. https://doi.org/10.1037/0002-9432.71.4.473

Simmel, C., Postmus, J.L., & Lee, I. (2012) Sexual revictimization in adult women: examining factors associated with their childhood and adulthood experiences. *Journal of Child Sexual Abuse, 21*(5), 593–611.

Simmons, H. (2020) *Surveillance of Modern Motherhood: Experiences of Universal Parenting Courses*. Basingstoke: Palgrave Macmillan.

Simon, B. (2001) Family involvement in high school: predictors and effects. *NASSP Bulletin, 85*, 8–19.

Sirvani, H. (2007) The effect of teacher communication with parents on students' mathematics achievement. *American Secondary Education, 36*(1), 31–46.

Skinner, G. C., Bywaters, P. W., Bilson, A., Duschinsky, R., Clements, K., & Hutchinson, D. (2021). The 'toxic trio' (domestic violence, substance misuse and mental ill-health): How good is the evidence base? *Children and Youth Services Review, 120*, 105678.

Smart, C. (2006) Children's narratives of post-divorce family life: from individual experience to ethical disposition. *The Sociological Review, 54*(1), 155–170. https://doi.org/10.1111/j.1467-954X.2006.00606

Smetana, J.G. (2017) Current research on parenting styles, dimensions, and beliefs. *Current Opinion in Psychology, 15*, 19–25.

Solberg, B., & Glavin, K. (2018) From man to father: Norwegian first-time fathers' experience of the transition to fatherhood. *Health Science Journal, 12*(3), 1–7.

Sonuga-Barke, E.J.S., Kennedy, M., Kumsta, R., Knights, N., Golm, D., Rutter, M., Maughan, B., Schlotz, W., & Kreppner, J. (2017) Child to-adult neurodevelopmental and mental health trajectories after early life deprivation: the young adult follow-up of the longitudinal English and Romanian Adoptees study. *Lancet, 389*(10078), 1539–1548.

Sorbring, E., & Gurdal, S. (2011) Attributions and attitudes of mothers and fathers in Sweden. *Parenting, 11*(2–3), 177–189.

Sousa, C., Herrenkohl, T. I., Moylan, C. A., Tajima, E. A., Klika, J. B., Herrenkohl, R. C., & Russo, M. J. (2011). Longitudinal study on the effects of child abuse and children's exposure to domestic violence, parent-child attachments, and antisocial behavior in adolescence. *Journal of Interpersonal Violence, 26*(1), 111–136.

Stadheim, J., Johns, A., Mitchell, M., Smith, C.J., Braden, B.B., & Matthews, N.L. (2022) A qualitative examination of the impact of the COVID-19 pandemic on children and adolescents with autism and their parents. *Research in Developmental Disabilities, 125*, 104232.

St-Amand, A., Servot, S., Pearson, J., & Bussières, È.-L. (2022) Effectiveness of interventions offered to non-offending caregivers of sexually abused children: a meta-analysis. *Canadian Psychology/Psychologie canadienne, 63*(3), 339–356. https://doi.org/10.1037/cap0000296

Sterne, A., & Poole, L. (2010) *Domestic Violence and Children.* Abingdon, UK: Routledge.

Stith, S. M., Topham, G. L., Spencer, C., Jones, B., Coburn, K., Kelly, L., & Langston, Z. (2022). Using systemic interventions to reduce intimate partner violence or child maltreatment: A systematic review of publications between 2010 and 2019. *Journal of Marital and Family Therapy, 48*(1), 231–250.

Stolz, H.E., Sizemore, K.M., Shideler, M.J., LaGraff, M.R., & Moran, H.B. (2017) Parenting together: evaluation of a parenting program for never-married parents. *Journal of Divorce and Remarriage, 58*(5), 358–370.

Straus, H., Cerulli, C., McNutt, L.A., Rhodes, K.V., Conner, K.R., Kemball, R.S., & Houry, D. (2009) Intimate partner violence and functional health status: associations with severity, danger, and self-advocacy behaviors. *Journal of Women's Health, 18*(5), 625–631.

Straus, M.A. (2000) Corporal punishment and primary prevention of physical abuse. *Child Abuse and Neglect, 24* (9), 1109-1114.

Stewart, E. (2000) Towards the social analysis of twinship. *The British Journal of Sociology, 51* (4), 719–737.

Sufna, J., Brandt, T., Secrist, M., Mesman, G., Sigel, B., & Kramer, T. (2019) Empirically-guided assessment of complex trauma for children in foster care: a focus on appropriate diagnosis of attachment concerns. *Psychological Services: Trauma Informed Care for Children and Families*, *16*(1), 120–133.

Supple, A.J., Ghazarian, S.R., & Peterson, G.W. (2009) Assessing the cross-cultural validity of a parental autonomy granting measure: comparing adolescents in the United States, China, Mexico and India. *Journal of Cross-Cultural Psychology*, *40*(5), 816–833.

Swenson, C.C., & Schaeffer, C.M. (2018) A multisystemic approach to the prevention and treatment of child abuse and neglect. *International Journal on Child Maltreatment: Research, Policy and Practice*, *1*(1), 97–120.

Syne, J., Green, R., & Dyer, J. (2012) Adoption: the lucky ones or the Cinderellas of children in care? *Educational and Child Psychology*, *29*(3), 93–106.

Takács, L., Smolík, F., Kaźmierczak, M., & Putnam, S.P. (2020) Early infant temperament shapes the nature of mother–infant bonding in the first postpartum year. *Infant Behavior and Development*, *58*, 101428.

Tamrouti-Makkink, I.D., Dubas, J.S., Gerris, J.R.M, & van Aken, M.A.G (2004) The relation between the absolute level of parenting and differential parental treatment with adolescent siblings' adjustment. *Journal of Child Psychology and Psychiatry*, *45* (8), 1397–1406

Tan, T.X., Gelley, C.D., & Dedrick, R.F. (2015) Non-child-related family stress, parenting styles, and behavior problems in school-age girls adopted from China. *Journal of Child and Family Studies*, *24*(10), 2881–2891. DOI: 10.1007/s10826-014-0092-4

Tang, E., Luyten, P., Casalin, S., & Vliegen, N. (2016) Parental personality, relationship stress, and child development: a stress generation perspective. *Infant and Child Development*, *25*(2), 179–197.

Taraban, L., & Shaw, D.S. (2018) Parenting in context: revisiting Belsky's classic process of parenting model in early childhood. *Developmental Review*, *48*, 55–81.

Tarullo, A.R., Bruce, J., & Gunar, M.R. (2007) False belief and emotion understanding in post-institutionalised children. *Social Development*, *16*, 57–78.

Tasker, F. (2005) Lesbian mothers, gay fathers, and their children: a review. *Journal of Developmental and Behavioural Pediatrics*, *26*(3), 224–240.

Teague, S.J., & Shatte, A.B. (2021) Peer support of fathers on Reddit: quantifying the stressors, behaviors, and drivers. *Psychology of Men & Masculinities*, *22*(4), 757.

The Children's Society. *Children's Society* [website]. Available at: www.childrenssociety.org.uk (accessed 26 January 23).

The Free Dictionary (2022) Family. *The Free Dictionary* [website]. Available at: www.thefreedictionary.com (accessed 26 January 23).

Timmons, L., Ekas, N.V., & Johnson, P. (2017) Thankful thinking: a thematic analysis of gratitude letters by mothers of children with autism spectrum disorder. *Research in Autism Spectrum Disorders*, *34*, 19–27.

Tomeny, T. S., Barry, T. D., Fair, E. C., & Riley, R. (2017). Parentification of adult siblings of individuals with autism spectrum disorder. *Journal of Child and Family Studies*, *26*, 1056–1067.

Tomeny, T.S., Ellis, B.M., Rankin, J.A., & Barry, T.D. (2017) Sibling relationship quality and psychosocial outcomes among adult siblings of individuals with autism spectrum disorder and individuals with intellectual disability without autism. *Research in Developmental Disabilities 62*, 104–114

Tooby, J., Cosmides, L., & Barrett, H.C. (2003) The second law of thermodynamics is the first law of psychology: evolutionary developmental psychology and the theory of tandem, coordinated inheritances: comment on Lickliter and Honeycutt (2003). *Psychological Bulletin, 129*(6), 858–865. https://psycnet.apa.org/doi/10.1037/0033-2909.129.6.858

Totsika, V., Hastings, R.P., Emerson, E., Lancaster, G.A., & Berridge, D.M. (2011) A population-based investigation of behavioural and emotional problems and maternal mental health: associations with autism spectrum disorder and intellectual disability. *Journal of Child Psychology and Psychiatry, 52*(1), 91–99.

Tozer, R., Atkin, K., & Wenham, A. (2013) Continuity, commitment and context: adult siblings of people with autism plus learning disability. *Health and Social Care in the Community, 21*, 480–488.

Trahan, M.H. (2018) Paternal self-efficacy and father involvement: a bi-directional relationship. *Psychology of Men & Masculinity, 19*(4), 624.

Tribotti, S.J. (1990) Effects of gentle touch on the premature infant. In N. Gunzenhauser (ed.), *Advances in Touch: New Implications in Human Development* (pp. 80–89). Skillman, NJ: Johnson & Johnson.

Triseliotis, J. (2002) Long-term foster care or adoption? The evidence examined. *Child and Family Social Work, 7*(1), 22–33.

Tucker, C.J., Finkelhor, D., Shattuck, A.M., & Turner, H. (2013) Prevalence and correlates of sibling victimization types, *Child Abuse & Neglect, 37* (4), 213-223 ISSN 0145-2134, https://doi.org/10.1016/j.chiabu.2013.01.006

Tucker, C.J., Finkelhor, D. & Turner, H. (2019) Patterns of sibling victimization as predictors of peer victimization in childhood and adolescence. *Journal of Family Violence 34*, 745–755. https://doi.org/10.1007/s10896-018-0021-1

Twigg, E. (2018) Safeguarding children. In J. Johnston, L. Nahmad-Williams, R. Oates, & V. Wood (eds), *Early Childhood Studies: Principles and Practice* (2nd edn). Abingdon, UK: Routledge.

United Nations Committee on the Rights of the Child (UNCRC) (2007) *General Comment No. 8 (2006): The Right of the Child to Protection from Corporal Punishment and Other Cruel or Degrading Forms of Punishment (Arts. 19; 28, Para. 2; and 37, inter alia),* 2 March 2007, CRC/C/GC/8. Available at: www.refworld.org/docid/460bc7772.html (accessed 5 May 2022).

UNICEF UK (1989) The United Nations convention on the rights of the child. *UNICEF* [website]. Available at: https://downloads.unicef.org.uk/wp-content/uploads/2010/05/UNCRC_PRESS200910web.pdf?_ga=2.78590034.795419542.1582474737-1972578648.1582474737 (accessed 5 May 2022).

UNICEF (2022) How we protect children's rights. *UNICEF* [website]. Available at: www.unicef.org.uk/what-we-do/un-convention-child-rights (accessed 17 January 22).

United Nations Convention on the Rights of the Child (UNCRC) (1992) Available at: www.unicef.org.uk/what-we-do/un-convention-child-rights

Urbiola Solís, A.E., Vázquez García, A.W, & Cázares Garrido, I.V. (2017) Expresión y trabajo de los Muxe' del Istmo de Tehuantepec, en Juchitán de Zaragoza, México. *Nova scientia, 9*(19), 502–527.

Valchanov, B.L., Parry, D.C., Glover, T.D., & Mulcahy, C.M. (2016) 'A whole new world': mothers' technologically mediated leisure. *Leisure Sciences, 38*(1), 50–67.

van Berkel, S., Tucker, C., & Finkelhor, D. (2018). The combination of sibling victimization and parental child maltreatment on mental health problems and delinquency. *Child Maltreatment, 23*(3), *244*. https://doi.org/10.1177/1077559517751670

van der Wal, R.C., Finkenauer, C., & Visser, M.M. (2019) Reconciling mixed findings on children's adjustment following high-conflict divorce. *Journal of Child and Family Studies, 28*, 468–478. https://doi.org/10.1007/s10826-018-1277-z

van Houdt, C.A., Oosterlaan, J., van Wassenaer-Leemhuis, A.G., van Kaam, A.H., & Aarnoudse-Moens, C.S. (2019) Executive function deficits in children born preterm or at low birthweight: a meta-analysis. *Developmental Medicine & Child Neurology, 61*(9), 1015–1024.

Vasa, R.A., Singh, V., Holingue, C., Kalb, L.G., Jang, Y., & Keefer, A. (2021) Psychiatric problems during the COVID-19 pandemic in children with autism spectrum disorder. *Autism Research, 14*(10), 2113–2119.

Verrier, N. (1993) *The Primal Wound: Understanding the Adopted Child*. Baltimore, MD: Gateway Press.

Vincent, C. (1996) *Parents and Teachers: Power and Participation*. London: Psychology Press.

Vygotsky, L.S. (1962) *Thought and Language*. Ed. E. Hanfmann & G. Vakar. Cambridge, MA: MIT Press.

Vygotsky, L.S. (1978) Interaction between learning and development. *Readings on the Development of Children, 23*(3), 34–41.

Vygotsky, L.S. (1979) Consciousness as a problem in the psychology of behavior. *Soviet Psychology, 17*(4), 3–35.

Vygotsky, L.S. (1987) *The Collected Works of L.S. Vygotsky: The Fundamentals of Defectology* (Vol. *2*). New York: Springer Science & Business Media.

Vygotsky, L.S. (2004) Imagination and creativity in childhood. *Journal of Russian & East European Psychology, 42*(1), 7–97.

Waite, L.J. (ed.) (2000) *The Ties that Bind: Perspectives on Marriage and Cohabitation*. New York: Aldine de Gruyter.

Waldfogel, J., Craigie, T.-A., & Brooks-Gunn, J. (2010) Fragile families and child wellbeing. *The Future of Children, 20*(2), 87–112.

Waldinger R.J., Vaillant G.E., Orav E.J. (2007) Childhood sibling relationships as a predictor of major depression in adulthood: a 30-year prospective study. *American Journal of Psychiatry. 164*(6), 949-54. DOI: 10.1176/ajp.2007.164.6.949

Waldron, J.C., Wilson, L.C., Patriquin, M.A., & Scarpa, A. (2015) Sexual victimization history, depression, and task physiology as predictors of sexual revictimization: results from a 6-month prospective pilot study. *Journal of Interpersonal Violence, 30*(4), 622–639.

Wall, G. (2010) Mothers' experiences with intensive parenting and brain development discourse. *Women's Studies International Forum, 33*(3), 253–263.

Waller, R., Gardner, F., Dishion, T., Sitnick, S.L., Shaw, D.S., Winter, C.E., et al. (2015) Early parental positive behavior support and childhood adjustment: addressing enduring questions with new methods. *Social Development, 24*(2), 304–322. http://dx.doi.org/10.1111/sode.12103

Wallis, C.R., & Woodworth, M.D. (2020) Child sexual abuse: an examination of individual and abuse characteristics that may impact delays of disclosure. *Child Abuse & Neglect, 107*, 104604.

Walton, K.M., Ingersoll, B.R. Psychosocial Adjustment and Sibling Relationships in Siblings of Children with Autism Spectrum Disorder: Risk and Protective Factors. *Journal of Autism and Developmental Disorders 45*, 2764–2778 (2015). https://doi.org/10.1007/s10803-015-2440-7

Wang CD, Hayslip B, Sun Q, Zhu W. (2019) Grandparents as the primary care providers for their grandchildren: A cross-cultural comparison of chinese and U.S. samples. *The International Journal of Aging and Human Development.* 2019;89(4):331-355. DOI: 10.1177/0091415018824722

Ward, B., Smith Tanner, B., Mandleco, B., Dyches, T.T., & Freeborn, D. (2016) Sibling experiences: living with young persons with autism spectrum disorders. *Paediatric Nursing, 42*(2), 69–76.

Ware, R.H. (1994) Developing a passion for pluralism: an expanded canon and teacher preparation. *ERIC* [website]. Available at: https://files.eric.ed.gov/fulltext/ED367602.pdf (accessed 3 December 2021).

Warren, J. (2020) Supporting men in their transition to fatherhood. *Journal of Prenatal & Perinatal Psychology and Health, 34*(3), 230–237.

Waters, E., & Deane, K.E. (1985) Defining and assessing individual differences in attachment relationships: Q-methodology and the organization of behavior in infancy and early childhood. *Monographs of the Society for Research in Child Development*, 41–65.

Waters, J. (2021) Families holding on: how will they bounce back after Covid? *Community Practitioner, 94*(3), 36–41.

Watson, D., Latter, S., & Bellow, R. (2015a) Adopted children and young people's views on their life storybooks: the role of narrative in the formation of identities. *Children and Youth Services Review, 58*, 90–98.

Watson, D., Latter, S., & Bellow, R. (2015b) Adopters' views on their children's life story books. *Adoption and Fostering, 39*(2), 119–134. https://doi.org/10.1177/0308575915588723

Watson, J.B. (1913) Psychology as the behaviorist views it. *Psychological Review, 20*(2), 158.

Watson, J.B., & Rayner, R. (1920) Conditioned emotional reactions. *Journal of Experimental Psychology, 3*(1), 1–14.

Watson, L., Hanna, P., & Jones, C.J. (2021) A systematic review of the experience of being a sibling of a child with an autism spectrum disorder. *Clinical Child Psychology and Psychiatry, 26*(3), 734–749.

Wayment, H.A., Brookshire, K.A. (2018) Mothers' Reactions to Their Child's ASD Diagnosis: Predictors That Discriminate Grief from Distress. *Journal of Autism and Developmental Disorders 48*, 1147–1158.

Weinfield, N. S., Sroufe, L. A., Egeland, B., & Carlson, E. A. (1999). The nature of individual differences in infant–caregiver attachment. In J. Cassidy & P. R. Shaver (Eds.), *Handbook of attachment: Theory, research, and clinical applications* (pp. 68–88). The Guilford Press.

Weiss, L.H., & Schwarz, J.C. (1996) The relationship between parenting types and older adolescents' personality, academic achievement, adjustment, and substance use. *Child Development, 67*(5), 2101–2114.

Weistra, S., & Luke, N. (2017) Adoptive parents' experiences of social support and attitudes towards adoption. *Adoption and Fostering, 41*(3), 228–241.

Wellard, S., Meakings, S., Farmer, E., & Hunt, J. (2017) *Growing Up in Kinship Care: Experiences as Adolescents and Outcomes in Young Adulthood.* Grandparents Plus [website]. Available at: www.grandparentsplus.org.uk/growing-up-in-kinship-care-experiences-as-adolescents-and-outcomes-in-young-adulthood (accessed 3 December 2021).

Wells, G. (2011) Making room for daddies: male couples creating families through adoption. *Journal of GLBT Family Studies, 7*(1–2), 155–181.

West Sussex County Council (2020) *Barriers to Developing an Effective Home School Partnership.* Local Offer [website]. Available at: https://schools.local-offer.org/childs-journey/home-school-partnership/top-tips-for-effective-home-school-partnership/barriers-to-developing-an-effective-home-school-partnership (accessed 3 December 2021).

Wheeler, H., Connor, J., & Goodwin, H. (2009) *Parents, Early Years and Learning: Parents as Partners in the Early Years Foundation Stage: Principles into Practice.* London: NCB.

White-Traut, R.C., Nelson, M.N., Silvestri, J.M., Cunnigham, N., & Patel, M. (1997) Responses of preterm infants to unimodal and multimodal sensory intervention. *Pediatric Nursing, 23*(2), 169–193.

White-Traut, R., Nelson, M.N., Silvestri, J., Vasan, U., Littau, S., & Meeledy-Rey, P. (2002) Effect of auditory, tactile, visual, and vestibular intervention on length of stay, alertness, and feeding progression in preterm infants. *Developmental Medicine and Child Neurology, 44*(2), 91–97.

WHO (2012) *Violence against Women.* World Health Organization [website]. Available at: www.who.int/news-room/fact-sheets/detail/violence-against-women (accessed 5 May 2022).

WHO (2020) *Global Status Report on Preventing Violence against Children 2020.* World Health Organization [website]. Available at: www.who.int/publications/i/item/9789240006379 (accessed 5 May 2022).

WHO (2022) *Child Maltreatment.* World Health Organization [website]. Available at: www.who.int/news-room/fact-sheets/detail/child-maltreatment (accessed 5 May 2022).

WHO (2022a) *Preterm Birth. Geneva: World Health Organization.* World Health Organization [website]. Available at: https://www.who.int/news-room/fact-sheets/detail/preterm-birth (accessed 19 January 2023).

WHO (2022b) *Violence against Children. Geneva: World Health Organization.* World Health Organization [website]. Available at: www.who.int/health-topics/violence-against-children#tab=tab_1 (accessed 5 May 2022).

Wiener, L., Devine, K.A., & Thompson, A.L. (2020) Advances in pediatric psycho-oncology. *Current Opinion in Pediatrics, 32*(1), 41–47.

Wiesner-Hanks, M.E. (2010) *Gender in History: Global Perspectives.* New York: Wiley-Blackwell.

Williams, K. (2003) Has the future of marriage arrived? A contemporary examination of gender, marriage, and psychological well-being. *Journal of Health and Social Behavior, 44*(4), 470–487. https://psycnet.apa.org/doi/10.2307/1519794

Willing, I., & Fronek, P. (2014) Constructing identities and issues of race in transnational adoption: the experiences of adoptive parents. *The British Journal of Social Work, 44*(5), 1129–1146.

Wilding, R., Baldassar, L., Gamage, S., Worrell, S., & Mohamud, S. (2020) Digital media and the affective economies of transnational families. *International Journal of Cultural Studies*, *23*(5), 639–655. https://doi.org/10.1177/1367877920920278

Wilson, S., & Durbin, C.E. (2010) Effects of paternal depression on fathers' parenting behaviors: a meta-analytic review. *Clinical Psychology Review*, *30*(2), 167–180.

Windholz, G. (1987) Pavlov as a psychologist. *The Pavlovian Journal of Biological Science*, *22*(3), 103–112.

Winnicott, D.W. (1953) Transitional objects and transitional phenomena: a study of the first not-me possession. *International Journal of Psychoanalysis*, *34*(2), 89–97. Reprinted in L. Caldwell & H. Taylor Robinson (eds) (2016), *The Collected Works of D.W. Winnicott*. Vol. *4: 1952–1955* (pp. 159–174). Oxford: Oxford University Press. https://doi.org/10.1093/med:psych/9780190271367.003.0034

Winnicott, D.W. (1960) The theory of the parent–infant relationship. *International Journal of Psycho-Analysis*, *41*, 585–595.

Wischerth, G.A., Mulvaney, M.K., Brackett, M.A., & Perkins, D. (2016) The adverse influence of permissive parenting on personal growth and the mediating role of emotional intelligence. *The Journal of Genetic Psychology*, *177*(5), 185–189.

Wolfe, J. (2002) *Learning from the Past: Historical Voices in Early Childhood Education*. Mayerthorpe, Alberta: Piney Branch Press.

Xia, Y.R., Wang, C., Li, W., Wilson, S., Bush, K.R., & Peterson, G. (2015) Chinese parenting behaviours, adolescent school adjustment, and problem behaviour. *Marriage and Family Review*, *51*(6), 489–515.

Yeh, C.J., Arora, A.K., & Wu, K.A. (2006) A new theoretical model of collectivistic coping. In P.T.P Wong & L.C.J. Wong (eds), *Handbook of Multicultural Perspectives on Stress and Coping* (pp. 55–72). Washington, DC: Spring Publications. http://dx.doi.org/10.1007/0-387-26238-5_3

Yeung, J.W., Cheung, C.K., Kwok, S.Y., & Leung, J.T. (2016) Socialization effects of authoritative parenting and its discrepancy on children. *Journal of Child and Family Studies*, *25*(6), 1980–1990.

Yu-wei, H. (2021) Filial piety and Chinese society. In H. Yu-wei, *The Chinese Mind* (pp. 167–187). Honolulu, HI: University of Hawaii Press. https://doi.org/10.1515/9780824844912-009

Zeitlin, M.F., Ghassemi, H., Mansour, M., Levine, R.A., Dillanneva, M., Carballo, M., & Sockalingam, S. (1990) *Positive Deviance in Child Nutrition: With Emphasis on Psychosocial and Behavioural Aspects and Implications for Development* (No. 14). Tokyo: United Nations University.

Zeleke, W.A., Koester, L.S., & Lock, G. (2018) Parents' understanding of adopted children's ways of being, belonging, and becoming. *Journal of Child and Family Studies*, *27*, 1428–1439.

Zephyr, L., Cyr, C., Monette, S., Archambault, M., Lehmann, S., & Minnis, H. (2021) Meta-analyses of the associations between disinhibited social engagement behaviors and child attachment insecurity or disorganization. *Research on Child and Adolescent Psychopathology*, *49*(7), 949–962.

Zigler, E. (1998). A place of value for applied and policy studies. *Child Development*, *69*(2), 532–542.

Zineldin M. (2019) TCS is to blame: the impact of divorce on physical and mental health. *International Journal of Preventive Medicine*, *10*, 141. https://doi.org/10.4103/ijpvm.IJPVM_472_18

GLOSSARY

Abuse   Any types of physical and/or emotional ill-treatment, sexual abuse, neglect, negligence and commercial or other exploitation, which results in actual or potential harm to the child's health, survival, development, or dignity in the context of a relationship of responsibility, trust, or power.

Adoption   The legal process through which a child is placed into the care of adoptive parents.

Adverse Childhood Experiences   Any "highly stressful, and potentially traumatic, events or situations that occur during childhood and/or adolescence. They can be a single event, or prolonged threats to, and breaches of, the young person's safety, security, trust, or bodily integrity." (Young Minds, 2018)

Attachment   A child's inbuilt drive to seek out a person who is available, attentive and responsive to their needs, which results in a lasting psychological connection between them (Bowlby, 1969). Generally involves an emotional, or affectional bond between the child and significant adult(s)

Attachment Disorder   A relatively rare clinical condition comprising two different forms (i) Reactive Attachment Disorder and (ii) Disinhibited Social Engagement Disorder, and linked to a range of psychiatric conditions or psychosocial problems.

Autism   A lifelong developmental disability which affects how people communicate and interact with the world (National Autistic Society)

Blended Families   A family unit where both of the adults have children from previous relationships, or where one partner has offspring from a previous relationship and the couple have additional children together.

Cognitive Developmental Theory   Is a theory of human development that focuses on how individuals acquire, integrate and use information, the mental processes this involves throughout their lifespan.

Collectivist Cultures   Traditional societies (e.g., China, Korea, Japan) where community, family and concern for the broader society are all extremely important. Compliance and social cohesion are usually emphasised.

Critical Period   A fixed point early in a child's development when they are particularly open to specific emotional, social or learning experiences. If conditions are not met at that point, it is not possible for the behaviour to develop later.

Custodial Grandparents   Grandparents who are formally acknowledged to be the primary caregivers for their grandchildren.

Dependent Children   Children who are aged under 16 years living and with at least one parent, or aged 16 to 18 years in full-time education, excluding all children who have a spouse, partner or child living in the household.

Determinants of Parenting   The model proposed by Jay Belsky that suggests the way in which people parent is influenced by their own characteristics, the child's characteristics, and the family's social context.

Developmental Systems Theory   Is a theoretical framework that emphasises the importance of contextual factors and interactions that exist between people and their environment.

Good Enough Parenting   The parenting style proposed by Donald Winnicott (1953) that acknowledges parenting will always be flawed and that children learn and benefit from these imperfections, provided their basic needs are met, and they are shown love, care and empaphy.

Horizontal Relationships   A relationship where the power, status and age are approximately equal (e.g. friends and siblings).

Individualism   Cultures (e.g. UK, USA) that emphasise individual and personal drives and achievement, leading to citizens leading largely independent lives.

Internal Working Model   John Bowlby's theory that, based on their emotional experiences with their primary caregiver, children form mental models which they then apply to new situations. The relationship with their caregiver leads the child to develop of a model of self, a model of others and a model of relationships.

Kinship Care   Where children live with a family member other than their parent. This is often done in order to avoid a move into local authority care.

Learning Theory   Is a theory that attempts to explain how humans and animals acquire new information and behaviour through learnt and mental processes.

Life Story Work   All adoptive children are provided with a life story book which documents details about the child's birth family, placements while in local authority care and transition to their adoptive placement.

Lone Parenting   A mother or a father living without a spouse but with his or her dependent child or children who are aged under 19 and undertaking full-time education (Gov.uk, 2010).

Multiple Birth   Where two or more children are born simultaneously to the same birth mother.

Non-dependent children   Young people who are living with their parent(s), and either aged 19 years or over, or aged 16 to 18 years and not in full-time education, or who have a spouse, partner or child living in the household.

Parental Sensitivity   Is the ability of parents to perceive and respond appropriately to the needs of their child.

Parental Style   Term associated with Diana Baumrind (1971) to describe common patterns of parental behaviours. She initially identified three parenting styles – authoritarian, authoritative and permissive. A fourth style – neglectful or disengaged was added later (Maccoby and Martin, 1983)

Prematurity   Refers to a baby born 37 weeks gestation age. A 'preterm' baby will also be of low birthweight (<2.5kg).

Psychoanalytic Theory   Pioneered by Sigmund Freud (1856–1939), who proposed that personality development, and the way parents manage their child's instinctual impulses, will affect the traits they later display. Includes the notion of the Id, Ego and Superego.

Secure Attachment   Where a children feels able to rely on their attachment figure to meet their needs, resulting in a warm affectional bond.

Sensitive Period   The times when the infant is particularly sensitive to environmental influences – making them the best times to develop specific behaviours.

Separation Anxiety   Term associated with James and Joyce Robertson to describe the distress children may experience when separated from their attachment figure.

Siblings   The gender-neutral term for brothers and sisters.

Stepfamilies   A family group where at least one child is biologically related to one of the adults, but not to that adult's partner.

Strange Situation   An experimental design pioneered by Mary Ainsworth and used to determine the nature of the attachment between a child and their caregiver.

Surrogacy   Embryos are generated in vitro, using the biological father's sperm and a donor egg. The embryo is then transferred to a gestational carrier who bears the child.

INDEX